THE REPRESENTATION OF THE OTTOMAN ORIENT IN EIGHTEENTH CENTURY ENGLISH LITERATURE

Ottoman Society and Culture in Pseudo-Oriental Letters, Oriental Tales and Travel Literature

by
HASAN BAKTIR

Hasan Baktir

THE REPRESENTATION OF THE OTTOMAN ORIENT IN EIGHTEENTH CENTURY ENGLISH LITERATURE

Ottoman Society and Culture in Pseudo-Oriental Letters, Oriental Tales and Travel Literature

Edited by Mustafa Kirca

ibidem-Verlag
Stuttgart

Bibliografische Information der Deutschen Nationalbibliothek
Die Deutsche Nationalbibliothek verzeichnet diese Publikation in der Deutschen Nationalbibliografie; detaillierte bibliografische Daten sind im Internet über http://dnb.d-nb.de abrufbar.

Bibliographic information published by the Deutsche Nationalbibliothek
Die Deutsche Nationalbibliothek lists this publication in the Deutsche Nationalbibliografie; detailed bibliographic data are available in the Internet at http://dnb.d-nb.de.

Coverbild: © Tokamuwi / PIXELIO

∞

Gedruckt auf alterungsbeständigem, säurefreien Papier
Printed on acid-free paper

ISBN-10: 3-8382-0132-9

ISBN-13: 978-3-8382-0132-0

© *ibidem*-Verlag
Stuttgart 2010

Alle Rechte vorbehalten

Das Werk einschließlich aller seiner Teile ist urheberrechtlich geschützt. Jede Verwertung außerhalb der engen Grenzen des Urheberrechtsgesetzes ist ohne Zustimmung des Verlages unzulässig und strafbar. Dies gilt insbesondere für Vervielfältigungen, Übersetzungen, Mikroverfilmungen und elektronische Speicherformen sowie die Einspeicherung und Verarbeitung in elektronischen Systemen.

All rights reserved. No part of this publication may be reproduced, stored in or introduced into a retrieval system, or transmitted, in any form, or by any means (electronic, mechanical, photocopying, recording or otherwise) without the prior written permission of the publisher. Any person who does any unauthorized act in relation to this publication may be liable to criminal prosecution and civil claims for damages.

Printed in Germany

To NURAY and RANA

Contents

Editor's Preface vii
Foreword (by Ian Almond) ix
Acknowledgements xi
Introduction 1
Orientalism and the Representation of the Ottoman Orient 3
The Representation of the Ottoman Empire from the International and Negotiating Perspective of 18th Century English Literature 18
Critical and Theoretical Assumptions of the Study 34

Interactions Between the Ottomans and English Society in the Pseudo-Oriental Letters and the Introduction of the Foreign Observer 37
The Representation of the Ottoman Orient in the Pseudo-oriental Letters and the Development of the Foreign Observer 38
The Pseudo-Oriental Letters and Persian Observers in the *Persian Letters* 52
The Negotiation of the *Turkish Spy* and the *Persian Letters* in England 67
Were the Ottomans Represented in Pseudo-oriental Letters? 77

The Representation of the Ottoman Orient 95
The *Arabian Nights* and Pseudo-oriental Tales in 18th Century England 96
Rasselas: The Prince of Abyssinia (1759) 104
Johnson's Idea of the Orient and the Source of *Rasselas* 107
Representation of the Middle Eastern Orient in *Vathek* (1786) 122
William Beckford's Biography and *Vathek* (1786) 123
William Beckford's Source of the Oriental Perspective in *Vathek* 128
Vathek's Difference from Other 18th Century Pseudo-oriental Tales 138

The Representation of the Ottoman World in 18th Century Travel-Writing in England 143
Barbary Captivity and Penelope Aubin's *Strange Adventure of Count de Vinevil* 146
Lady Mary Wortley Montagu: *Turkish Embassy Letters* (1769) 156
Elizabeth Craven: *A Journey Through Crimea to Constantinople* (1789) 173

Conclusion 185
References 193

Editor's Preface

In the letter to Warren Hastings, Samuel Johnson wrote Europeans had either deficient thinking or uncertain conjecture about the region. With an unusual interest in ancient and Christian civilizations of the East, he once said Eastern civilizations had a great influence on the advancement of European civilization: "East had provided almost all that sets European society above savages". In another letter to Boswell, Johnson wrote the English public had an unusual interest in oriental countries and therefore such studies might be made part of the college curriculum. In this book, Hasan Baktir, following this argument, studies the representation of the "Ottoman Orient" in 18th century English literature. He claims that a comprehensive understanding of the representation of the Ottoman Orient in 18th century English literature requires a new perspective; therefore, he investigates in his book different aspects of the interaction between the Ottoman Orient and 18th century Europe. Said's *Orientalism* discusses how European writers created a separate discourse to represent the Orient. The present study does not completely reject Said's argument; rather, it shows us that there was also a dialogic and negotiating tendency which did not make a radical distinction between the East and the West. Relying his argument on 18th century pseudo-oriental letters, oriental tales and oriental travelogues, the author tries to indicate here that the representation of the Ottoman Orient in 18th century English literature was different from earlier centuries because developing critical and liberal spirit established a negotiation between the two worlds. The negotiation of the two worlds has been studied as a significant theme of the pseudo-oriental letters, oriental tales and oriental travelogues. The present study has tried to indicate how the critical and inquisitive spirit of the age of Enlightenment interanimated Oriental and European cultures.

Mustafa Kirca

Foreword

The history of the study of the representation of Islam/the Muslim Orient in Western literature has almost become a genre in itself. Said may have been the first to bring a Gramscian/Foucauldian perspective to such an approach, but undoubtedly histories of such representations go back to at least the turn of the century. Baktir's study of eighteenth century representations of Islam adds to this genre, and its contribution brings together some critical attention on the major Orientalist/Orientalizing figures of the period – Johnson, Montagu, Beckford, Montesqieu. A number of questions continue to arise in the wake of Said's 1978 landmark study, *Orientalism*. How monodirectional was the flow of power in such representations? To what extent did the travelling observer also participate and become influenced by the phenomena he tried to depict without attachment? What variety of motivations lay behind the desire to know and represent the Oriental other –was it simply a question of political control? Or were there deeper, more enigmatic factors at play –sexuality, existential affirmation, even utter idiosyncrasy? How various and diverse was the Western response to the East –can we discern degrees of sympathy, knowledge and difference in the various Orients offered up to us by the canonical and non-canonical figures of 18th century English letters?

Baktir's study certainly attempts to answer some of these questions, through a detailed examination of very different texts. One of the consequences, as he points out in his conclusion, is that to insist on the autonomy of Orientalism is to overlook the large, interstitial areas of hybridity where existed between the spaces we somewhat naively term "the Muslim world" and "the Christian world". The extent, for example, to which non-classical,

Ottoman Greeks offered a kind of tertiary, inbetween Oriental, Christian but not quite Western, indicates the difficulties involved for Western travelers. When Hegel glimpsed a Greek prince at the opera in Vienna in the 1820s, he thought he was a Persian or a Turk. The Italian-speaking Arabs of the Hohenstaufen period would offer another example of such hybrid and problematic entities. Baktir's attempt to examine and analyse some crucial 18th century English texts in this light clearly illustrates his awareness of the complexities he is taking on.

Ian Almond

Acknowledgements

This project has been developed out of my studies on travel writing submitted as a dissertation at Middle East Technical University in Ankara. I am greatly indebted to Prof. Dr. Nursel İçöz for her invaluable help and guidance throughout the study, and also for her constant moral support and encouragement. I should extend my sincere thanks to Prof. Dr. Belgin Elbir, Assist. Prof. Dr. Margaret Sönmez, Assist. Prof. Dr. Nurten Birlik and Assist. Prof. Dr. Dogan Bulut for their positive and reassuring attitude and suggestions. I would like to thank Prof. Ian Almond for his valuable effort to write a foreword to this book and also to Dr. Mustafa Kirca for his efforts in editing the manuscript. Finally, to my wife, Nuray, I offer sincere thanks for her unshakable faith in me and her willingness to endure with me my endeavors.

Introduction

In eighteenth century European texts the Orient signifies Turkey, the Levant and the Arabian Peninsula occupied by the Ottoman Empire[1] (Lowe 7). The present study aims to discuss the representation of the Ottoman Orient in 18th century English literature. The texts in the present study consist of three literary genres: pseudo-oriental letters, oriental tales and travel writing. A chapter will be devoted to each of these genres, but there will not be a strictly formal and generic interpretation. The first chapter explores the historical context of the foreign observer in eighteenth century pseudo-oriental letters. The significance of the foreign oriental observer in pseudo-oriental letters has not been explored in the context of European and Ottoman interaction. Critics like Arthur Weitzman and Martha Pike Conant undermined the significance of the observer[2]. The foreign observer is not only a mask for eighteenth century writers to attack contemporary political corruptions but is also significant for his critical perspective on the European and Oriental world. The critical perception and perspective of the oriental observer helps to re-identify the Europeans' idea of their society and of Oriental society.

---

[1] There are two different ideas about the Orient. Lisa Lowe's idea of the Orient signifies the Middle East and Levant; Edward Said's Orient also includes the Far East. In 18th century England the Orient used to signify the Middle East and Levant, the Far East was part of the East and Asia.

[2] Martha Pike Conant in *The Oriental Tale in England in 18th century* (1965) and Arthur Weitzman in the *Turkish Spy* (i-viii) consider the foreign observer as a literary device employed by contemporary writers to criticize political and social issues.

The critical perspective of the oriental observer influenced the development of the critical and liberal view about the Oriental world. Martha Pike Conant considers pseudo-oriental letters a precursor of 18th century oriental tales[3]. The pseudo-oriental letters and Oriental tales have certain similarities. Observation of the Oriental world through a distant perspective is a significant literary device the tales inherited from the letters. The perspective of the distant observer in the letters was taken further by the tales to discuss cultural and social aspects of the Oriental world. The tales replaced the critical spirit of the foreign observer with the inquisitive spirit of the enlightenment writers who recognized, discussed, and valued the contribution of the Orient to the European civilization. Travel writing is also significant for its embodiment of the Orient through authentic human observation and experience. Pseudo-oriental letters and oriental tales can be considered as characteristically 18th century genres, but travel writing about describing the Ottoman Orient has a long historical past. Travels to the Ottoman Levant from England began in the 16th century and went on unbroken until the end of the 18th century. In the accounts of the Levant travelers from the Levant Company we come across different ideas about the Ottoman world. In addition, the ideas of the Levant travelers and of the free adventurers about the Ottoman Orient are not the same. For instance, English travelers before the 18th century, though many of them recognized and admired the superiority of the social and political structure of the Ottomans, considered the Ottoman Empire as a threat to and an enemy of European civilization, but 18th century travelers were less concerned with the Ottoman threat. In particular, 18th century female travelers asserted that the earlier male travelers had misrepresented the Ottoman world. They claimed to have a more intimate observation and more critical view of the Ottoman Empire than those of the male travelers.

---

[3] Conant categorized the *Turkish Spy* and *Persian Letters* as the precursors of the Oriental tales in the introduction to *The Oriental Tales in 18th Century in England* (1965). In the following chapter she evaluates them as a separate genre.

Orientalism and the Representation of the Ottoman Orient

Edward Said investigates the underlying historical and cultural prejudice in *Orientalism* (1972). He deals with how Western writers from ancient Greece to the present age have created the image of the Orient as the "deepest and recurring image of the Other" (Said 1). It is "regarded as a manner of regularized writing vision" dominated by imperatives, perspectives and ideological biases (60). It is argued that the Orient has been a particular discursive framework and it remains a "network of interest" and a "peculiar entity" (Said 3). The "framing of the Orient in European discourse" is based on certain classifications influenced by politics, ideology, scientific studies, culture, history and literature; therefore, Orientalist discourse comprehends interdisciplinary approaches. Said argues this as follows:

> My principle operating assumptions were that fields of learning as much as the works of even the most eccentric artist, are constrained and acted upon by society, by cultural tradition, by worldly circumstance, and by stabilizing influences like schools, libraries, and governments; moreover, that both learned and imaginative writings are never free, but are limited in their imagery, assumptions, intentions; and finally that advances made by 'science' like Orientalism in its academic form are less objectively true than we often like to think. In short my study hitherto has tried to describe the economy that makes Orientalism a coherent subject matter, even while allowing that as an idea, a concept, or image the word *Orient* has a considerable and interesting cultural resonance in the West. (59)

Said argues that different disciplines have framed the discursive strategies of Oriental studies throughout the history in Europe. According to Said, the Orientalist attitude has transformed the Orient from a spatial destination into a scientific-fictitious field. A "mobile army of metaphors, metonymy, and anthropomorphisms, and sum of human relations are posed and embellished poetically and rhetorically" to signify the Orient (Said 60). Therefore, everyone who scrutinizes the Orient "locates himself vis-à-vis the orient" and frames his research within a certain discourse which includes "the kinds of narrative voice he adopts, the type of structure he builds, the kinds of images, themes, motifs that circulate in his texts" (Said 20). Macfie states that

Said's Orient occupies a particular place in European discourse as one of its deepest and most recurring images of the "other" to make an ontological and epistemological distinction. The distinction is made by European orientalists in order to develop a "particular policy" for dominating, restructuring and having an authority over the Orient (Macfie 85).

Said's extensive critical approach in *Orientalism*, though valuable in many ways, constructs the representation of the East upon the notion of a presumed continuity of actual Europe vs. fictional Orient. Thus, he skips what might be significant in different historical periods. On the contrary, the representation of the Ottoman Orient in 18th century English literature – namely in pseudo-oriental letters, oriental tales and travel writings– relies on extensive familiarity and knowledge due to a long process of actual interactions. Travelers, ambassadors, adventurers, missionaries and scholars, from the Crusades to the Renaissance and to the 18th century, visited the Ottoman Orient and observed the Ottoman world in its own context. They observed and wrote about different aspects of the Ottoman world. There are similarities as well as differences between travelers' opinions, and none of these texts is identical in approach to the Orient.

In the 18th century, the Ottoman world was not a mysterious, strange and unknown land to English writers and the reading public thanks to travelers' accounts from the 16th century onward. Here I find it illuminating to review some of the accounts written before the 18th century by travelers to the Ottoman world, to show that there is not one homogenous discourse. Although there was an earlier military contact between English and Turkish states, the real, actual contact between England and the Ottoman Empire began with the 1396 Crusade, with the Lord of Lancaster's support of the Hungarian king Sigismund with 1000 English soldiers against the Ottoman progress in Europe[4]. However, it was Queen Elizabeth[5] who initiated a long and peaceful interaction between the Ottomans and the English when she

---

[4] Nazan Aksoy surveys English-Ottoman relation between the 14th and 17th centuries in *Turk in English Renaissance Literature* (1985).
[5] She was fascinated with the oriental fashion and asked her ambassador to buy a Turkish dress from Constantinople.

sent Richard Harbourne to Sultan Murat III to cooperate openly in the Mediterranean. She considered that the Ottoman and English cooperation against Catholic Spain would be beneficial to expand the influence of the English trade in the open seas against the Spanish armada. In her letter to the Sultan, Queen Elizabeth first addressed him as the "unconquered and most passionate defender of the true faith," and then asked for support against the "idolaters (the Spanish and Catholics) who falsely professed the name of Christ"[6]. The same desire to cooperate against the king of Spain, who relied on the help of the Pope and all other "idolater princes" to crush the Queen of England and destroy the Ottoman Sultan, was conveyed by the ambassador in 1587 to Sultan Amurath III, who, in return, promised support. The Queen went on and sent Edward Burton in 1588 as the first resident ambassador of England to Constantinople with a "jewel of her Majesty's picture set with rubies and diamonds" together with "three pieces of gilt plate, ten garments of cloth of gold" and other "fine gifts" (qtd. in Bent viii-x).

The Queen's strategy worked and the agreement opened the Ottoman seas to British merchants. The alliance was created between the two states. They cooperated against the Spaniards in the sea. The reward of this correspondence between the Ottoman Sultan and Queen Elizabeth in 1579 was the Levant Company which provided English merchants with three hundred and fifty years of safe and free trade in the open sea. Mattar writes that "the English fleet attacked Cadiz with the support of five galleys from Barbary" in 1596. After the attack, the English fleet "released thirty-eight poor, wretched Turks" who had been galley-slaves. They were "furnished with money and all necessaries," and safely sent to Turkey ("The Age of Discovery" 20). During the seventeenth century a lot of visiting Ottoman merchants escaped from the Spaniards to the British mainland which aroused the suspicion of a secret plan by the Queen to allow Turks into Western Europe. She was accused of a

---

[6] Mattar argues in *Turks, Moors and Englishmen in the Age of Discovery* (1999) that there were people in England who believed that the Ottoman could protect them from the evil of the Pope (Mattar 498). The Ottomans were a threat to Europe until the defeat of Vienna in 1683, which according to Defoe had been a disappointment for English Wigs. According to Defoe, the English Wigs had such a strong resentment that there was an abundance of people in England who wished everyday the Turks should take Vienna (Weight 52).

confederacy with the Turk by the Pope. But the protest did not prevent the continuation of this agreement up until the 18th century. Turks kept on using the English and Welsh harbors during this period. Some of the Turkish merchants and sailors visited and lived in England during the period of cooperation. There were also captive Turks who escaped and resided in England, and some even chose Anglicanism. It is recorded in 1605 that a "Chinano Turke converted," and "became a priest" (21). Another Turk, Rigep Dandulo, who visited Lady Lawrence of Chelsea in 1650, became the center of the community's interest with his Turkish dress. It was written that he later converted to Christianity and settled in England. John Evelyn, in *The Diary De Beer* (1654), writes about an Ottoman Rope-dancer. He calls him a Turk and identifies him as an "Albion Blackamore [...] who was skilled in Dancing on the Ropes" (22).

The Levant Company, in addition to providing wealth, went on sending merchants and ambassadors who became mediators of economic, cultural, social and political interactions between England and the Ottoman Empire. Edward Burton was the 2nd of the Queen's ambassador to Constantinople. He lived in Constantinople for five years and became very close to the Sultan during his residence, accompanying him in the victory of Cerestes and dying on his return to Constantinople from this battle. Upon the death of Burton, the Ottoman Sultan sent a letter to the Queen and expressed his grief:

> As to your highness's well-beloved Ambassador at our blessed Porte, Edward Burton, one of the nation of Messiah, he having been enjoyed by us to follow our imperial camp without having been enabled previously to obtain your highness's permission to go with my imperial Staff, we have reason to be satisfied, and to hope that also your highness will know how to appreciate the services he has thus rendered to us in our imperial camp. (qtd. in Bent xi)

The political and economic alliance between the Queen and the Ottoman Sultan continued successfully through ambassadors and merchants. The Queen sent to each succession of a new Sultan an outstanding gift to strengthen this relation. Among many, the gift accompanying Thomas Dallam, who served as intermediary to maintain the support of the Sultan against the Catholic enemies and to further the interests of the Levant Company in the

Ottoman states, is prominent. The gift Dallam took was referred to in the *State Papers* of January 31 as follows: "A great and curious present is going to the Grand Turk, which will scandalize other nations" (qtd. in Bent xvi).

Thomas Dallam was sent by the British court to Constantinople to make an organ for the Ottoman Sultan. His impressions are important in terms of being a memory of a simple organ-maker who met the Sultan. He writes that the introduction to the Sultan was amazing and frightening. He was told by the English ambassador in Constantinople not to expect any gift for his service from the Sultan. Dallam reports this as follows:

> [It was] never known that upon receiving of any present he gave any reward unto any Christian [...] you would think that for long and wearisome voyage, with danger of life, that you were worthy to have a little sight of him; but that you must not look for neither. (65)

Dallam must have been frightened by the ambassador. However, his report also reflects that he was excited by the diversity in the Seraglio. He writes that he met people who were once Christian in addition to dumb people, and dwarfs, and big bodied men with a low stature all in exotic costumes (Dallam 65). As he was not educated about the oriental customs and manners and had no earlier acquaintance with Turkish people, the ceremonial acceptance and the extraordinary customs and manners of Turks must have struck him very forcefully. His experience at the Turkish Seraglio indicates how bewildered he was. He felt almost in another world when he stood behind the Sultan. He writes of his amazement and anxiety:

> Coming into the house where I was appointed to set up the presents or instruments; it seemed to be rather a church than a dwelling house; to say the truth, it was not a dwelling house but a house of pleasure, and likewise a house of slaughter; for in that house [...] [the Emperor] had ninety brothers put to death. (62-3)

The Great Signor's interest had not been enough to reassure him. What he heard from Lello, the ambassador, about the cruelty of the Sultan made him anxious while he was setting up the organ. Dallam writes this instance as follow:

> He (the Sultan) sat right behind me that he could not see what I did; therefore he stood up, and his Coppagaw (Kapıcıbaşı) removed his chair to one side, where he might see my hands; but in his rising from the chair [...] he sat so near me; but I thought he had been drawing his sword to cut off my head. (71)

When Dallam's organ began to strike, the Sultan was so happy that he rewarded Dallam with a handful of gold. The Sultan's pleasure made Dallam a very important man. He became a constant visitor to the Seraglio to enjoy himself, to eat and to see women in the Harem (Dallam 75). He was also asked by Mehmed III to stay at the Seraglio to practice his art, but since he did not feel free and comfortable in Constantinople, he gave the excuse of family back home, though he was not married. The courtiers in the Seraglio told him that the Great Signor would give him two wives from the two best virgins of the Harem. The English ambassador, Thomas Lello, also wanted to convince him to stay. But he insisted on going back. The Ottoman court was not a very safe place for a man like Thomas Dallam who did not want to engage himself in political and commercial affairs. He wanted to escape to Christendom as soon as possible and therefore secretly made a plan to go. He found an Englishman, who had been born in "Chorlaye in Lancashier," but had stayed long enough to learn how to escape safely from the Janissaries. He was taken home by this Englishman whom he calls a "trustie frende" (qtd. in MacLean 9). According to Dallam, this man, though his name was Finche, was in religion a perfect Turk; therefore, he calls him "our Turk" (9). He took Dallam with him as far as the Greek border, and Dallam escaped from the Ottoman Empire. His graphic account of the Ottoman court, his description of Sultan Mehmed III and records of the incidents in the seafaring-life of the period add to the sum of our knowledge of the past of the English concerning their relations with and opinions about the Levant and Turks.

Dr. John Covel, unlike Dallam, was a man of learning who served in Constantinople from 1670 to 1677 as a chaplain to the ambassador. His diary was published in 1679. It seems that he was happy to see the Ottomans in everyday life and to enter their world as an observer. Covel noted curiosities of the Turkish society, and the English public read from Covel's diary about the costumes, manner and life of the Turks in Constantinople, the great celebration in honor of Prince Mustapha, and marriage of the Sultan's daughter. Covel also set some Turkish songs to music which he considered very good in terms of sense and sound, but foreign in terms of language (qtd. in Bent xxvii). The description of Sultan Mustapha in Covel's account must have created much curiosity in the readers. He realized that the Ottomans were multicultural and ethnically a much diversified society in which Christian and Muslim values, beliefs, and life-styles were mixed. Another of his works, *Some Account of the Present Greek Church* ... (1685), was based on his observation of the Greek Church in Constantinople. It is a work of long observation and careful scholarship that Dr. Covel wrote after he returned to England from Constantinople. This is the earliest scholarly study in this field which first time talks about the possibility of a union between Eastern and Western churches, an idea which must have frightened the Protestants (xxxi).

Dudley North, another English visitor to the Levant, went further in adapting himself to the Turkish way of life. He was later to be identified by his family with his Levant costume, Cordubee hat, and his mustachios in the Turkish manner and by his habit of breaking into the Turkish tongue when much provoked (qtd. in Bowen 16). He was a careful observer of the Ottoman court. He learnt about the legal system in Turkey. Whenever he had a problem, he used to defend his own case in Turkish at the Ottoman Court. His knowledge of the Ottoman system made him treasurer of the Levant Company. Harold Bowen in *British Contributions to Turkish Study* expresses this as follows:

> North has many observations to make on Turkish justice, which in view of his great experience of its own workings, are of particular interest. He admitted that Turkish judges had to be kept in a good temper by being given small presents at regular intervals, but maintained that these should be regarded as fees rather than as bribes. For the rest, he found the procedure simpler and more expeditious than in English courts and extolled the regard paid to reason and equity. (17)

According to Bowen, he did not hesitate to converse with the native inhabitants. He gave descriptive accounts of Turkish methods of building, of dervishes, superstitions, Jewish brokers, trade guilds, and of slaves. He was fluent in Turkish; therefore, he had access to common people's lives. But he was nevertheless dependent on his culture and English identity, which led him to evaluate certain things that seemed normal to the native Ottoman people as superstitious. He prospered in the Levant, and when he returned home he advocated free trade with England. All his experience and observation in the Levant contributed to his success in life; he first became sheriff of the City, then a Member of Parliament (Bowen 18).

William Biddulph, known as the Lavender, was one of the few English clergymen in the Ottoman Empire who wrote accounts of his experiences there. Biddulph's experience in the Levant is interesting for two major reasons. He observed the Ottoman society from the perspective of a clergyman and mainly dealt with the interactions and relationships among the Britons then living in the Ottoman Empire. From his accounts, we learn about the gossip and conflicts between English citizens in the Ottoman country. The English public for the first time heard about Coxden's and Glovers' affairs through Biddulph who accused Coxden of "prostituting his wife to the Great Turk" (qtd. in McLean 59). He also blamed the English agent Thomas Glover, though he did not openly name him, for having many children from an "infamous" Greek woman (63). The debates concerning the corruptions of English citizens in the infidel country well served the purpose of the writer to attract attention in England. But to avoid the anger and hatred of English people in the Levant and their acquaintances in England, Biddulph assumed an editorial persona, Teophilus Lavender. In the preface, the editor says that he compiled these composite epistles by editing several letters sent from abroad by William Biddulph and his brother. He argued that English people would appreciate more what they had when they read about the Ottoman state. He thinks that English people must be thankful for their good king, English women for their husbands and English servants for their benevolent English masters. In England the rich could enjoy their wealth and the poor have better conditions than those of the poor in the Ottoman Empire. Biddulph also pointed to the general view that "Turks were followers of the Devil and a false prophet" and that they "were defending blasphemies against God". For instance, he interpreted the hybridity of the Turk's religion as the source of evil. Their language was hybrid, like their religion. The confusion was reflected in the way the Ottoman society was structured.

Biddulph thinks that the Jews, the Armenian and the Greek Churches were part of the Ottoman diversity and it was not possible in such a mixture for a true religion to survive. Biddulph had probably for the first time in his life encountered such diverse and different religions co-existing. He could not find any convenient term in his own religious and scholarly traditions to compare with or to explain the Ottoman society. Therefore, he sometimes contradicted himself. He claimed that there was nothing true and holy in the Turks. While considering "to be good to one and others, to fast, to give charity as virtuous," he still thinks that "to pray five times a day" is evil (qtd. in Mclean 88). But it was amazing for Biddulph *never* to see or hear "two Turks in their private quarrels, strike one another" (58). Whenever he walked in the streets, all the nations of the Ottoman society saluted him reverently after the manner of their country. He says: "If the like order were in England women would be more dutiful and faithful to their husbands" (55). In spite of this, he thought that the English would be the happiest of all nations if only they knew the miseries of other people living under the tyranny of the Ottomans. They would know the value of their country and religion if they had been in the "Heathen Country" (Mclean 85).

Henry Blount was one of the rare travelers to the Ottoman Empire to claim and to achieve a certain degree of Renaissance perspective. He promised to avoid the general tendency of the voyagers to describe other nations "by their own silly[7] education". He also promised to consider the advancement of the Ottoman nation. He admits this as follows:

> I who had often proved the Barbarisme of other Nations at Sea, and above all others, of our owne, supposed my selfe amongst beares, till by experience, I found the contrary; and that not only in ordinary ci-

---

[7] Here "silly" means naïve, innocent and lacking.

vility, but with so ready service, such a patience, so sweet, and gentle a way, generally through them all, as made me doubt, whether it was a dreame, or reall; if at any time I stood in the way, or encombred their ropes, they would call me with a Janum, or Benum, terms of most affection. (75)

Unlike many European travelers, he uses the "sword" as a metaphor to interpret the advancement and victory of the Ottoman Empire. He says: "The Turkish religion favors hope above fear and paradise above hell thus fills the mind with courage for the military purpose" (Blount 78); the permission for polygamy "makes numerous People" and the prohibition of wine "hardens the Soldier, prevents disorder, and facilitates public provision" (82-3). Since the Ottomans inhabit countries once filled with wits, wise men and "the greatest Divines, Philosophers and Poets in the world" it seems likely that marriage with the ancient, local and Ottoman culture will in the process of time "gentlize" the military spirit of the Ottoman Empire. Blount also thinks that the things that seem ridiculous and strange to the Europeans and Christians are received as natural by Turks because there is a difference between Turkish and English mentality[8]. He admires the severity, speediness and arbitrariness of the Ottoman justice. He argues that absolute power of the Sultan is necessary and reasonable considering that the Ottoman Empire expanded by constant fighting (93). Blount believes that human actions are not always motivated by beliefs; certain conditions may motivate them. Our beliefs sometimes appeal to passionate ignorance rather than rational understanding; therefore, they cannot be free from criticism. It seems that Blount was conscious of the cultural difference between the Ottoman Empire and European society. This is very apparent in his encounter with the Ottoman armies who recognize him as a Christian. As he recounts, when the soldiers came he

[s]tood still, till they menacing their weapons, rose, and came to me, with looks very ugly; I smiling met them, and taking him who seemed of most port, by the hand, layed it to my forehead, which with them is the greatest sign of love, and honor, then, often calling him Sultanum, spoke English, which though none of the kindest, yet gave it such a sound, as to them who understood no further, might seem af-

---

[8] He uses the following expression to explain the difference: "our very Reason differs" (85).

fectionate, humble and hearty; which so appeased them, as they made me sit and eat together, and parted loving. (98)

According to Blount, Turks were in general admirable for their cleanliness and social institutions. Yet, he says that the Turk's "habit of catching a Christian to enslave and sell" is "beastly" (102). Blount observed that people from different ethnic and cultural backgrounds in the Ottoman society identified others from the way they dressed. Therefore, he suggested that travelers to the Ottoman territories would be safer if they made suitable preparations, learned about the customs and expectations of the Ottomans, and wore suitable clothes.

There were also accounts by English citizens who were enslaved at sea and taken as prisoners to the Ottoman Empire. Their accounts also present a different and interesting side of the interaction between England and the Ottoman society. T. S., known only by these initials, was captivated by slave-masters, sold to several masters and entered the service of Haly Mamiz Reis. He traveled in the North African territories of the Ottoman Empire with an Ottoman tax-collector and became one of the major agents of the Ottoman Empire there. His interesting accounts indicate the flexible and adventurous working opportunities provided for Europeans in the Ottoman Empire. We learn from T. S.'s accounts the British point of view about the imperial administration of the Ottomans and the local culture of the tribes, then living in Algeria. The strange animals he saw and the extraordinarily beautiful nature were some of the experiences he wanted to share with the English public. He first gives accounts of some "English Turk[s]" and then shifts his attention to several accidents. In one of these adventures, one of the soldiers attacks a lion with a "Cymeter in his hand" and would have died if they had not shot the lion (qtd. in Mclean 202). He gives in *The Adventure* conventional, fascinating but strange encounters in Eastern countries. He claims to have witnessed very strange occurrences:

> I saw a flying serpent, about the bigness of an ordinary Dog, with a long Tail, and a head like an Ape, with a larger mouth, and a longer tongue, the body had about four foot in length; we shot at it, but could not kill: It threatened some of our men when they ventured to

> come near it, and could not be obliged to depart until a great number of us were arrived at the Place. I saw it near the pleasant fountain that did rise in one side of the furthermost Grove. I enquired of the Name, but could not learn it; it had Wings of divers colors, the chief were red and white: It hovered long over our heads, and had not the noise of our gun frightened it away, I think it had ventured among us again [...] I imagined it to be [...] a desperate Serpent. (qtd. in Mclean 73-75)

In *The Adventure* the readers are given the conventional image of the Orient and Africa as bizarre and strange locations with unusual creatures. This perspective locates the Ottomans in a different order of beings in which men are savage and sometimes not different from beasts. McLean states this as follows:

> Reports of beastly encounters belong to a strategy that, by shifting, blurring or even erasing the border between nature and culture in strange Islamic locations, brought local peoples and animals into a common register below the superior human level which Europeans imagined for themselves. What this strategy permitted early travelers [and fiction writers like William Beckford, Penelope Aubin], who perhaps only partly understood what they were seeing, was the ability to feel less threatened and humbled by their potentially subordinate position within the exotic Ottoman Emperium. Regular reports of infestation by invisible perils, alien insects and other vermin not before seen by Englishmen, contributed to previously existing structures of xenophobic prejudice. (204)

Yet, there were some incidents which really happened. Such incidents contributed much to the perception of Islamic and oriental customs as "strange and superstitious". We see several interesting anecdotes in *The Adventure*. For instance, in one of them T. S. speaks of the clever trick of the rebellious chief of a North African village to prevent rebellion and establish government's legitimate authority. The rebellious chief circulated a so-called dream of a man who had just returned from a pilgrimage to provoke people against the Ottoman authority. Isha Muker, the chief, declared that Turks were not true Mohammedans. They were heretical in thought and deed; it was not lawful to submit to the Ottoman authority. McLean quotes this as follows:

> Finding 'the multitude' still reluctant to fight, Isha Muker resolved upon a clever 'Strategem'. He persuaded one Elmswar Tapnez, recently returned from the pilgrimage to Mecca, to feign lameness. Next, he produced a letter purporting to be from 'the Keeper of Mohamet's Temple, certifying that Elmswar Tapnez had been visited while there by a vision of the prophet who had commanded him to signify unto them that it was his pleasure to assist them this year in a notable manner, and free them from the slavery of the Turk. News of this letter attracted the attention of the local grandies who met in the council. Once Elmswar Tapnez, appearing before them, was miraculously cured from his lameness, all doubts vanished; the Arab leaders declared him a Holy Man and resolved they would no longer pay tribute to the Turk. (206)

T. S. took the Ottoman side and fought against the rebellious tribes with Ben Osman Butcher. He says, for instance, "we lost 50 men and 435 of the Arabians were killed" (qtd. in Mclean 102). The readers not only learn about the fights and struggles between the superstitious villagers and "villainous" Ottoman soldiers but also read about ordinary social events. T. S. and his commander win the battle against the tribe. They visit a local marriage ceremony and honor the landlord to re-establish the authority. They go to the place, honor the solemnity with their presence and pay respects to the Bride and Bridegroom to create peace among the tribes and Ottomans (Mclean 135). T. S. also entertains the readers with some amusing details: "The bride receives a Cock and a Dog, to teach her diligence and watchfulness" and the bride does not open the veil until she is taken to her husband's house (137-38). He claims that he eye-witnessed all these incidents.

It was not only adventurers and travelers from Britain who gave information about the Ottomans. The English public also saw and read about the Ottoman adventurers, captives, merchants and pirates who visited England. Sometimes, Turks captured in an open sea-fight were imprisoned. Sometimes they were exchanged with English captives. For instance, Nabil Mattar quotes from Sir John Eliot's report the execution of twenty captives and the reprieve of five, among whom there was a young boy and a little baby ("The Age of Discovery" 25). Some were lucky to be employed as tailors, shoemakers, button makers, menders and solicitors.

The ambassadors from the Ottoman and other Muslim countries were the luckiest minority thanks to the protection of the English monarchs. They were free to practice their religion, dietary rules and dress in their local clothes. The first ambassador from the Ottoman Empire came with lions, Turkish scimitars, horses and unicorn horns as a gift to the English king in 1583. Another ambassador from Morocco (Alkaid) made a great impact on the English public when he brought with him from Morocco 366 British captives as a sign of good will. The London public saw the picture of this ambassador and read about him in a weekly publication. For instance, the arrival of Mohammed bin Hadou –another ambassador from Morocco– was recorded in the *London Gazette,* described in diaries and celebrated in poems written upon the occasion. He visited the Royal Society, attended banquets and concerts and engaged in public activities (Mattar, "The Age of Discovery" 38-40). In return, the arrival of the ambassadors was celebrated by the king who exhibited his wealth and fine English products in the court when he met them.

It is not known whether the English authority and Turkish ambassadors had a meeting in London. But an English man, Finet, who was once the British ambassador to Constantinople, used to invite Lord Marshall and the Lord Chamberlain to eat Turkish food. Customs, manners, eating habits and religious practices of the Ottomans then living in London must have been exotic to the Londoners. For example, their so-called animal slaughter was a matter of curiosity and wonder for many English citizens: "They killed all their own meate within their house as sheepe, lambes, poultrie, and such like, and they turned their face eastward when they killed any thing" (Mattar, "The Age of Discovery" 34). There are also some records of marital relations between Turks, Moors and British women. In 1614, the marriage of the Sultan of Sumatra and the daughter of an English gentleman were conducted. The Turks, who went to England, have occupied the literary imagination, the streets, courts, markets, and jails of England after the age of discovery. These people probably introduced to the London community the first Muslim community infrastructure (42). But it is unfortunate that they left no records of their native observations of the British context; therefore, the British public does not know what they thought about England.

It is obvious that there was an English traveler like Henry Blount who admired the Ottoman order and sobriety as well as others, like John Covel and Thomas Dallam, who took the opposite view and considered the Ottomans as the enemy of European civilization. In the context of this long historical interaction and the heterogonous views of the English travelers, it must be an incomplete argument to say that there was a historical and rhetorical discourse which constructed the Ottomans as "the deepest and recurrent image of the European other". Said's Orientalism may be illuminating in discussing the aspects of "otherness" of the Ottoman Orient; we dare not challenge such an argument. However, there was a long cultural, political, economic, and social interaction between the Ottomans and European nations, when we look at the representations of the Ottomans from this perspective; it can be argued that the Ottoman world, though different and complex, was a familiar and knowable reality to the Europeans. This familiarity and knowledge were used by 18th century writers to look at the Orient from the perspective of a foreign oriental observer who knew both Europe and the Orient and who could view them from a more critical and liberal perspective. According to Said's *Orientalism*, it is not possible to construe the 18th century context, and the critical and liberal perspective because Said's theory ignores the disruptions and diverse aspects of the representation of the Ottoman Empire in English literature. I find it necessary here to review the critical and liberal aspect of the 18th century context from a comprehensive historical point of view in order to see the changing face of the interactions between England and the Ottoman Empire.

The Representation of the Ottoman Empire from the International and Negotiating Perspective of 18th Century English Literature

Daniel Defoe writes about the 18th century England's commercial relation with the world in the *Review*; 1707: Vol. 4, No. 21. He says: "the subject of trade [...] has one Excellency in it [...]. It is impossible that coffee, tea and chocolate can be advanced in consumption without an eminent increase of those trades that attend them" (1). Tobacco from America, textiles and silk from the Mediterranean, coffee from the Caribbean Islands and Turkey, and tea from China were brought to English markets. International commerce began to bring wealth and peace, and made the world more familiar to English people than ever before. Johnson noted that commerce was one of the significant aspects of European civilization. A country does not only borrow new and beneficial goods through trade but also learns new things about other nations which change and enrich a language. He says: "the Language most likely to continue long without alteration would be that of a nation raised little above barbarity" ("A Dictionary" 26). John Dryden also noted in the "Annus Mirabilis" that trade would bring "the eastern wealth" to London (1210-15). The most notable shops and valuable utensils like drugs, coffee, tea and chocolate were supplied and brought to London through trade by means of which the English public began to feel the changing face of interaction between the growing British Colonialism and the world.

Henry Fielding admitted that commerce with the world "had indeed given a new face to the nation" (qtd. in Sherman and Zwicker 2073). The English merchants also profited spectacularly from the capture, transport, sale and labor of African slaves in current and former colonies. By 1763 Britain had got control of Bengal and India, the Caribbean and North America and earned great profits and wealth through trade with new colonies. In the atmosphere of the rapidly changing face of the nation, intellectual context began to change too. Richard Rolt published the first British commercial dictionary in 1756. He writes in the preface to the dictionary that commerce "transforms" the British world "from war to peace" (qtd. in Dierks 476). Joseph Addison also writes about the influence of international trade in the *Spectator* May 1711: No. 69. The periodical character, Mr. Spectator, visits the Royal Exchange in London and observes the commercial exchange between Britain and other countries. Having visited the Royal Exchange and seen the products of various nations, Mr. Spectator realizes that he is a citizen of the world who observes mankind.

Hume writes that from a more open commerce of the world, people have learned to compare the popular principles of different nations and ages, and have changed their whole system of philosophy ("Natural Religion" 14). In the context of interaction with the world, orthodox beliefs were re-questioned by 18th century scholars like John Locke, David Hume, and Michel Montaigne who argued that the Christian view of man was false[9]. In the search for the universal source of the human mind and civilization, there were two opposite answers to the question of human progress. Recognizing the limits of man, the diversity and goodness of human nature, some skeptics like Rousseau and Montaigne developed a sentimental view which stressed that the human being is naturally good and his goodness is instinctive. Challenging the conventional idea of progress, they believed that civilization corrupts the natural genius, thus the form of primitive society is better than civilization. The second group of 18th century scholars like David Hume and Edward Gibbon argued that civilization develops and progresses in historical diversity. Human nature might be uniform but at the same time might cele-

---

[9] Deism and natural religion had a wider appeal to the abovementioned enlightenment writers than medieval scholasticism did. Deists were dissenters in the Enlightenment Christian society; they used scientific methods to verify their belief about the world and God. They applied hypothesis, observation, deduction, generalization, and experiments to discuss and solve social, political and moral problems. Theory of religion and knowledge were transformed into general science of man by deists who were very skeptical about universal truth. They "maintained that in vast welter of diverse human beliefs and practices no universal rules could possibly be found" (Berlin 71). According to Locke, "all the knowledge we have can never be well made known"; it is better to remember that most of our beliefs are guided by philosophical, traditional and religious beliefs, which are "mere opinions". Thus it is safer "to affirm nothing as absolutely true" (Locke "Understanding" 292-317). 18th century Enlightenment writers argued that "only that is true which any rational observer, at any time, in any place, can, in principle discover" (Berlin 70). David Hume, for instance, challenged in his *An Inquiry Concerning Human Understanding* the idea that human nature remains the same in principles. He insisted on testing all the moral values and emotions to prove whether they are true or false (306-18). Detailed information can be found in Berlin's book *The Crooked Timber of Humanity* (1992). Ekhtiar also discusses the representation of the Orient with a reference to the Enlightenment context in *Fictions of Enlightenment: The Oriental Tale in Eighteenth-Century England* (1985).

brate itself in infinite variety. Therefore, one should find the particulars which best represent the human being. John Dryden, Samuel Johnson and Alexander Pope represented the second group. For instance, Dryden identifies Shakespeare's characters as natural because "he was the man who [...] had the largest and most comprehensive soul. All images of Nature were still present to him" ("Dramatic Poesy" 231). Pope's idea of a critic indicates the idea of "comprehensive soul". According to Pope, a critic is the one "who sees with equal eye as God of all" ("Essay on Man" 87). A critic is "a perfect judge" who "reads each work of wit with the same spirit that its author writ" ("Essay on Criticism" 233). In these lines, Pope implies a necessity to replace personal views with a more comprehensive and liberal perspective. Observing from a more comprehensive perspective, Alexander Pope admits and admires the contribution of Oriental scripture to European literature. He says: "the pure and noble simplicity is nowhere in such perfection as in the scripture [...] one may affirm with all respect to inspired writings, that the divine spirit made use of no other words but what were intelligible and common to men at that time and in that part of the world" ("The Iliad" 28).

Samuel Johnson also emphasized the value of the accurate observation of the living world in the *Rambler* 1750: No. 4 on Fiction. Praising James Thomson for his ability to observe the particular in the external nature, Johnson argues that the observation of the living world provides a writer with the knowledge of the world. Admitting that the known world was even larger than it was when the ancient writers wrote about it, he argues that mankind is naturally curious to learn the sentiments, manners and condition of people in distant countries. He thinks that every mind that has leisure and power to extend its views has to be desirous to learn about the advantages and privileges of at least several nations on the earth. Knowledge about the other nations will improve the condition of men and can enlarge his view about the world. An enlightened mind can offer something to be avoided or imitated, or can say something new and interesting to the readers. Every nation has a certain peculiar sense of genius, valuable manners and customs, useful policy and agriculture. One should observe and learn about the conditions of the distant countries in order to bring home something by which his country may benefit. He writes in the "Vanity of Human Wishes": "Let Observation, with extensive view, / Survey mankind, from China to Peru / Remark each anxious toil, each eager strife, / And watch the busy scenes of crowded life" (1-5).

John Locke thinks that the spirit of inquiry is an inquiry into the nature of understanding. Locke wanted to see how far human understanding could reach for self-discovery. In "An Essay Concerning Human Understanding" (1690), he deals with how man, through senses and reflection, creates all his beliefs about the world. To Locke, the human mind has a complete freedom to create associations, impressions and ideas. He says: "I cannot avoid [...] ideas produced in my mind" (303). Tracing the source of ideas to sensation and reflection, Locke argues that it is not possible to be certain of the existence of the general truth. Another empiricist, David Hume writes about the difference between the perceptions of ignorant and civilized people. Seeing the propensity of mankind towards unfamiliar objects as a natural inclination, Hume thinks that he should be concerned to investigate the learned world ("Inquiry" 307). Hume must have felt an ambition to contribute to the investigation of human reasoning. He says: "the observation of human blindness and weakness is the result of all philosophy, and meets us, at every turn, in spite of our endeavors to elude or avoid it" ("Inquiry" 307). According to Hume, a philosophical discovery can change one's idea about the world. He says:

> when we peruse the first histories of all nations, we are apt to imagine ourselves transported into some new world, where the whole frame of nature is disjointed, and every element performs its operations in a different manner from what it does at present [...] [as we advance and become more enlightened] we soon learn that there is nothing mysterious or supernatural in the case. (qtd. in Zwicker and Sherman, "Understanding" 2679)

There was also a growing desire in the 18th century to learn about the unknown world. This desire was also represented by the members of the Royal Society which consisted of merchants, politicians, scientists, dukes, monarchs, and courtiers. Members of the society worked for the progress of the nation and submitted their experiments, observations and journals to the

King. Certain members were qualified as virtuoso, new inquirers, who were dissociated from any profession to guarantee the objectivity of their observations and inquiry. The Society created a universal slogan by claiming "to serve the glory of God and the good of mankind" (qtd. in Sherman and Zwicker 2124). They enquired into and introduced some curiosities of the world to the 18th century English public. For instance, a member of the Royal Society wrote about his meeting with a man who told him about the nature of grease amber. He wrote of the inquiry of the man in the Philosophical transaction of the Royal Society. In the paper entitled *A Letter of the Honorable Robert Boyle of Sept. 13, 1673, to the publisher concerning Amber Greece and its being a vegetable production,* the writer says:

> Amber greece is not the scum or excrement of the whale, etc., but issues out of the root of a tree, which tree how far so ever it stands on the land, always shoots forth its roots towards the sea, seeking the warmth of it, thereby to deliver the fattest gum that comes out of it, which tree otherwise by its copious fatness might be burnt and destroyed. (qtd. in Sherman and Zwicker 2130)

Here, the observation of the unknown object [grease-amber-Substance] from a distance becomes a significant experience to learn about the nature and reality of the unknown object. Another member of the Royal Society, Robert Hook, considered the observation of unknown objects and doing an experiment as serviceable to mankind and a remedy for the distraction of senses. He explained this with a physiological description of the body and a description *Of the Point of a Sharp Small Needle* through magnifying glasses [microscope]. In the *Micrographia* he expressed that a microscope made it possible to learn about the things which are unreachable by eyes and mind alone thus it extended the knowledge and observations of men[10] (2153).

Inquiry and curiosity were the essentials of the eighteenth century England. Observations of the world and of contemporary society from a distance

---

[10] Margaret Cavendish rejects Hook's argument and claims that the microscope and such dioptrically glasses did the world more injury than benefit because they intoxicated men's brain with the appearance of the objects and useful studies were laid aside (qtd. in Sherman and Zwicker 2152).

were a popular tendency of the entire 18th century. The popular press like newspapers, periodicals and novels were especially designed to reflect the observation of the curious mind. Defoe argued that the function of periodicals was "to make due Inquisition" (qtd. in Demaria 532). The Renaissance stage was replaced in the 18th century by periodicals which promulgated the new cultural awareness. Mr. Spectator, the fictitious voice of *The Spectator*, made all London a kind of theatrical playhouse in which he enjoyed the privilege of making observation and judgment[11]. This inquisitive spirit was available to novelists, poets and writers like Joseph Addison, Richard Steel, Lady Mary Wortley Montagu, Thomas Gray and William Cowper. Prose became a special style to convey abstract and general ideas in a simple but effective language. Dialogues were also significant in that they made the co-existence of different voices possible for writers because they best express the spirit of the age (Richetti 42). The newspaper, the periodical essay, and the magazines had become confirmed habits in the lives of almost everyone who could read. In daily rituals of drinking and smoking people read in the periodicals about the variety of tobacco from Virginia, tea from China, coffee from the Caribbean, textile from Turkey, which was comparatively inexpensive and enormously popular.

As a result of free print and comparatively inexpensive access to periodicals and novels, ideas were circulated very fast. News from all over the world and about any contemporary issue could be found in the periodicals. For instance, in *The Spectator* 1712: No. 21, the public read about Indian American Kings, and Japanese merchants who visited London. The expansion of reading publics created a new sense of the social and political knowledge, and people began to see and judge the world in the light of a new and a more liberal perspective. Introducing themselves as citizens of the world, Mr. Spectator and Mr. Bickerstaff claimed that they were spectators and lovers of mankind. They addressed everyone from any segment of social strata.

The spirit of the age could also be seen in travel literature. Like the periodical persona, travelers wrote from a distant perspective, had a spirit of

---

[11] "Addison claimed a daily readership of 60.000," which must have been higher than the audiences of the theaters (Demaria 529).

inquiry and a genuine desire for knowledge. European people began to travel throughout Europe for self-discovery and they also journeyed outside Europe to observe and bring home the unique values of the countries they visited. Travel books and travel letters sold by the thousands. Fabricant writes that travel books in the eighteenth century were among the most popular genres, outselling novels many times over (708). But there was a difference between 18th century travel-writers and their predecessors in that the enlightenment skepticism, the critical spirit of inquiry and the exploration re-framed the content and perspective of the 18th century writers. Fabricant thinks that Don Quixote's reply "To all corners of the globe [earth]" to Sancho Panza's question "Where then, my dear country man are you going?" best reflects the spirit of 18th century travel writing (707).

Addison transmitted travel letters in *The Spectator*. He wrote about the historical, geographical and cultural aspects of the eastern nations of the world from Egypt and China to the Turkish Empire (qtd. in Fabricant, 711). George Anson's *A Voyage round the World* (1748) was one of the popular travel writings which made more than three editions. Anson dealt in the *Voyage* with the manners of people in the Far East. China, Chinese commodities and the irregular forms of Chinese landscape were popular descriptions in the *Voyage*. Fabricant argues that Sir William Chamber used Angon's description in his *Dissertation on Oriental Gardening* (1772) which is significant because many English people, who had never been to China, created a fantasy world of Oriental beauty from Chamber's *Gardening* in the gardens of their homes in the midst of England (Fabricant 730). Richard Pococke's *Description of the East* (1743) reports the five years of his journey in the Ottoman Near East. Pococke supplied descriptions of Bursa and the southern coasts of the Sea of Marmora and of the roads from the capital through Silivri to Adrianople. He was in Constantinople when the Ottomans signed the Treaty of Belgrade. He thinks that the Treaty created peace between Turks and foreigners (qtd. in Bowen 27). He describes the two-thousand year old ancient Egyptian ruins of the Valley of the Kings and the Colossi of Memnon. James Bruce was a British Consul-General who studied Arabic and wrote a report about Ottoman Egypt in 1790. His *Travels to Discover the Source of*

Nile (1772) introduced the intimate details of the Abyssinian country which was little known having been isolated for centuries. According to Fabricant, there was a great parallel between Johnson's *Rasselas* and Bruce's description of Abyssinia so that it was very difficult to distinguish truth from fiction (Fabricant 737). Sir James Porter was an English ambassador in Constantinople from 1746 to 1762. He wrote *Observation on the Religion, Law, Government and Manners of Turks* in 1768. According to Bowen, the book produced curiosity due to the sympathetic picture of the common people. He says: "the true Turks, particularly the *Yürüks* of Anatolia– were so perfectly honest that police were almost superfluous" (qtd. in Bowen 29). Porter criticized the English authors who investigated Ottoman cultures from books written by Arabian authors. It is evidential that 18th century writers either went to or wrote about almost all corners of the world with much curiosity. They crossed the boundary of national culture and culminated in diversity.

There was a parallel between fiction and historical writing in the eighteenth century in terms of perspective. Both historians and fiction writers, particularly those who wrote about the Ottoman Orient, dealt with the social and cultural context and tried to understand the lived experience of the people (Richetti 381). O'Brien says that history "was regarded as a branch of literature" in the 18th century. She argues that writers and readers crafted historical and literary narratives in a way that "was fundamentally at odds with their presentation of historical truth" ("History and Literature" 365). The sense of history as a lived experience was replaced by a more inquisitive spirit which investigated unforeseen "aspects of the past" (368). In the search for the cultural roots of human civilization the ancient Oriental culture was given a particular significance. Thomas Blackwell, for instance, claimed that Thales and Homer had studied in Egypt before they founded a school in Greece. He says: "Greece had scarcely emerged from barbarism when the Egyptians were living in Peace and Splendor [...]. It was widely accepted that the Hebrew patriarchs, too, learned their religion in Egypt" (qtd. in Sambrook 216). 18th century writers like Voltaire, Montesquieu and Gibbon were also aware of ancient Oriental influence on the progress of civilization: "whether drawn by congenial style or devotional content," early eighteenth century

English [writers] referred to the ancient Oriental and Judeo-Christian source of the European civilization (Sambrook 217). Gibbon and Hume, who were less interested in national history and more concerned to detect underlying patterns of social evolution, were exponents of the 18th century historical writing. They dealt with social forces which transformed the old world into the modern and enlightened one (Richetti 377). It was considered as an intellectual achievement to write about history in the 18th century. For historians like Hume and Gibbon it was more significant to write about civilization than about religious history. This cosmopolitan outlook proceeded from the skeptical and inquisitive perspective of the age in which writers moved from a national history towards more global, secular and materialistic notions of the social and cultural world. The customs, manners, gender relations and family structure of people became a popular subject of the 18th century historical writing. James Boswell's character Monboddo states this as follows: "the history of manners is the most valuable [...]. I never set a high value on any other history" (qtd. in Richetti 381).

Hume and Gibbon represented the new attitude in England. Gibbon's *History of the Decline and Fall of the Roman Empire* (1776) is among the representative secular historical inquiries of the 18th century which presents an interesting case study about the social and cultural context of the falling empire. O'Brien says: "*The History of the Decline and Fall of the Roman Empire* far exceeded all other histories of this period in historical erudition and narrative mastery, and it garnered even greater critical praise [...] Gibbon was able to extend to [...] the long, unfamiliar history of the Byzantine Empire and its Arab, Persian, Central Asian and Latin neighbors" ("Books and Their Readers" 121). Robertson's prediction that the apparently irreligious content of chapters 15 and 16 would hurt the sale had proved inaccurate and the first edition sold more than 1000 copies within a few months. Gibbon remarks: "My book was on every table and almost on every toilette" (qtd. in O'Brien, "Books and Their Readers" 122). Influenced by Hume, he adopted a cosmopolitan and skeptical attitude. Gibbon says: "a philosopher [should] enlarge his views and present the history of various people with the same level of politeness" (qtd. in O'Brien, "History and Literature" 388). Having surveyed the

Roman and Byzantine Empires from this perspective, he considered Christianity as the major cause of the decline of the Roman Empire. He argued that "Christianity was largely responsible for the decay of Rome's once tolerant and sociable religious and civic culture" (389). According to Gibbon, the new religion re-structured the social and political world of the Roman Empire and was less tolerant of the diversity. Richetti states that Gibbon, like Hume, had a distance from the world he described. As a detached observer, he surveyed the causes that changed and prepared the fall of the two empires. He also added to the last chapter the birth of a new Empire, that of the Ottomans. Bowen says that Gibbon paid attention to the rise of the Ottoman power, which must have been interesting for the growing British Empire (Bowen 374). Gibbon seems to be implying that the developing British Empire might inevitably fall like the ancient empires if it does not establish wisdom, liberty and balance.

The gendered division of labors and education was also spelled out. Women began to proclaim their own rights. Mary Carleton says:

> I could instance in many other customs of nearer nations, in respect to female right and propriety in their own dowers, as well as in their husbands' estates: but, I will quarrel with the English laws, which I question not are calculated and well accommodated to the genius and temper of people. (qtd. in Sherman and Zwicker 2121)

She claims that a wife should share an equal portion with her husband in all things of weal and woe, and should be free to bring an action, begin a transaction, and finish a suit in her own name. In the *Case of Madam Mary Carleton* (1673), she writes that she learnt Latin, Greek, French, Italian, Spanish and some Oriental tongues to earn a better fortune. In 1694, Mary Astell had written in the *Serious Proposal to Ladies* that women should withdraw to pursue the pleasure of learning and escape the drudgeries of marriage (qtd. in Sherman and Zwicker 2072). She also stated in *Some Reflections upon Marriage* (1700) that "he who should say the people were made for the prince who is set over them, would be thought to be out of his senses as well as his politics [...] one person is not in reality better than another" (qtd. in Sherman and Zwicker 2357). The idea of self-made free woman had an immediate effect on contemporary female writers like Lady Mary Montagu and Mary Chudleigh who began to challenge men with their own perspective and style. The difference between men and women was particularly apparent in female travel-writing. They wrote with a desire and ambition to represent the world in a different way from that of their contemporary male writers. Lady Mary Wortley Montagu, Elizabeth Craven and the characters in Aubin's *Strange Adventure of Count de Vinevil* (1721) courageously wandered the streets and town of Constantinople alone to indicate that the Ottoman world had many things that escaped from the view of the male travelers. The issues they discussed were mostly about women. Lady Mary Montagu discussed in her letters how male traveler misinterpreted the Ottoman world. She interpreted veiling, baths, harem, and marriage from a perspective which challenged the earlier male travelers' description. For instance, Lady Mary identified *entari* as a practical clothe and satirized the Christian chastity belt.

Women's perception of the world and their perspective were similarly critical in eighteenth century England. Although writers like Goldsmith, Gibbon, and Hume were aware of the female readership, and deployed techniques and strategies to sustain their interest, 18th century women developed a separate critical perspective (O'Brien, "Books and Their Readers" 126). Eliza Haywood criticized the condition of women in England in the *Female Spectator* 1745: Vol. 2, No. 10 with respect to Oriental women. As a female observer, she thinks that the case of English women is worse than that of women who are taught to believe that they are inferior. She says: "while we live in a free country and assured from our excellent Christian principles that we are capable of those refined pleasures [...]. [O]ur minds [...] are left wholly uncultivated and like a rich soil neglected" (qtd. in Sherman and Zwicker 2436). The author of the *Female Spectator* recognized the fact that the taste of the "gentle sex" is different from that of men. Claiming to be a mouthpiece of the female readers, the author states in Volume 1 of the paper that the *Female Spectator* is a new paper which aims to address the curiosity and diverse interests of female readers. The author will use in the *Female Spectator* three different personas; by the name of Mira, the author will be addressing the curiosity of family life. The widow-persona will address gallantry and Euphrosyne [another persona] will discuss curious intellectual issues (1-2).

The female perspective was not less critical and inquisitive in spirit than that of the male writers in the 18th century. They evidenced the wealth of the empire and freely consumed their fathers' and husbands' economic gains. Women not only consumed but also produced. Female periodicals were immensely profitable. They manifested female autonomy and innovations. Female writers "deployed their words and wit as a kind of cultural capital" to look at the world from their own perspective. Poems, books and precepts by women became a commonplace in the 18th century (Sherman and Zwicker 2071). Women began to express themselves more freely than in earlier centuries. They protested their secondary status in the letters, journals, and diaries.

It was recognized by male and female writers in the 18th century that the human world was extensive and consisted of diversity. Richetti argues that writers and historians in eighteenth century England could only construct a critical narrative "from a detached or cosmopolitan vantage point" to keep the wider, comparative context in view (384). The "Enlightenment cosmopolitanism" made critical and inquisitive "inferences" and observed human diversity from this vantage point. The similarities and differences of people's customs and manners were brought into view (O'Brien, "Books and Their Readers" 117). In the critical and inquisitive context of the 18th century, the Ottoman Orient was negotiated with the spirit of the age.

It is possible to see the negotiation and dialogy of the Orient and Europe in eighteenth century English literature. Here, "negotiation" is used with a particular meaning to convey the new force which revolutionized the conventional perception of the Ottoman Orient and challenged the idea that European society was superior to the rest of the world. Negotiation has a very specific meaning in new historical literary terminology where it is taken as indispensable from cultural poetics. Although literary criticism has a familiar set of terms like allusions, symbolization, allegory, representation and mimesis for the relationship between a work of art and the historical events it refers to, they become inadequate to explain the critical perspective and cultural change that took place in the 18th century. New terms are needed to describe the new atmosphere of the 18th century in which the relations between writer, society and a work of art were transferred into a more critical sphere than in previous centuries. When we see a work of art as the product of negotiation between a creator and a class of creators, equipped with a complex and communally shared repertoire of conventions, we can discover the process of adjustment and transformation in a work of art.

Stephen Greenblatt, leading new historicist, argues that "the convenient working distinction between cultural texts that are social and political and those that are not becomes something worse than an error: namely, a symptom and a reinforcement of the reification and privatization of contemporary life" ("Learning to Curse" 147). The new historical critics emphasize "an intensified willingness to read all of the textual traces of the past with the attention traditionally conferred only on literary texts" (qtd. in Hawthorn 197). The process of new historical reading works with an assumption that a reader should avoid value judgment and venerate the past tradition to find the relation between different forms of art (Hawthorn 198). Literary and non-literary texts can intersect at certain points to create currency, which in return brings about negotiation. Here, the term "negotiation" becomes significant. It can be used to identify the currency which identifies the critical and inquisitive spirit of the 18th century.

The complex and negotiating relation between a work of art and society can be observed in the introduction of coffee-houses in England in the late 17th century[12]. When Turkish coffee was first introduced by merchants[13], it

---

[12] In New Historical terminology, negotiation is a process of change and re-appropriation in the form of narrative. Greenblatt explains this process in the example of the story of the convict Gary Gilmore. He was a convict (a subject). Norman Mailer wrote about his life and prison-experience in a novel, which became a best-seller and in turn was made into a movie. The movie led Mailer to contact another convict, Jack Abbott, and to write another book which led to the release of Abbott, who committed another murder, and this murder later was made into a play called *In the Belly of the Beast*. This particular instance indicates the interaction between artistic [novel], political [rejudgement and release], social [best seller book] and economic [circulation of money in the production and consumption of this single event] terrains in the society. A work of art, then, "is the product of a negotiation between a creator or class of

was identified as a Turkish beverage. A metaphorical relation in those early days was established between coffee and Turks. There were people who considered coffee as an ugly, black, evil beverage and a Turkish enchantment that spoiled the pure Christian spirit. It was, however, very popular: "there appeared at this time a Turkish drink to be sold, almost in every street, called coffee" (Aytoun 48). There were people who had "scarce Two pence" to buy bread but spent "a penny each evening" in the coffee-house. By the end of the 17th century, any Londoner had only to walk to the end of the street to see a hanging sign of the coffee-pot or the Turk's head (51). Then, there began to develop a particular form of negotiation between coffee and English people. The "Turkish Novelty" [coffeehouses] created a currency and transformed the social imagination. Turkish coffee had for some time been a dominant subject for discussion. Different social institutions and discourses interacted and negotiated on coffee and coffeehouses. There appeared eight pamphlets between 1652 and 1675; and a number of poems, judicial letters, about coffee and the characters of the coffee-house (Aytoun 15-6). Women claimed in a vulgar and obscene language that the whole English race was in danger of extinction due to this "unhappy berry" and "Turkish Enchantment". They asked the court to forbid "Drinking COFFEE" with severe penalties (17). The powerful resistance and hostile attitude towards coffeehouses led the government to take precautions. The King was informed of the inconveniency of the coffee-houses. He asked the Lord Keeper and the Judge to proceed against coffee-houses. It was decided that coffee was used in the

---

creators, equipped with a complex, communally shared repertoire of conventions" (Greenblatt, "Negotiation" 158). In order to achieve the negotiation, an artist needs to create a currency that is valid for a meaningful, mutually profitable exchange. Here, the "currency" metaphorically designates the systematic adjustments, symbolizations and lines of credit necessary to enable any exchange to take place (158). The *currency* firstly mediates the production and circulation of a work of art. Secondly, it designates representations and adjusts different discursive practices modeled as a process of exchange. The texts (movie and novels) and contexts (judgment, release, murder) enter into interlocking dialectics to create political, poetic, legal, and economic discourses to bring together a complex web of "currency" between the writer and the society. This web constitutes what Greenblatt calls the "poetics of culture". In the matrix of this web different discourses coalesce to produce, affect, and change the matrix of the social context.

[13] Pasqua [Ottoman citizen from Greece] and Jacob [Jewish-ottoman] first opened coffee-houses in England (Aytoun, *A History of the Coffee-Houses* 32).

common assembly "to nurse the idleness and pragmaticalism," so it "might be thought as common nuisance" (Aytoun 89). It was claimed that the coffee-houses "effeminate Majesty's subjects by broaching lies, insinuating the people's ears a prejudice" against each other and against government and rulers; therefore, if they remain too long, they will be very "pernicious and destructive" (89). The king signed a "Royal Proclamation" in the Christmas of 1675 to "suppress" and "put down" all the coffee-houses.

There was a protest against coffee by orthodox people, and the English king declaimed against people who loved coffee and coffeehouses. But, the King's proclamation was also protested by people as a sign of "despotism and tyranny" (Aytoun 93-94). There were also judges at the English courts who found the Royal Proclamation wrong. For instance, Judge Rumsey had the same opinion with the protesting public and decided:

> Whereas formerly Apprentices and clerks with others used to take their morning's draught in Ale, Beer, or Wine, which by the dizziness they cause in the Brain, made many unfit for business, they use now to play the Good-fellows in this wakeful and civil drink: Therefore, that worthy gentleman […] who introduced the practice hereof first to London, deserves much respect of the whole nation. ("Anonymous Paper" 7)

The judicial decision became the turning point for the acceptance of the coffee-houses in England. It is evident that coffee and coffee-houses created currency and negotiation between different social and cultural practices in early 18th century England. The coffeehouses were transformed into a center of literary and aesthetic works of eminent English writers like John Dryden, Samuel Pepys, Joseph Addison and Richard Steele. William Urwin's coffee-house, known as *Will*'s, which was near the Ling Theatre, inspired many poets and writers. It was for more than forty years a center of public taste and education. Players and writers were the frequent visitors of *Will*'s coffee-house. The coffee-houses also led to exchange between intellectuals and publics. They were a birthplace of periodicals. Periodicals and coffeehouses together established a civil social sphere in late 17th century Britain; and they together prepared the ground for an age of democratic revolutions (Cowan

361). In 18th century London, Addison and Steel found in the coffeehouses a virtual stage on which they might expose the false arts of life, disguises of cunning, vanity and affection, the general simplicity of dress and discourse to "reform the public manners and enlighten the citizens of the Commonwealth" (362). Coffee-houses accomplished what the theater in Renaissance England had done for the public. In the introduction and negotiation of coffee-houses, it is possible to see the interaction of different discourses and social practices as part of the poetics of culture.

We need to look at the representation of the Ottoman Orient from the negotiating perspective of 18th century England in order to see the transformation of the restrictive national point of view into a more liberal one. Developing colonialism and trade in the 18th century made England open to the world. The novel became a new form of representing the national and foreign world. Bakhtin suggests in the *Epic and Novel* that the novel was born into a new and creative polyglot world in which the national perspective was replaced by dialogic ones. The dialogic perspective of the novel had a peaceful co-existence with local and universal languages (12). Seeing the early examples of the novelistic discourse in Xenophon's work, the ancient Greek writer, Bakhtin writes that Xenophon replaced the monolithic and closed world of the ancient Greek with the great and new world of "the [Oriental] others". According to Bakhtin, Xenophon had a desire to renovate Greek political forms in a spirit closer to oriental autocracy. Bakhtin considers Xenophon's desire as a new light which interanimated the interaction between European and Eastern cultures. The dialogy and co-existence of the alien and national worlds developed a particular way of seeing. The temporal model of the world changed and the world unfolded as an unconcluded historical process into future (Bakhtin 30).

The symptom of changes in 18th century England and its negotiating relation with the other [Ottoman] world appeared in the pseudo-oriental letters, Oriental tales and travel accounts. Such genres mixed the national and alien worlds by replacing the historical image of the Ottoman with the negotiating and dialogic spirit of the age in which English people's view of themselves coincided to a certain extent with their view of the Orient. This new perspective established a particular creative dimension and threw light on the new liberal representation of the Orient in 18th century English literature. This negotiation will be discussed in the following chapter to explain the transformation of a foreign observer of pseudo-oriental letters into a local observer in 18th century periodicals. It is argued that there is a reorientation and restructuring of the old relations with the Ottoman orient in 18th century English literature that deals with specific historical and cultural features of the Oriental countries and reflects very broad and varied relations with the Ottoman, Egyptian and Ethiopian worlds. As Greenblatt argues, the pattern of classifications of discursive practices that each individual learns gives a sense of what we consider as the same and different. This is what makes the world seem natural to us. Once the imperatives that mask the discursive framing and modifications are unmasked, the existing difference disappears. Different metaphors and symbols begin to negotiate exchange and circulate in the communally shared repertoire of conventions, practices and institutions of society ("Towards a Poetics of Culture" 158).

Critical and Theoretical Assumptions of the Study

The critical and liberal spirit of the enlightenment made the negotiation of local and global perspectives possible. In this study, I will first survey the historical past of the point of view of the foreign observer. It is an important fact that the foreign observer did not participate in the society he observed; nevertheless, looking at one's own society from a distant perspective had a great potential to negotiate the global and local perspectives. It will be argued in the present study that the oriental observer of the letters and the local observer in 18th century periodicals developed in negotiation and coincided to a certain extent. In addition, the critical and negotiating perspective in the letters anticipated the inquisitive spirit of the Oriental tales which in turn paved the way for the recognition of the diversity of the Oriental Ottoman world. Such an attitude indicates an inquisitive and scholarly interest in ancient and contemporary Oriental civilizations. Apart from pseudo-oriental letters and Oriental tales, I think female Oriental travel-writings should also be given a distinct place in 18th century English literature because contemporary women writers challenged the male predecessors and claimed to present a better understanding of the Oriental world. This claim will also be investigated in the present study.

It is presumed that the critical and inquisitive perspective of the Enlightenment developed a more liberal and universal outlook in English literature than in any other period. This critical orientalism transformed the image of the Ottoman Orient. The idea that the Ottomans were a threat to or enemy of the European civilization was replaced with the idea that the Ottoman Orient was similar to and, at the same time, different from Europe in cultural, historical and political aspects.

The investigation of the representation of the Ottoman Orient in 18th century English literature is restricted in this study to pseudo-oriental letters, Oriental tales and female travel writings. The argument is restricted to the ideas of negotiation and dialogy, terms thought to be illuminating to discuss the critical aspects of this topic. While limiting the scope of the book to pseudo-oriental letters, oriental tales and travel literature, many references to other materials and information which are not relevant have been excluded. I focus on the critical and inquisitive aspects of the 18th century perspective; therefore, this study may inevitably neglect what is irrelevant to the argument. For instance, historical criticism is not used to deal with each political, economic, social and cultural subject separately. Only the subjects which are related to the argument are emphasized.

Interactions Between the Ottomans and English Society in the Pseudo-Oriental Letters and the Introduction of the Foreign Observer to 18th Century England

This chapter deals with the representation of the Ottoman Orient in pseudo-oriental letters. It is commonly held that pseudo-oriental letters used an Oriental mask to comment on contemporary European society and manners; Eastern contexts, proverbs, customs and culture were thought to be supplementary to the central theme. Therefore, the representation of the Ottoman Orient in the letters was taken as mostly illustrative (Conant 157-61). We can find more than illustration in the letters in terms of the representation of the Ottoman Orient. I will survey in this chapter the historical process which can disclose the interaction between Europe and the Orient, and unravel the consistent spirit which reinforced the negotiation between East and West. This moving spirit disguised itself within the liberating critical perspective of the foreign body in the letters which re-presents Eastern and Western world as an experimental human space. I will trace the historical antecedents of the oriental observer and discuss Jean Paulo Marana's *Turkish Spy* (1684) and C. de S. Baron Montesquieu's *Persian Letters* (1621). The critical perspectives in the *Turkish Spy* and the *Persian Letters* blended the positive and negative aspects of the two worlds and amalgamated the familiar and unfamiliar, ridiculous and serious facets of Eastern and Western cultures. The use of Oriental narrators worked as a metaphor for the intellectual and cultural transformation of Eastern and Western perceptions of each other. This transformation created a critical narrative tradition where Eastern and Western values had contact, clashed, and found a way to get rid of religious prejudice. Using Bakhtin's terminology, it can be said that the critical view of the two continents interanimated each other by disclosing the serious and absurd aspects of the two cultures. For instance, the Oriental narrator Rica established a correlation between European and Oriental intolerance in the *Persian Letters*. When the negotiating perspective is taken into consideration, relations between the Orient and Occident can be seen to have been transformed into a more accessible and familiar context which motivated a critical, inquisitive and cosmopolitan view.

The Representation of the Ottoman Orient in the Pseudo-oriental Letters and the Development of the Foreign Observer

The idea of an un-interrupted, consistent orientalizing tendency has been extensively excavated in Said's *Orientalism* and Homi Bhaba's post-colonial criticism. However, the Ottoman orient has not been taken into account in their study, though the Middle Eastern Orient was part of the Ottoman Empire until almost the end of the 19th century. The interaction between the Ottoman Empire and Europe has certainly been more than a continuation of un-interrupted narrative tradition. We cannot trace the five long centuries of European and Ottoman interaction in this study to justify our argument. However, a focus on 18th century English literary texts can lead to claim that the Ottoman Orient occupied a significant position in 18th century English literature. There are three different narrative forms which specifically deal with the Ottoman Orient, namely, pseudo-oriental letters, oriental tales, and oriental travelogues. Considering that these three forms all deal with the Ottoman Orient, there should be resemblances and continuity between such diversely constructed works and the cultural context which motivated them. Such texts were written in France and England, in French and English cultural contexts, in the French and English languages, and were read by French and English readers. But they cultivated Oriental and European cultures with a critical spirit. Once the literary representation of the Ottoman Orient in 18th century pseudo-oriental letters, Oriental tales and Oriental travelogues is situated in a dialogic interpretive context, it is possible to explore and discover the significance of this critical spirit. The persistent critical spirit of the letters did not only anticipate the popularity and formal-structure of the Oriental tales and travelogues but also influenced the 18th century perception of the world. Thus, an extensive and elaborate study of the pseudo-oriental-letters is necessary to see the development of the critical perspective.

Pseudo-oriental letters became popular with the publication of *Letters Written by A Turkish Spy* (1684). The *Turkish Spy* has an interesting and extraordinary history. The work was first written in Italian by Jean Paulo Marana who was originally from Genoa but fled to Paris as a political refugee after taking part in the conspiracy against Spanish hegemony in Genoa. Marana's migration to Paris and the publication of the *Turkish Spy* overlap. The editor implies in the preface to the work that he found the documents of "Arabic Letters" after he moved his lodging to Paris. It was difficult for the editor to find someone to translate the letters in a proper discourse which would appeal to the contemporary European readerships. But he found someone and had the letters translated into French. He understood that they had been written by a Turkish spy, Mahmut, who resided between 1637 and 1688 in Paris, to inform the Ottoman Divan about the condition of French and European society. The editor published the letters in a certain order. He decided to publish the first thirty letters in the first volume. Having seen the popularity of the letters, the editor published the remaining seventy-two letters in the second and third editions.

The *Turkish Spy* became very popular in France, Italy, Holland and England. The Dutch edition was published between 1684 and 1686. It was translated into English and appeared in England between 1691 and 1694. The *Turkish Spy* made more than twenty-two editions from 1687 to 1734 in England. Extensive numbers of letters were added and the number of the volumes of the *Turkish Spy* rose to seven[1]. The seven volumes of the *Spy* were not French or Italian in origin. Writers like William Bradshaw, Robert Midgley and Sir Roger Manley claimed the honor of its authorship (McBurney 915). Therefore, it is argued that the last seven volumes of the *Spy* may not have

---

[1] The *Turkish Spy* has eight volumes in total.

been written by Marana. As Robin Howells states, "the notion of a single author may itself be misleading" (155).

There are different arguments about the authorship of the letters in the *Turkish Spy*. The first one is that the letters were written by an ambiguous Italian writer and Marana claimed the authorship. This claim still remains unresolved. The second claim is based on Marana's statement at the preface that the letters were originally written by a real Turkish spy and Marana had them translated into Italian. The third claim is that the 102 letters in the earlier volumes were written by Marana and the rest of the letters were written anonymously by different authors. It is commonly believed that Marana created Mahmut to avoid the censor, to create a sense of reality and a particular form of wit and that the true aim was to invite the readers to go beyond the surface meaning of the letters. In my argument, I will not deal with the problem of authorship and the secret aim of the writer. I will first trace the historical background of the foreignness of the narrative character and his role as the observer, reporter, and critic of contemporary society. Secondly, I will discuss the direct and indirect literary achievement and the influence of the narrative voice on 18th century English literature. Then, I will deal with the significance and consistency of the narrative-voice as the forerunner of a more liberal form of representing the Ottoman Orient in 18th century oriental tales and oriental travelogues. I am going to use in my argument Arthur J. Weitzman's selected edition of 1970, published by Temple University.

Paolo Giovanni Marana's *Letters Writ by a Turkish Spy* (1694) made pseudo-oriental letter writing and foreign-mask a popular literary achievement. The Oriental machinery in the *Turkish Spy* made the discussion of contemporary 18th century issues, such as the neoclassical consensus which refutes religious orthodoxy, the desire to find natural principles for every man, and to make a peaceful trade across the world, more popular and easier: "The spirit of Enlightenment has been more fully realized in Marana's *Turkish Spy* than in the writings of Bayle and Locke" (Weitzman vii). The foreign mask and the critical voice of the oriental observer became a new popular voice of common sense in 18th century culture. Secondly, the *Spy* cultivated oriental documents with a more liberal and critical spirit and anticipated free interplay of interaction between the Orient and Europe in the Oriental tales and Oriental travelogues. The Enlightenment attacks on religious prejudice, the end of the long period of Ottoman progress in Europe, and extensive travel and missionary documents which introduced the diversity of the Oriental world to European readers, contributed to the narrative context of the *Turkish Spy*. 18th century writers had a sufficient stock of knowledge and of materials to write oriental letters. Marana made use of this stock to create an Oriental observer to compare and contrast the beliefs, morals, customs and manners of Oriental and European countries. What Marana revealed was not distant and imaginary Oriental countries. It was Europe itself visited, observed and criticized by a distant and intelligent observer. It is implied in the preface that the distant oriental observer has more objective views about the customs of and corruptions in the contemporary society than the natives of Europe. Here, two terms become significant: "observation" and "criticism". "Observation" relates itself to the development of the public voice in the periodicals. "Criticism" refers to the interpretation of the contemporary European society from a critical and intellectual distance. Giovanni Paolo Marana's *The Letters Writ by a Turkish Spy* (1684) documented Oriental knowledge with the liberal spirit and inspired 18th century writers to create a more critical point of view to discuss contemporary issues.

Although the pseudo-oriental letter writing and foreign mask became popular with the *Turkish Spy*, the genre achieved great popularity with the publication of Montesquieu's *Persian Letters* in French language in 1717. Yet neither Marana nor Montesquieu was the first to use the oriental mask though they were the first to write pseudo-oriental letters. Roosbroeck in the *Persian Letters before Montesquieu* (1972) traces the historical background of the foreign mask in French literature. He argues that the mask was first used in the fourteenth century in Honore Bonet's satirical poem *Apparicion Maistre Jehan de Meun*. The title of the poem is explained by its general structure. In a dream, Jean de Meun appears to the author. He reproaches him bitterly for not protesting against the evils that are destroying both France and Christianity. The assumed oriental observer travels in Europe. The poet supposes that a Saracen is traveling through the Christian states as a spy, and he is sending his impressions of the Christian Western world to his Mohammedan overlord (Roosbroeck 23). The Saracen travels in Christian lands as a spy. He carefully maintains the distance between himself and the native people which provides him with light and freedom to criticize the evils and admire the virtues of people. He mocks the Pope's ambition, despises religious controversies, and condemns the luxury of the nobility. The Saracen spy thinks that such corruptions can make it easier for the Saracens to conquer the Christian territories. The foreign observer also witnesses that France is worn out by its own armies and the exaggerated expenses of the administration (24-5).

Roosbroeck thinks that Ibn Tofail's the *Original Man* (published in the 16th century in Spain) can be considered as an earlier piece of prose that utilized a similar narrative-device to criticize society. Hay ben Yaqzhan, the main character of the *Original Man*, was a man born out of wedlock and lived a primitive life in a deserted island until he became twenty-one years of age. Then, a traveller came to the island and took Yaqzhan with him to teach him the truth. They together travelled around the world as foreigners. They represented in their own ways natural free-minds confronted with a degenerate civilization (Roosbroeck 28). Baltasar Gracian, a Spanish writer, rewrote Tofail's story of Hay ben Yaqzhan in the 17th century in *El Criticon* (1650). Baltasar's Andrenio is a primitive man who embarks on a journey of self-discovery. The ridiculousness and follies of men perplex him during this journey among human beings. Critilo, his master and friend, explains to him the absurdities and countless evils of mankind. They compare and contrast different societies, customs and manners. In the end, they discover that

> virtue is hunted, vice applauded, truth mute, falsehood has three tongues, the wise men have no books and the ignorant have whole collections. The books are without a doctor and the doctor is without books. The discretion of the poor man is nonsense, and the nonsense of the powerful one is applauded. Those who should give life, kill. The young men wither and the old grow young. (qtd. in Roosbroeck 30)

Critilo and his master use the foreign mask to criticize the customs and manners of each society they visit. Through the foreign mask they are able to criticize the follies and correct the mistakes of people. The foreign masks in the *Apparicion Maistre Jehan de Meun, Original Man,* and in the *El Criticon* "represented the critical intellect confronted with the diversity of human life, with social stupidities and ineradicable animality, – and in the ironical laughter of both, there sounds an undertone of hidden bitterness" (Roosbroeck 32). *Apparicion Maistre Jehan de Meun* was written in verse; *Original Man* was the first prose work to use the foreign mask and it was written by the Arabic writer Ibn Tofail. *El Criticon* was a copy of Tofail's work. The invention and appropriation of the foreign mask indicate intertextual and intercontinental influences.

Ferrante Pallavicino became the first writer to reconcile the foreign mask with pseudo-oriental letters. He used them neither in poetry nor in story. Pallavicino used pseudo-oriental letters and foreign masks in his pamphlets *Il Corriere Svalligiato* (1643). They were written as pamphlets to discuss the corruption and follies of the Church under Pope Urban VIII. Pallavicino uses an Armenian as the foreign observer in the pamphlet. The Armenian visits Rome and is perplexed with the condition of the church under the rule of the Pope. In the letters the Armenian foreign observer expresses "bitterness about the luxurious life of the Cardinals, of the tyranny masquerading as Christian zeal, of intriguing ambition hidden under the cloak of Christian humility, of slanderous insinuations passed off as pure-minded charity" (qtd. in Roosbroeck 35). The foreign visitor's attack is restricted to the papal court only; he does not survey the whole Western society and its institutions. Thus, the scope and influence of Pallavicino's pamphlets have remained very limited.

With the *Turkish Spy* Paulo Giovanni Marana became a popular writer and achieved fame as a precursor-author who reconciled pseudo-oriental letters and foreign observer. He brought together in one genre the "all-important" crossing of the "foreign observer" device and "the critical mind of the Enlightenment". Marana was born in Genoa in 1642. His Genoese background is significant. Genoa had established an early colony in the Galata district of Constantinople at the beginning of the 15th century. After the fall of Constantinople, the Genoese settlement in Galata was not interrupted. The

Genoese merchants had privileges in the Ottoman open seas and became allies with the Ottomans against Spain and Venice. Alliance and active interactions between the Ottoman Empire and Genoa continued until the invasion of Genoa by France in 1805 (Özkan 8-10). Although Marana did not during his life-time visit the Ottoman Empire, as a Genoese he must have had a great deal of information about the Ottomans due to his occupation. He was a journalist in Italy before he moved to France. McBurney also argues that the bulk of Oriental knowledge in the *Turkish Spy* indicates that Marana must have been engaged in reading about the Ottoman culture; McBurney says that Marana probably ripened "the idea of having a Turk visit Paris and write his observation" out of his readings (925). In addition, Marana's own experiences and adventures as a political agent of Count Rafaello must have contributed to the framing of the *Spy*. Due to his participation and role in the rebellion, he was imprisoned in Paris for spying[2] (Weitzman vii). Mahmut's letter in Book I Volume VI refers to the prison experience in the *Turkish Spy*. He dreams of Cardinal Mazarin in his dream while he is in prison:

> I dream of nothing but racks, wheels, saws, gibbets and such like instruments of human cruelty. Or that I am in some dark dungeon, condemned to more insufferable tortures by order of the state with Cardinal Mazarin sitting by me like a Spanish inquisitor and in the most tyrannical manner threatening me with pains to which the damned themselves are wholly strangers if I will not confess what I am and reveal the secret which I am entrusted. (*Turkish Spy* 140)

Mahmut was arrested by the guardians of the Cardinal. He was suspected of spying and was sent to Cardinal Mazarin who carefully questioned him about his country, religion, business and political matters. The Cardinal

---

[2] Marana before the age of thirty endured a four-year imprisonment because he was accused of either being involved in or at least failing to expose Count Rafaello Della Torre's plot to give the Duke of Savoy control of Savona. After the imprisonment he left Genoa for Spain and received patronage to write about the Della Torre conspiracy but could not complete it due to the war against France. He took refuge in Monaco and with royal patronage wrote the political history of Louis XIV. The initial segment of the *Turkish Spy* was the first project of this history (McBurney 925-26).

sent him to the Bastille[3] where he stayed for "six moons imprisonment" (*Turkish Spy* 69). According to Roosbroeck, the lonely and unsociable Turkish spy of this letter is "after all, a transparent symbol for a Genoese exile of Marana. In the complaints of Mahmut's isolation and melancholy we may observe a complaint about Marana's own suffering from mal-adaptation to his French surroundings and his imprisonment in Palermo"[4] (46).

Marana must have been very successful in transforming his oriental readings and personal experiences into literary narrative in the *Turkish Spy*. He creates a foreign spy to write pseudo-oriental letters. His choice of a Turkish spy who visits Paris also helped Marana to escape from the political censure which he faced several times in Italy and France (Weitzman ix). The majority of the letters in the *Turkish Spy* are about contemporary issues and the so-called Turkish origin of the letters is used as machinery to smuggle the truth under the guise of the oriental foreign mask which was a device to make readers feel that the letters were really written by a Turk[5]. This is highlighted at the preface to the first edition. After introducing him as a Turk, Mahmut begins his first letter with a reference to his mission in Paris as a spy of the Ottoman Divan on the French military, social and political activities (*Turkish Spy* 1). Then, he goes on writing about his arrival and his first impressions of Paris. For instance, he writes about Paris in Letter VIII of Book I:

> We must not expect here in Paris the great tranquillity which is at Constantinople. The town is so full of coaches, of horses and wagons, that the noise surpasses their imaginations. Thou will certainly find it strange that men who are in Health […] should cause themselves to be driven in an engine with four wheels. The more moderate French, which do not approve this luxury, say, that, in the time of Henry III,

---

[3] Like Mahmut, Marana had been a captive in Palermo for four years, four months. Mahmut states that during his imprisonment he studied Plutarch, Livy and Tacitus and was beaten for reading Seneca. There is a contingency between Mahmut and Marana's prison experiences. Mahmut was beaten for reading Seneca; Marana translated Seneca's works during his own imprisonment (McBurney 929).
[4] Marana was twice imprisoned; once he was imprisoned in Italy due to his support in a rebellion against Spanish authority in Italy. He escaped from Italy and fled to France where he was also imprisoned due to his revolutionary political thought.
[5] Weitzman discuses the historical process concerning the authorship of the *Turkish Spy* in the introduction to the letters. He also refers to texts which deal with the same topics.

there were but three coaches in Paris whereof two were the King's. But the number is so great that they are not to be counted. I can tell thee no more of the Genius of the French. [...] There is in all their actions a spirit very delicate and Activity like that of fire. It seems none but they knew the short durations of man's life. They do everything with so much haste as if they had but one day to live. If they go on foot, they run: if they ride they fly; and if they speak, they eat up half their word. They love new innovations passionately [...] they love money, which they look upon as the first matter, and second cause of all things. (4)

Mahmut informs the Divan about the general condition of the Parisians. He engages himself in ordinary events and common human relations in Paris. He noted that the French nobles prefer coaches whereas common people ride horses. The Parisians have a delicate and quick spirit along with their love for innovations.

Mahmut also compares the present Paris to its past. He carefully distinguishes Constantinople from Paris and writes that one must not expect here in Paris "the great tranquillity" which is at Constantinople. The tranquillity of Constantinople is first implied in this letter. The present character of Constantinople reflects the general attitude of Mahmut towards the Ottoman Orient. He leaves the Ottoman world many times in "tranquillity" in the rest of the letters. Descriptions of Paris and of contemporary French society are fascinating, realistic and attractive. The present letter implies that Mahmut will concern himself more with European manners and customs than with the Ottoman world. He admits this in the first letter: "I observed all the motions [...] as I was ordered" (*Turkish Spy* 1). During his residence in Paris, Mahmut goes on investigating and reporting the most remarkable transactions in Europe, several secrets and the intrigues that he observes against the Divan in Constantinople. Sometimes he forgets that he is in Paris and behaves according to oriental habits. For instance, when he meets someone he knows, he is apt to forget that he has a hat on and instead of taking off his hat according to the French manner, he lays his hand on his breast and bows; or if he addresses a man of quality he kisses the cloak as the custom is in the East. He often uses Oriental proverbs when he forgets that he is in Paris. He is suspected, questioned and even imprisoned; but since he is careful enough not to leave any evidence that may unmask his identity and secret mission in Paris, he is released (*Turkish Spy* 68).

Mahmut's point of view is remote. He goes from place to place. He visits taverns, coffeehouses, churches and courts, and observes groups of people in different social settings. He writes on all sorts of subjects as long as he finds them interesting and trivial. He speaks of new things as a foreigner to whom things appear different from the way they do to the natives of the country. Mahmut's situation is comparable to the role of a priest as described in letter 5, volume IV. In this letter he writes about how ancient Greeks discovered the taste of roasted meat:

> The historians say that the first inhabitants of the earth, far above two thousand years, lived together on the vegetable products, of which they offered the first fruits to God –it being esteemed an inexpiable wickedness to shed the blood of any animal, though it were in sacrifice, much more to eat their flesh. To this end they relate the first slaughter of a bull to have been made in Athens. [...] In process of time a certain priest, in the midst of his bloody sacrifice, taking up a piece of the broiled flesh which had fallen from the altar to the ground, and burning his fingers therewith, suddenly clapped them to his mouth to mitigate the pain. But when he had once tasted the sweetness of the fat, he not only longed for more of it, but gave a piece to his assistant, and he to others, who, all pleased with the new found dainties, fell to eating flesh greedily, hence this species of gluttony was taught to other mortals[6]. (qtd. in Conant 161-62)

The Priest is the prime agent and the central figure of the ritual in the anecdote. He changes the long-existing beliefs and habits of human beings with the discovery, though coincidental, he makes. In the story, by means of the priest the whole Greek civilization is transformed from being a vegetable eating to a flesh-eating community. The priest, as the leader of the ceremony, burnt his finger and suffered the pain. But he was the one who could introduce the discovery. The role of the priest in this anecdote seems insignificant but the discovery emerges as crucial. Yet, it is obvious that the sweetness of the fat could not be discovered without the agent. The presence of the priest and the coincidence together led to the discovery. The priest was also given a prime role in the introduction of the "new found sweetness of the fat". The pleasing dainties were taught to other mortals by the priest. Likewise, Mahmut assumes the role of the ancient Greek Priest in the letters to introduce the delightful and absurd aspects of life in France. Mahmut lives in the midst of Parisians; he participates in the community, observes people in the "midst" of their life, "tastes the sweetness" and bitterness of human experience. Since he is an outsider in Paris, he transmits such experiences as new discoveries through letters to his correspondents. Yet, in the entire observation and discovery Mahmut does not assume any active role. Like the priest, he introduces new things about unknown people and societies to his correspondents. His curiosity and discoveries are more important than his existence.

Mahmut is very curious about the French world, manners and customs. He desires more and more to learn about this world. He writes and presents to his correspondents in Constantinople his discovery and observations. He also criticizes the corruptions in contemporary French society, and denounces the political and moral condition of people. Certain letters satirize the follies of society, academicians, churches and institutions. He admits that the more he learns about Parisians and about the town the more he realizes that Paris is in a "thriving condition" (*Turkish Spy* 79) but is a "hospital of fools" (*Turkish Spy* 26). Sometimes, Parisians are ridiculed through the levity of their discourse and actions (*Turkish Spy* 133). For example, Mahmut considers it as a corruption that Parisians believe it is women in the brothels that "restrain libidinous youth from falling into greater enormities". He learns from the French community that the Pope himself "tolerates an infinite number of them in Rome," which makes "prostitution a memorable custom" (*Turkish Spy* 79). Mahmut also ridicules the nobility. He regards dueling as

---

[6] This anecdote is taken from Conant's *The Oriental Tales in England in the Eighteenth Century* (1965). It was taken by Conant from the *Turkish Spy* but it does not exist in Weitzman's edition.

"foolish" and finds it strange that "[t]he greatest affairs as well as the smallest are therein decided by the sword" (*Turkish Spy* 40). Follies and corruptions are sometimes caricatured and sometimes ridiculed, but always observed with similar critical remoteness. Although Mahmut considers certain customs as foolish, he nevertheless finds European foolishness beneficial. He thinks that wars between Christian princes help the Ottoman Empire in different ways. He says:

> I cannot but call these Christians fools, who suffer such customs among them and yet adore a Messiah who is a God of Peace, and they call us barbarians, when they are the only people that teach us and all other nations the art of single combats, which is the most pernicious custom that can be introduced amongst men, who cut one another's throats oftentimes on slight occasion and become prodigals of that treasure with which the Immortal has intrusted them. (*Turkish Spy* 44)

Conflicts and fights between Christian princes make it easier for the Ottomans to take dominions in Europe. Mahmut suggests to the Ottoman court that they should attack Europe while the European princes are engaged in war against one another.

Mahmut observes the corruptions of the church and thinks that French ecclesiasts are responsible for follies and corruptions. He observes that the high priests exploit the poor prelates and other ecclesiastics. They are invested with empty titles and among them poverty becomes as remarkable as to become a proverb. He learnt that it is common in the mouths of the Romans to say "the Pope's mule fares better than the bishop of Orvieto" (*Turkish Spy* 111). There is hardly one priest in ten who does not keep two or three harlots. They masquerade and revel about the streets with a company of whores in the time of carnivals (*Turkish Spy* 153). They are "the most glozing hypocrites in the world, mere devils in the city and abounding in wicked thoughts and practices" (*Turkish Spy* 154). There are some men amongst the ecclesiastics who "raise a dust in the eyes of those that give heed to them, play fast and loose with human reason as it serves a turn" (*Turkish Spy* 205). They divert people from the way of God. They leave men "in the labyrinth of errors" (206). Mahmut argues that the Europeans consider cruelty as noble. They are ignorant of morality and justice, due to their pride. And they do not actually believe in the Day of Judgment (*Turkish Spy* 113). The court of France is a "perfect theatre of fraud, dissimulation, envy, malice and a thousand vices, which there act their various parts under the habit and disguises of seeming virtues" (*Turkish Spy* 115). The daily life, customs, institutions, religion and court in France are re-presented to the readers of the century by Mahmut from a curious and critical perspective in the *Letters Writ by a Turkish Spy*. He enjoys observing and discovering new things and denouncing the follies and corruptions of the contemporary society.

Mahmut's journey and experience become an opportunity for him not only to realize the follies of French society, but also in this way to get to know certain aspects of his oriental identity which he would otherwise not have realized. He speaks, judges, criticizes other people. Yet his learning and his ongoing encounter with the other identities (French people) cause disturbing changes in his life and opinions. He attains a higher awareness by meeting the otherness of French society but this awareness is reciprocal. The more he learns about good and bad qualities of people the more psychological conflict he has: "Why was I made a man to endure these cruel agonies?" (*Turkish Spy* 178). In Letter XVII of Volume-VI Book IV he complains about the "surly rugged looks of proud and wealthy infidels" (*Turkish Spy* 177). He feels that he is "forced to imitate the fox" to pass undiscovered in Paris (*Turkish Spy* 140). He seems unhappy, to "have a veil upon veil" and "to have a mask with a natural face outside" (*Turkish Spy* 74). He peeps into the life of the "infidels" and freely observes their "inveterate hatred" against each other. But he feels lucky because he can easily conceal his identity: "Being of low stature, of an ill-favored countenance […] and by nature not given to talkativeness, [he] shall better conceal himself" (*Turkish Spy* 1). He learns that he is in between the habitation of danger and border of security. But he believes that he should be able to do an acceptable service to the Ottoman Empire (*Turkish Spy* 67).

The epistolary form and the oriental mask are two significant features of the *Turkish Spy*. The mask provides critical freedom and the epistolary form of the letters creates a narrative space to negotiate social, political, historical, personal, commercial subjects and the intrigues of everyday life of the French people. The co-existence of satire and entertainment must have pleased the readers. Contemporary readers of the *Spy* enjoyed thinking that the letter writer was a Turk who resided in Paris for some time to spy for the Sublime Court. The arrangement of the letters and seriousness of the tone in each letter were strategically employed to strengthen this atmosphere. Mahmut's letters to a political officer in the Ottoman Empire were about politics; to a dervish or imam the subject was religion or philosophy; to his family and friends he sent personal letters. In addition, Mahmut was an unusual character and a new protagonist in the literature of Europe with his realistic, witty, critical, free-minded point of view. Mahmut is taken by Weitzman as the first literary figure to demonstrate so much diversity:

> He is sensitive to the hypocrisy and fanaticism around him, but does not effect changes. And he can be a warm advocate of liberal sentiments. In an eloquent passage he defends the liberal education of women. 'Their senses are as quick as ours, their Reason as nervous, their judgment as mature and solid. Add but to this natural perfection, the advantages of acquired learning, what polite and charming Creatures will they prove'. These sentiments, considering that a Moslem uttered them –add to the attractiveness of his character. He reveals himself as vegetarian, the result of this benevolent impulse. Tender-hearted about the treatment of animals, he writes some letters against the prevailing notion that animals have no souls. He insinuates himself quietly, the observer of society and events rather than the initiator of them. (qtd. in Weitzman xiii)

But what makes him particularly significant in 18th century English literature is not his ability to use the Oriental mask to negotiate contemporary social issues. His importance in the literature of 18th century England lies in the "mask" which occupies an important role in the reflection and circulation of 18th century contemporary debates from a critical distance. The foreign mask was taken further and improved by contemporary writers. In English literature the foreign observer was transformed in the periodicals into a local observer who intentionally creates a critical distance to discuss social and political subject matters. This process will be discussed later in this chapter.

The Pseudo-Oriental Letters and Persian Observers in the *Persian Letters*

Marana's *Turkish Spy* made the pseudo-oriental letter-writing a popular literary engagement in 18th century English and French literature. The epistolary form and the foreign mask became a convenient machinery to discuss and criticize various political, social, economic, personal and psychological issues. The *Turkish Spy* was the earlier example of this genre but Montesquieu's *Persian Letters*[7] (1721) became more popular than the *Turkish Spy*. After the first publication of the *Persian Letters*, the excessive demands by the readers encouraged the book publishers to ask writers for the continuation of the pseudo-oriental-letters: "They [the publishers] pulled every author they met by the sleeve, and said, Sir I must beg the favor of you to write me a collection of Persian Letters" (Conant 176). The curiosity and demand of the contemporary readers for the letters motivated 18th century writers to produce such texts. Oliver Goldsmith, Richard Steel and Joseph Addison wrote pseudo-letters but Montesquieu's *Persian Letters*, among many imitations, remained as the most popular text.

Montesquieu's *Persian Letters* was written with the same spirit and in the same form as Marana's *Turkish Spy*. Like Mahmut, the Persian observers are gradually enlightened and have an identity conflict. Rica, like Mahmut, questions certain oriental values. For instance, in Letter LXXXIX Rica argues that freedom and glory are more abundant in France than in Persia. He imitates the preface to the *Turkish Spy* in the *Persian Letters*. Like the editor of the *Spy*, the editor of the *Persian Letters* claims in the preface that he discovered manuscripts of letters left by two Persian visitors[8]. But unlike the editor of the *Turkish Spy*, the editor of the *Persian Letters* claims a personal acquaintance with the Persian visitors, Usbek and Rica; and unlike Mahmut, Rica and Usbek do not conceal their Persian identities. They openly declare their Persian identity to the Parisians and walk in the streets in their native

---

[7] Persia was also considered as part of the Ottoman Orient. Rica and Usbek, the Persians in the letter, were from Ispahan, which was then occupied by the Ottoman Empire.
[8] The editor of the *Turkish Spy* claimed that he discovered the manuscripts of letters in his room after he moved to his new pension in Paris. But the editor of the *Persian Letters* admits that he knew the Persians by sight. They were his neighbors. The Persians sometimes shared letters with the editor.

Persian clothes[9]. Rica admits that it is fascinating for the French public to see him in the Persian habit. The oriental clothes locate him, in the eyes of the native people, in another order of existence. In Letter XXX Usbek says:

> when I arrived they looked at me as though I had been sent from Heaven; old men and young, women and children, they all wanted to see me. If I went out, everyone perched at the windows: If I was in the Tuileris, I experienced immediately a circle gathering around me. (*Persian Letters* 41)

The editor claims that it took time for him to omit trifling matters and alter the Asiatic phraseology in order to adapt the work to the taste of French readers. The editor, who cooperated with the Persian visitors to read and copy the letters, eliminated signs of Oriental jealousy against Europeans. In this process, he realized that the Persians were very careful observers who discerned the particulars of the manners and customs of the French nation that may have escaped the native's observation. The editor decided to publish the letters to share the foreigners' ideas about France with French people. Thus, after Usbek and Rica left France for Persia, the editor eventually had the letters translated. He thought that the publication of the letters would introduce oriental customs, mentality and exoticism to French people who would not only be instructed and delighted by the romantic and sensual intrigues of the Oriental seraglio, tyranny and despotism but would also learn about the values of good government, justice and law, the greediness of the clergy, conceit of the academy, the caprices of fashion and the moral corruptions of men and women in France through a distant critical point of view (*Persian Letters* 4-5).

There are two levels of structuring narrative points of view in the letters. As the editor admits in the preface to the work, the oriental visitors will not only introduce oriental society to the contemporary readers but they will also re-present those aspects of French society which escape the natives'

---

[9] It can be argued that Montesquieu's transformation of the Oriental spy of Marana into the Oriental observer and his use of the Persian clothes to reinforce the Oriental identity indicate that the French public recognized distinct Oriental (here Persian) customs and evaluates the Orient with respect to its cultural symbols.

point of view. The oriental mask and the variety of subjects implemented in the letters anticipate these diversities. This diversity is implied in Letter LXXXII. Rica meets a man who talks about "morality," "historical problems," "natural philosophy," "sciences," "news of the times," and even about the "streets in Ispahan" competently. Rica identifies this man as someone who is very much pleased with himself but he decides not to compete with this man: "I soon determined what part to take: I was silent, I left him to talk; and he yet decides"[10] (*Persian Letters* 177). The meeting between Rica and this strange man takes place in a street of Paris. There is a cynical criticism which masks this speech. Rica mocks the man who claims to have competence on every subject. Yet the criticism also betrays Rica's role. He writes on all subjects with confidence and competence. He locates himself in the position of the man he met in the street. Like the man who contradicted Rica upon Persia, Rica claims competence on French community. The editor implies that this exchange and interaction between the Oriental visitors and the public will show French people the contradictions in their perception of the Orient and their own community. Then, it is implied in the letters by Rica and also openly declared at the preface by the editor that the foreign observer may show the minute particulars and ridiculousness of our native habits to us better than we see them. With this aim, the role of the foreign observer in the *Persian Letters*, like Marana's *Turkish Spy*, is to re-present the contemporary society from a critical point of view to the readers' attention. In addition, the foreign mask is a strategy to avoid the censure and penalty of the French court. In order to avoid censure, Montesquieu had the first edition of the *Persian Letters* published in Holland in 1721 as an anonymous work. The choice of two oriental Persian characters also masks the critical attitude of the actual writer towards religion, customs, and politics.

Through the letters of the oriental visitors, Rica and Usbek, the contemporary public is given access to a diversity of thoughts and beliefs, to the historical conflicts between East and West, to religious convictions and superstitions. Spatial distance from the Oriental Persia provides Rica and Usbek with

---

[10] The present anecdote may also be taken as a satire on pseudo-oriental letters and the oriental mask. The man contradicts him upon Persia with French sources.

freedom to re-evaluate and question the Orient; intellectual and cultural distance from the contemporary French society enables Rica and Usbek to obtain a new perspective to criticize the absurdities and vices of Parisians. As Roosboeck states, the oriental observers present the junction of East and West "with the critical spirit of the eighteenth century [enlightenment]" (21). The present junction creates a narrative flexibility, individualization and sensibility. Bayle argues that the oriental machinery in the *Turkish Spy* and the *Persian Letters*

> gives a greater flexibility in the presentation than any other form of expression. In particular, letters could be added (and substituted if necessary) quickly, so as to enhance the work's scope and degree of contemporary relevance and spontaneity. Furthermore, this could be done right up to the month of publication, without fundamentally altering the rest of narrative. This narrative form [also] gives particular ease to Marana and Montesquieu for dating the letters according to Muslim chronology [...] [T]ake for example CXL, which refers, albeit obliquely, to the financial ruin which beset many people in the week of 21st-28th May 1720, when John Law's Compagnie des Indes collapsed in panic of speculation. This event did not occur until three or four months before Montesquieu carried his manuscripts to Paris. Only through the epistolary form could Montesquieu [and certainly Marana and others who used pseudo-letters] have integrated such a contemporaneous event with such ease. Montesquieu carried out commentary on current events –victories over Turks, The Cellamore Conspiracy, the death of Charles XII. The pseudo-letter genre again made it easy to deal with such events separately. (38-39)

According to Bayle, it became easier and safer for Marana and Montesquieu to discuss the contemporary events in pseudo-oriental letters. Contemporary events are presented in two ways; they are either presented from the critical perspective of the oriental characters or they are located in the Orient and presented as if they took place in Persia. For instance, the intrigue in the Seraglio in the *Persian Letters* and the revolution that brought about the collapse of the Harem are analogues to actual history. It is based on a wedding between a Mongolian prince and a Persian princess, which caused conflict and rebellion in the Persian court. Montesquieu writes in the *Spicilege* that a marriage between the Mongol king and beautiful Persian princess took place in the Persian court. This wedding was considered as an insult by the Persian nobles due to religious difference. The Mongolian king was an infidel according to the Persian religion. Since the Persian Princess was Muslim, the Persian religion did not allow such a union. Therefore, orthodox Persian nobles of court poisoned the king and drove out the pagans [Mongols] from their lands. The news about this catastrophe was written in France in 1719 (qtd. in Bayle 39). Montesquieu must have used this news in the *Persian Letters* to disclose the violent face of orthodox beliefs. He also implied the active role of the nobility in the government. Contemporary readers could compare this incident to the power of the Church and of French nobles over their own king.

The extension of commercial enterprise between the European and oriental countries and of long-existing historical relations changed the nature and aspects of interaction between East and West. 18th century readers could read about social and historical events which took place in Oriental countries. Political and commercial alliances of ambassadors, merchants and scholars from Europe and the Middle East mediated the political and cultural interactions between Oriental and European countries. The news about the wedding catastrophe at the Persian court was not the only incident that the Parisians read about in the news. There are other examples of this process in France. The arrival of Mehmet Riza Bey in Paris as an ambassador of the Persian Shah created anxiety and scandals. His manners, free behavior, and complete disregard for financial matters created in the Parisian society of 1721 a proper background for satirical works concerning the manners and customs of Persia. Mehmet Riza Bey became a model for contemporary writers after it was discovered that he was an impostor and had no credentials from the court of Persia (Baum 36). His scandalous behavior "filled for many years pages of the *Chronique Scandaleuse*" (Roosboeck 19). This scandal also became the subject of Letter XCI in the *Persian Letters*. The arrival of Peter the Great of Prussia in Paris in 1717 was another incident which provided an opportunity for the people of Paris "to see the legendary oriental despot in the flesh" (Roosboeck 36). News from oriental countries, the arrival and intrigues of Mehmet Riza Bey, and the visit of the Prussian despot supplied

Montesquieu with lively examples and rich materials for the *Persian Letters*. The Construction and intrigues of the Seraglio in the Letters, the presentation of Usbek as an exiled despot like Peter the Great of Prussia owed much to the contemporary context. Montesquieu carefully cultivated such events in the *Letters*. Since the contemporary readers were familiar with all these events and read about them in the newspaper, it was not difficult for Montesquieu to project his idea of a tyrannical government upon the Persian Seraglio and explain to contemporary readers what it was to be a despot. The concept of despotism was easily substantiated in the "typical conduct and fantasies of oriental characters" (Shklar 31). This playful presentation and re-figuration of the contemporary events gave Montesquieu psychological force to mask his attacks on the politics of the French king for his despot-like rule over France. Once the intertextual relation is unmasked, the *Persian Letters* illustrates "largely an unprejudiced account of the France of Regency, seething with the conflict between the tottering old order and the dawning enlightenment [...] [and] deeper criticism of all human values from the intellectualist point of view" (Roosboeck 11).

However, such re-figuration and intertextuality are not allowed to permeate the oriental atmosphere in the work. Montesquieu uses the foreign mask as a strategy to give his work oriental coloring. The Persian settings and characters, the sensuality and exoticism and the dating of the letters according to the Islamic calendar create a sense of reality. This is what Ian Watt calls "formal realism" which is the prevailing tendency of 18th century novel (Watt, 30-34). The epistolary form has three main advantages. Firstly, each letter by a different correspondent reflects the character's subjective views and saves the author from accusation and formal punishment. Secondly, the form provides the writer with flexibility to discuss social, historical, political and local issues at the same time. Lastly, the pseudo-oriental letters re-fashion and popularize sensuality and passion in the highly rational neoclassical age. Montesquieu benefits from these for his own purpose. He utilizes the epistolary form to avoid political sanction and to personify sensuality. For instance, he uses the oriental harem as a metaphor to personify human passions and sensuality which would otherwise not be brought into the view. Bayle quotes Robert Shackleton to argue how Montesquieu serves the public interest in the *Persian Letters*. According to Shackleton, "the emotional part of the *Lettres Persanes* is handled by Montesquieu in such a way that he is able, at least in the rakish society of the Orleans Regency, to make sensibility respectable" (qtd. in Bayle 42). According to Bayle, the *Persian Letters* contains the sociology of contemporary society, its modes, customs, and institutions. He argues this as follows:

> Society is seen by Montesquieu in *Lettres Persanes* as a reality [...] much in the manner of Durkheim; for Montesquieu, as for Durkheim, society exists external to individual, constraining him to act and think in certain ways. The term 'society' is meaningful to Montesquieu, as a concept it exists in his thought reified. Montesquieu, in fact, goes one step further than Durkheim; not only does society constrain the individual, it prevents him from evaluating his position in society with any degree of objectivity; the Frenchman is prevented from seeing his true position in society, his understanding of its values, norms, and institutions. [...] They are not part of the French society, they are not constrained by it and they can assess its worth objectively. The choice of two oriental visitors as a means by which the author can comment upon contemporary social processes is neither accidental nor fortuitous. Montesquieu's use of an increasingly popular literary device has the latent function of allowing him the degree of disinterestedness necessary to his art. Usbek and Rica, paradoxically alarming as it may seem, are proved capable of understanding French society, about which they had virtually no prior knowledge at all, and completely incapable of understanding their own Persian society, among which they had been brought up. (Bayle 42)

The native and foreign perspectives are compared in the *Persian Letters*. A native is blinded by subjectivity and a foreigner is skilled with discernment. In the context of the *Letters* Usbek and Rica cannot foresee the revolution in the Seraglio because they are restricted and constrained by the society they live in to the extent that they cannot discern any idea of what is happening in their native environment. It is the policy of the author in the *Letters* to show that the native citizen is blindfolded by identity, roles and responsibilities bestowed on him in society; the native context threatens and represses the spontaneity of men and subverts the natural character of the individual. There are two Persian characters that are represented as citizens of oriental Persia and individuals of a despotic political country. They are obliged to live under a political system which constrains and subverts the individual freedom of men and women. Usbek is an oriental man. He is blinded by his Persian identity, therefore, he cannot grasp his own despotism until finally he loses what he has in Persia, and Roxane betrays him. The narrative-voice integrates itself into the frame-tale to look at the French society from a distant, foreign perspective.

The readers do not only see that Usbek has to run away from such a restrictive Persian Seraglio, which subverts the identity and constrains human freedom but also see the French society and institutions from a very critical point of view half a century before the revolution. The author makes this obvious by choosing a foreign-observer to judge French society and institutions in the *Persian Letters*. Behind "the all-wise foreign observer" there is a personality that intellectually remains a stranger to his time and land (Roosboeck 13); Montesquieu, who became mentally or temporarily "a foreigner to his race and civilization; one who with a guileless lucidity could deny all its values; one who became the unprejudiced free-mind" offers an image of the Western mind in conflict with fundamental notions (Roosboeck 14). This can be observed in the treatment of different subjects. For instance, Montesquieu discusses love from a moral and philosophical perspective. According to Montesquieu, society and institutions determine the form of love between sexes. Kettler's argument concerning Montesquieu's treatment of love illuminates love between man and woman in the *Persian Letters*. He says:

> In fact it is truer to say that almost never can man find true love, for the institutions of society deprive man of the capability for love. This is a crucial point; Montesquieu tells us not only that social conditions may preclude the fruition of love but that men's perception of themselves and others is so decisively influenced by the habits they acquire in society that the very emotion of love will be denied them or be transformed into parody of that love which fulfils man. (qtd. in Bayle 46)

Institutions by means of legislations control human society and determine the limits and meaning of an individual's feeling; therefore, in the context of social relations the individual is unable to create his own form of love. He is not given freedom to decide on the nature of sexual relations. This attitude is made clear in the context of the Persian Seraglio. Montesquieu indicates through the Seraglio how institutions determine and limit the natural feeling. Love between men and women in the Seraglio is a despotic (institutional) one which denies equal role and authenticity. Women in this relation are considered as sexual objects, which is made clear in Letter II by Usbek. He writes to the black eunuch:

> You are the faithful keeper of the loveliest women in Persia. I have entrusted you with what in this world is most dear to me: you bear the keys of those fatal doors, which are opened only for me. While you watch over this precious storehouse of my affections, my heart, at rest, enjoys an absolute freedom from care [...] should the women whom you guard incline to swerve from their duty; you should destroy their hopes in the bud. (*Persian Letters* 16)

The choice of Eunuchs to discuss love between man and woman is strategic. Rica and Usbek were chosen to discuss the absurdities, vices and virtues of French society, though they were not French. Here spatial and cultural distance of the observers became significant. Eunuchs have a similar significance. They are neither men nor women. They have a certain distance to both sexes, but they are familiar with the feelings and desire of both sexes. The eunuchs are made responsible for women and watchers of the precious storehouse (harem). Men make the law at the Seraglio but eunuchs apply them. Men have feelings and attachment but eunuchs are given authority at the Seraglio to punish women if they show any "slackening of the laws of chastity" (*Persian Letters* 17). By the rules of the Seraglio, women are denied freedom and individuality. They live under men's laws in a state of dependence, their will belongs to men and this condition arouses dissensions between the sexes. They are imprisoned not to be seen by anybody. A letter from Zachi, Usbek's wife, reflects the general condition of women in the seraglio:

> We had carried our desire to please you. But you soon made those borrowed graces give way to more natural charms. You destroyed the results of our labours: we were compelled to despoil ourselves [...] [M]y triumph was the despair of my rivals [...] [Y]ou [Usbek, her husband] do not even know what it is to lose [...] [Y]our insensibility takes you further and further. (*Persian Letters* 16-7)

The rules of the Seraglio work on behalf of men. Men are given the authority to rule over it and women are denied any role and feeling. Eunuchs, who are in between, have more power and freedom than women. The Seraglio is the institutionalized empire of men where their ambitions find their utmost gratification. The eunuchs are the executers in the Seraglio. Oriental men use the "black monsters" (eunuchs) to destroy the freedom and happiness of their women. In Letter LXIII Rica discusses this issue. He writes to Usbek that he has really known about women only since arriving in Paris. What he learnt in Paris in a month about women, he could not possibly learn in thirty years if he was in the Seraglio:

> I knew nothing of women until I came here [France]; I have learnt more about them in one month of Paris, than I could have done in thirty years of a seraglio: with us character is uniform, because it is constrained: we do not see people as they are, but as they are obliged to be; in that slavery of heart and mind, it is only fear that utters a dull routine of words, very different from the language of nature which expresses itself so variously. (*Persian Letters* 68-9)

The letters about the condition of women in Persia and in Paris present two different attitudes. Persian women, irritated by eunuchs, are not given freedom and are tormented by the tyranny of Persian men. Women in the West, on the other hand, have liberty to express themselves to men. They also have sexual freedom. The condition of women in Paris prevents domination and repression. There are no mediators, like eunuchs, and there is no barrier, like the seraglio, in France. Thus, French women are given right to resist discrimination. French women have power to change the course of social events, which is observed by Rica as follows:

> The women are the prime movers of the rebellion, which divides the court, the kingdom, and every family in the land; because the document prohibits them from reading a book which all the Christians assert is of divine origin: it is indeed their Koran. The women [...] have brought over to their side all the men who are not anxious about their privilege in the matter. (*Persian Letters* 35)

Rica finds men's confidence in women more natural and civil. Men's peace of mind and happiness in Paris do not depend on the confidence they have in their wives: "The Parisians believe a husband who loves his wife and insists on keeping her to himself is a man lacking the attraction to make himself loved by another woman". Everybody in France hates a "jealous husband," and thinks that they are the "most miserable men". Husbands accept their lot with grace and the "infidelities of their wives seem as inevitable as fate" (*Persian Letters* 62). Love and relation between men and women in France are of willing compliance and not of eternal love. The concept of platonic or eternal love is ridiculous and unnatural to Parisians:

> After what I have told you of the morals and manners of this country, you will easily imagine that the French do not altogether plume themselves upon their constancy. They believe that it is as ridiculous to swear eternal love to a woman, as to insist that one will always be in the best of health, or as happy as the day is long. (*Persian Letters* 62)

In the context of the letters the women of Paris are not like the women of Persia; women in Persia lose nothing because they have nothing to lose. The Persians talk a lot about their wives whereas men in Paris talk seldom about their wives (*Persian Letters* 63). A close-reading of the *Letters* can reveal the critical and dialogic aspects in the letters. At the surface level, by contrasting the Oriental Persia to Occidental France, Montesquieu draws two different images. Montesquieu, in a sense, finds both France and Persia corrupted in different ways. For instance, the tyranny of the Persian is not very different from that of the French government. The cruelty of the eunuchs is not very much different from that of French aristocracy and law. There is also criticism of French women. Women in Persia are enslaved but they are still faithful. French women are freer but they are unfaithful. The Persian society is structured to constrain what is most natural in human character. The French society does not deny freedom and authenticity but cannot prevent corruption. Human rights and freedom are restricted in Persia. In France there are privileged classes like the church, army and high ministers, each of which has such a sovereign contempt for the other that sometimes a man is despised only because he is a lawyer. "They all resemble more or less a certain woman of the province of Erivan, who, having received some favor from one of our monarchs, wishes a thousand times [...] that the heaven would make him governor of Erivan" (*Persian Letters* 50). In Letter XXVI to Roxana Usbek illustrates this:

> How happy you are, Roxana, to be in the delightful country of Persia, and not in these poisonous regions, where shame and virtue are alike unknown. How happy, indeed! In my Seraglio you live as in the abode of innocence, inaccessible to the attacks of all mankind; you rejoice in the good fortune which makes it impossible for you to fall. (*Persian Letters* 36)

The concept of enforced chastity in the Persian Seraglio is compared to the absurd freedom of women in Paris. Persia reinforces institutionalized violence, French society mediates corruptive freedom. Persia is a "delightful country" of men; France is a "poisonous region" of women. Persia is violent, Paris is shameful. It is easier to fall in Paris; it is possible to live in good fortune in Persia. Then, there are two different images of corruptions. One is about the Persian institution (Seraglio and the law of Seraglio) which subjugates women. The other one is French society which changes women in a different way. The present dichotomy indicates that there are varying social and institutional norms and values in Eastern and Western world which cause the decline and corruptions of natural bonds between men and women. It is not marriage but love that keeps men and women together in a respectful union. If the natural bond between sexes is transformed into a formal union, love disappears. Usbek discusses this with respect to the Church's denial of the right for divorce. He says:

> Divorce, which has been permitted in the Pagan religion, was forbidden by Christianity. This change, which appears at first of such slight

importance, produced by degrees consequences so terrible, that one can hardly believe them. (*Persian Letters* 120)

Montesquieu plays with the conventional Western criticism of the Eastern family structure to attack the European family. He thinks that prohibition of divorce takes loyalty and respect out of marriage, though the intention behind this prohibition is to strengthen the bonds of marriage. The prohibition is a constitutional enforcement, thus, unnatural. In certain cases this prohibition causes disaster for the couple and for the country. When they cannot make a child, the couples are left to everlasting sorrow. This is the reason why "such a large number of marriages provide such a small number of citizens" (*Persian Letters* 121). The population of the country does not increase, thus, the power of the government decreases. Since divorce and polygamy are allowed in the East, the population and power of the government in oriental countries increase. The comparison of positive and negative aspects of laws and gender relations in France and oriental Persia illuminates the different social and political norms of different countries. The purpose must be to highlight different aspects and customs of dissimilar societies in order to reform the contemporary government and develop universal perspectives which may bring new and enlightening ideas that may contribute to the advancement of civilization.

The intimate access of the oriental visitors to French society, manners and customs is strategic. The Persian foreign observers' acquaintance with the "minute particulars" of French society in the letters aims to bring these particulars into the view of the contemporary readers from a very different perspective. This narrative-frame and allegory give the readers of the letters enough space to look at the contemporary society and institutions from a critical point of view. Baum discusses this as follows:

> Despite the fact that the largest numbers of letters deal with one country [the Persian seraglio and society], the most thoroughly documented society is that of Paris from the years 1711 to 1720. The political history of France during the nine or ten years is clearly reflected in the text of *Lettres Persanes*, with all the changes in other

social institutions, moral, economic, religious as well as political. (Baum 49)

Here, Baum considers the Persian mask as "a new venture" in order to shock people to take a critical and objective view of their situation. By means of the Persian mask Usbek "reflects" the orthodox mind and Rica reflects social objectivity. The contrasting viewpoints and arguments of Rica and Usbek bear witness to the satire and allegory of the work. Rica, the less serious of the two Persians, enhances satire and allegory, and heightens the awareness of the readers through which Montesquieu touches upon the "most sacred prejudices of French society". It is Rica who calls the Pope an idiot; makes fun of the sacred dogmas of the Catholic Church, academy and its members, and ministers (Baum 51).

The pseudo-oriental letters and foreign observer became parts of 18th century narrative politics which provided security and freedom to challenge certain political and cultural notions. They re-presented the "other" face of the Enlightenment in that radical ideals were presented; morals and manners were questioned and a desire for reform was implied. The foreign-mask and oriental machinery became instrumental to the criticism of society, to the presentation of new and radical thoughts. East and West were employed interchangeably and the binaries between different values were challenged. Just as English novels based on the fiction of travel –such as Thomas Moore's *Utopia* (1516) and Swift's *Gulliver Travels* (1726) portrayed England's internal and external social and political struggles in the displaced and imaginary locales of the land of Lilliputians, Brobdignag Giants, and Laputans, so too did 18th century imaginary French pseudo-oriental letters present internal domestic challenges. However, it is apparent that the nature of the internal struggles was determined by different forces and factors in England and France. Montesquieu in the *Lettres Persanes* employs the theme of travel to signify the desire for empire as well as to veil more urgent preoccupations with the diminishing stability and coherence of the national culture itself. Thus, not only does the literary trope of travel express French preoccupations with the land and empire, but travel as a representation of imagined territorial expansion becomes an available discursive means of registering and regulating the domestic culture's concern with internal social differences and change (Lowe 54-55). Montesquieu carefully integrates satire and allegory with the frame-story and narrative technique to bring into discussion subject matters ranging from religion and metaphysics to political and social issues. This integration gives him flexibility on the one hand to demonstrate the relativity of customs and norms and all social organizations in different climates, and on the other hand to justify his arguments. That is, the epistolary form and foreign observers provide the author of the *Persian Letters* with an effective and flexible narrative opportunity to bring social, political, colonial and metaphysical issues into discussion which would otherwise remain untouched.

Then, it can be argued that in the *Persian Letters* Montesquieu comments on French institutions and practices as a foreign observer by staging Persia as France's other. The letters describe France from an invented foreign viewpoint of Persian travellers. Rica's and Uzbek's oriental identities serve as the observing other in the letters and gives them a crucial role to create what it means to be French. The Persian characters stand as "the other" with their clothes, beliefs, language, and their attitude towards women. The exchange of the letters between different correspondents brings into foreground different arguments such as the condition of slaves, tyranny of masters and oppression of women. The eunuchs are enslaved by the master and they are commanded to exercise the master's power. Their castration is a physical sign of their enslavement and of the political tyranny. Women in the Harem and eunuchs realize that they have no power of their own. The masters' distance and detachment from the harem indicates that the ruler and the ruled do not trust one another. The Persian Harem and the relations between eunuchs, Usbek's wives and Usbek are used as a representation of the relation between people and rulers as viewed by the French writer, Montesquieu. The instrumental use of pseudo-oriental-letters and oriental foreign observers indicates that there are considerable social, political, economic and cultural interactions between the Ottomans and Europe. The Orient becomes the pretext without which the con-text would not exist.

The Negotiation of the *Turkish Spy* and the *Persian Letters* in England

Marana and Montesquieu achieved a great popularity at the beginning of the century as pseudo-oriental letter writers. Mahmut, Rica and Usbek instructed and entertained the contemporary readers from behind the mask by setting a critical comparison between the oriental and occidental customs. The oriental world behind the *letters* and *observers* remained a shadow; but the follies and corruptions of actual people were relocated into the social world again. Representation and criticism of the contemporary society from the perspective of the Oriental observers were used by contemporary English writers in a way similar to that utilized by Marana and Montesquieu. This long-lasting influence on the literature of 18th century England is explained by Conant as follows:

> The similar idea of description of England as if by foreigner was suggested [first] by Swift as a good and original one in the journal of Stella, and was utilized by many successors, but Montesquieu's *Persian Letters* is the best example. Many subsequent writers, including Charles Lamb, have been under obligations to the letters. Dufrensy's influence as well as Marana's on the development of the genre of pseudo-letters is clearly visible. [...] [T]he chief difference between French and English writers is the clever way in which the English writers enrich the brief, generalized, mildly satirical comments of [...] French [writers'] concrete sketches of street life. (163)

This narrative strategy gave rise to a large number of imitations and applications in England during the 18th century. The first collection of pseudo-letters written in imitation of Montesquieu and his predecessors was the *Persian Letters* of Lord Lyttelton (1735), which directly influenced Goldsmith's *Citizen of the World*. Like the *Turkish Spy* and the *Persian Letters*, in Goldsmith's and Lyttelton's prefatory notes the letters are claimed to have been written by an oriental visitor, in these cases to England, and translated from the original language. Lyttelton creates two Persian characters, Selim and Mirza. They exchange letters during Selim's journey in England. There are stock phrases and expressions that give the letters an oriental coloring like "the resplendent palace of the empire," a garden "adorned with the finest flowers in the East," "jasmine of Persia, tulip of Candahar" etc. (Conant

180). Conant argues that Lyttelton had the same aims with Marana and Montesquieu. Like Marana and Montesquieu

> [h]e uses the pseudo-letter merely as a means to a definite satirical end. He comments freely upon the unhappy victims of injustice in debtor's prison; upon the courts of law, parliament, the evils of parties, 'the abuse of the thing called eloquence,' the growth and value of constitutions, the faults of the educational system, the soporific effects of fashionable opera, and the immorality of society. He depicts various types of characters. There is a set of people in this country, whose activity is more useless than the idleness of monks. They are like those troublesome dreams which often agitate and perplex our sleep, but have no impression behind them when we wake. I have sent thee an epitaph made by one of those men of business, who ended his life [...] not long, ago; [...] 'Here lies [...] who lived three-score and ten years in a continual hurry. He had the honor of sitting in six parliaments, of being chairman in twenty-five comities, and of making three hundred and fifty speeches'. (Conant 181)

Character-sketches like these and the integration of social satire are a means to an end. They teach the proper manners by setting a comparison between oriental Persia and occidental England. They also delight the 18th century readers through the depiction of intrigues and sensuality. For instance, the meeting of Selim and an old lady in Letter III indicates the popularity and parody of the genre; Selim is invited by an English Lady. He imagines that the lady who invited him is a fair young English woman. Instead, he meets a very dirty, little old woman who is curious to know all the mysteries of the Koran in order to perfect her theology. He is disappointed and replies to her with his lack of knowledge about the Koran. Instead of the Koran, he suggests telling a Persian tale which makes her so angry as to retire to her closet (Conant 185).

Goldsmith's *Citizen of the World* is considered as a leading text in this genre in 18th century England. The book was published in 1762 under the title *Citizen of the World or Letters from a Chinese Philosopher Residing in London to his Friend in the East*. The title is related to the French writer Fougeret de Monbron's work *Le Citoyen du Monde* published in 1752. It is obvious that Goldsmith imitates Marana's *Turkish Spy* and Montesquieu's *Persian Letters*.

Like the *Persian Letters* and the *Turkish Spy*, *The Citizen of the World* consists of letters written by an oriental observer who describes and criticizes the manners, customs, and absurdities of English society. However, Goldsmith is more satirical than Marana and Montesquieu. Conant states this as follow:

> The ideals of feminine beauty are all the more acutely and quizzically described by praising absolutely opposite Chinese standards. The justice of literary patronage in China is contrasted with the bribery and falsity of the English customs. Absurd English fashions in dress and household decoration, cruelty to animals, and inconsistent funeral rites are freely criticized. Goldsmith employs effectively the indirect method of the satirist [like Marana and Montesquieu] to condemn one custom by praising its opposite. (193)

Letter XXV about "The Rise and Decline of the Kingdom of Lao" in the *Citizen of the World* apparently confirms Goldsmith's copying of Montesquieu's the "History of the Troglodytes" in the *Persian Letters*. "It is a moralistic tale about political evils modeled on Montesquieu's History of the Troglodytes" (Conant 193). In the story of the Troglodytes, Montesquieu refutes the idea of natural government. In the story each citizen behaves according to his natural appetite in complete selfishness which leads to the destruction of the whole nation. The fictional Chinese observer Lien Chi Altangi introduces himself to the English public of the 18th century exactly in the same way as Uzbek in the *Persian Letters* and Mahmut in the *Turkish Spy* introduced them to French society. Uzbek writes to his wives, eunuchs, and friends in Persia, Mahmut writes mostly to his friend Osman, Lien Chi Altangi writes to his friend Fum-Hoam.

Conant argues that Chi Altangi, like Mahmut, sometimes forgets to keep the mask before his face and makes comments that give the Chinese character more of a native view than the views of the foreign observer. Conant writes: "The picture of London streets where 'a great lazy puddle moves muddily along' is more vivid by contrast to Lie Chi's memory of the golden streets of Nankin" (191-92). Goldsmith admits that he creates an intimacy between himself as an English citizen and his character Lie Chin as a Chinese character by using Eastern metaphors and allusions together with English "colloquial ease" (193). Goldsmith's confession quoted by Conant in the *Oriental Tales in England in the Eighteen Century* indicates how the intimacy between the English author behind the mask and the Chinese character who observes 18th century England works in *The Citizen of the World*. Goldsmith says:

> I have written many a sheet of Eastern tale myself [...] and I defy the severest critic to say but that I have stuck close to the true manner. I have compared a lady's chin to the snow upon the mountains Bomek; a soldier's sword to the clouds that obscure the face of heaven. If riches are mentioned, I compare them to the flocks that graze the verdant Tefflis; if poverty, to the mists that veil the mount of Baku. I have used thee and thou upon all occasions, I have described the fallen stars, and splitting mountains, not forgetting the little Houris who make a pretty figure in every description. (qtd. in Conant 222)

Although he writes numbers of oriental tales, he is conscious of his English identity; he knows that he is not Chinese, nor Persian. He is a poet, a man of literature and a true Christian in religion. Like his contemporaries Goldsmith's purpose is to teach and to delight the public. To this purpose he creates in the *Citizen of the World* the foreign observer of the contemporary English society from China. The Chinese character Lien Chi is converted into a central narrative medium to create a sense of humor, to express the attitude of polite society by setting a comparison between China and England. The narrative creates a sense of sympathy towards all men, Chinese and English, far and near. It helps Goldsmith to display the changing mind of the Enlightenment towards other people in the world.

Stuart Sherman states that the major change in the relations between the public and writers in the 18th century was a new form of social transaction. This change shaped and bridged the distance between the social and individual world. Sherman admits that this relation is represented by "the mix of the solitary and the social" (2076). The foreign observer, as a solitary figure, visits the social world of contemporary people and conveys his social experiences. He writes about contemporary social issues and reflects the developing spirit of expansion, trade and imperialism. The paradox of seeing one's own familiar social world from the perspective of the solitary oriental observer fascinates the readers with new ideas, learning, countries and customs. Joseph Addison and Richard Steele used pseudo-letters in their periodicals. Steel used letters by four Indian kings, whose sojourn awoke wide popular interest in London, to "instruct the public of natural justice" in 1710: May 13, issue of *The Spectator*. In his story, the Indian Kings fall ill and they are taken care of during their illness by a kind-hearted upholsterer. In return they ennoble this generous man of lowly birth for acting according to the dictates of natural justice. In *The Spectator* of 1712: November 25, Steele also published a sharply critical pseudo-letter from the so-called Emperor of China to suggest the forming of a treaty of alliance between oriental and Roman churches by arranging a marriage between a noble lady of Europe and the Chinese monarch, which, metaphorically, indicates that the oriental countries engaged the imagination of 18th century public to such an extent as to suggest a political and cultural coalition between Eastern and Western monarchs. The Indians and Chinese characters introduced their culture to the English public but the readers already knew that the man behind the mask was a true Englishman. This became apparent in the letters when the narrator ridiculed the politics of the Whigs, haughtiness of English women, banality of common people and the narrow-mindedness to appreciate the manners and values of other people.

The oriental observer first displayed himself as a spy in the *Turkish Spy*. The mission of Marana's spy was to inform the Ottoman court about European society. The role of the spy as an observer of contemporary society influenced 18th century literary narratives in two ways; firstly, writers like Marana, Montesquieu, Lyttelton, and Goldsmith produced pseudo-oriental letters in which they discussed social, political and philosophical issues. Secondly, the characterization of the oriental observer influenced an extraordinary number of "spy" books. Gatien de Courtilz's *French Spy* appeared in 1700; the *York Spy* of Captain Bland was published in 1713; there were some other imitations like the *German Spy* (1738) and the *Jewish Spy* (1739). One of the testimonials to the popularity of the *Turkish Spy,* and merely a derivative of it, was Ned Ward's monthly issued periodical *London Spy*, which borrowed *Spy* from Marana's title. Ward shifted the attention from the oriental origin of the observer into a witty, urban one (Weitzman xvi). But, like Mahmut and Rica, Ward's spy is an outsider who observes the follies and corruptions in contemporary London from a critical distance. Mahmut, Rica and the other oriental observers mainly deal with serious political and social issues whereas Ward's spy exposes the underworld of "pimps, pickpockets, hirelings, drunkards, gamblers and gunman" to the readers (Roosbroeck 52).

The shift from the explorations of serious political, social and philosophical matters into trivial daily issues was a ground-breaking exploration, which indicates the other face of life and literary narrative in the early modern period. 18th century writers like Montesquieu and Goldsmith used pseudo-oriental letters to discuss serious subjects; Ward, on the other hand, transformed the observer into a narrative space of periodicals to discuss less political issues. Money, manners, appetites and the taste of common people came to be perceived as interesting and worthy by the spy to be observed and to be written about. He visited the seamier side of life in order to entertain and instruct the readers. The fictional social setting in Ward's periodical was London Bridge, the Coffeehouse and Bedlam, where the spy could meet and portray almost every seamy side of society. The spy is objective because he is a stranger to Londoners as an urban character. Like Mahmut and Rica, the spy uses detachment to look at contemporary London from a critical point of view. He does not present political retrospect or historical discussion. Roosbroeck says: "The Spy's vivid and scurrilous sketches of the lower layers of London life formed a more effective critic of this pool of hell than any intellectual theorizing" (Roosbroeck 53).

The London spy popularized the observation and re-production of the trivial daily experiences of town people. The naïve urban-observer of the *London Spy* is replaced by the inquisitive Indian in Tom Brown's *Amusements Serious and Comical* (1700). Like Marana and Montesquieu, Brown chooses an Indian identity for his character but he relies on Ward for the description of London life. Brown's character in the *Amusement Serious and Comical* visits various towns and draws pictures of different lives and people in London and sends the letters to his friends. Roosbroeck states that Brown adds a second part to his adaptation in which the author and his hero wander around the upper and underworld of London:

> In so doing, he found occasion to write over sixty pages of sarcastic comment on European civilization viewed through the Indian's eye. The very variety of several halting places where the Indian reveals his wisdom reminds one strongly of the mobility of Montesquieu's *Persian Letters*. The innocent simplicity and natural wit of this intellectually gifted 'savage' finds full occasion for censure in successive visits to a London tavern, St. Paul's Cathedral, a Presbyterian meeting house, a Quaker's church, a bawdy house, Westminster Abbey, the coffee houses, etc. (Roosbroeck 54)

Ned Ward and Thomas Brown transformed the "foreign observer" into another space of narrative. The oriental observers who dealt with serious issues in the pseudo-oriental letters became local observers who dealt with public life and events. The local observers of the periodicals gave practical knowledge to the urban-visitors on how to survive in the conflicting world of London. The local observers were witty, innocent but privileged with natural wisdom. They did not concern themselves with serious political and philosophical issues. Such observers transmitted the comical and serious lives of common people with critical and bawdy language. If we consider Mahmut as an ideal Renaissance man of the 18th century, we can consider Brown's and Wards' heroes in the monthly periodicals as the first periodical personae, who discussed the daily issues as detached observers.

There was a paradigm shift in characterization and in subject matter with Ward's replacement of the foreign observer with the urban one. This transformation was taken further to create a "periodical personae" by Joseph Addison and Richard Steele. Mahmut and Ward's spy had a significant influence on the characterization of Mr. Spectator and Mr. Bickerstaff. It may be too much to claim that *The Spectator* and *The Tatler* were written after the form and structure of the *Turkish Spy* and *London Spy,* but "there was an obvious need for some kind of journalistic commentary on the society of Queen Anne, and Mahmut and London spy prepared the taste for genial satire and ironic mode of *The Tatler* and later *The Spectator*" (Weitzman xviii).

As Sherman stated the solitary and the social were re-united. The homeless Mahmut and London spy were transformed by Addison and Steele into social characters. "Mr. Bickerstaff" and "Mr. Spectator" are "critical observers" like Ned's London spy, and Mahmut but they are social figures who take great pleasure from being among people.

Although the origins of the periodical persona have been sought in writers' desire to conceal their identity and to expand controversial arguments, pseudo-oriental letters and the foreign voice are the predecessors of the periodical persona in certain aspects. Steele argues that "Isac Bickerstaff" first appears in the pamphlets prepared by Jonathan Swift to demolish John Partridge's positive and vague predictions. Once he prophesizes that Partridge will die of a fever at eleven o'clock on the night of May 29. It is reported that Partridge was indeed dead but four hours ahead of the scheduled time. This prophecy and event afterward become a public issue. Partridge himself enlarges the debate by denying the report of his death, which becomes an occasion for much merriment and "Isac Bickerstaff" becomes a public figure and a hero. In the present argument Isaac Bickerstaff is presented as "a mask ready for Steele to gain a large number of audiences who had any taste for wit" (qtd. in Bond 8). But Mr. Bickerstaff is no more than a continuation and cultivation of the London spy in the sense that he is urban, witty and, like the London spy, a public-spirited, political person of strong zeal and weak intellect. They both offer "something worthy whereby well-effected members of commonwealth may be instructed" (9). Like Ward's spy, in the earlier paper the objects of Bickerstaff's "reforming satire had for the most part been types found about the Town as he knew it in his own particular London" (Bond 90). The spy and Mr. Bickerstaff go to similar public places, like coffee-houses, to observe and comment on the manners and customs. They include moral and social issues, and criticize the conventional practices they encounter around the public places. The varied topical scope of these miscellaneous essays makes, first the *London Spy*, then *The Tatler* appeal more to a diverse reading public.

If "Mr. Bickerstaff" resembles Ned Ward's London spy, "Mr. Spectator" is very much like Marana's Mahmut. He is a curious, intelligent, and cunning character and has a very different character from native French people. This extraordinariness also becomes a part of Addison's "Mr. Spectator," as a curious and cunning person. He claims that he is more a spectator of mankind than one of the species (*The Spectator*, 1711: 1 March). It is reported by his mother that "he had thrown away his 'Rattle' before he was two months old" (2). Like Mahmut, he traveled everywhere to search for wisdom. He was a very sullen youth who upon the death of his father left the university to travel into foreign countries with a Fellow of great deal of learning:

> An insatiable Thirst after Knowledge carried me into all the countries of Europe, in which there was any thing new or strange to be seen; nay to such a degree was my curiosity raised, that having read the controversies of some great men concerning the antiquities of Egypt, I made a voyage to grand Cairo, on purpose to take measure of a Pyramid; and as soon as I had set myself right in that Particular, returned to my native country with great satisfaction. (1711: March 1, No. 1)

His visit to grand Cairo is frequently referred to: it was there, for example, that he picked up several oriental manuscripts, including the vision of Mirza (*The Spectator*: No. 159), and it was there that he met the good-natured "Mussulman," who promised him so many favours (No. 604). He also travelled in France where he delighted in listening to the songs of the people; at Rome he saw the Pope officiate at St. Peter's (Bond 31). When Mr. Spectator returned, he decided to be a spectator of public places and share his experience with people before he died: "I have passed my latter years in this city, where I am frequently seen in most public Places" (qtd. in Bond 32). But he does no longer feel like a common Londoner. As he admits, he is not one of the species. He is a speculative statesman, soldier, merchant and artesian. He feels like a citizen of the world. Mr. Spectator best identifies himself with the Royal Exchange. In *The Spectator* 1711: May, No. 69, Mr. Spectator discusses his visit to the Royal Exchange where he takes secret pleasure in observing the assembly of countrymen and foreigners. People come from all over the world to the Royal Exchange to consult upon the private business of mankind. This diversity makes Royal Exchange "a kind of emporium for the whole earth". People of different origin and background come together to "negotiate affairs, conclude treaties, and maintain good correspondence between [...] wealthy societies of men that are divided from one another by seas and oceans, or [people who] live on different extremities of a continent". Mr. Spectator, very much pleased with this diversity, goes on to describe The Royal Exchange:

> [...] to hear disputes adjusted between an inhabitant of Japan and an alderman of London, [...] to see a subject of the Great Mogul entering into a league with one of Czar Muscovy. I am infinitely delighted in mixing with these several ministers of commerce, as they are distinguished by their different walks and different languages. Sometimes I am jostled among a body of Armenians: sometimes I am lost in a crowd of Jews, and sometimes make one in a group of Dutchmen. I am a Dane, Swede, or Frenchman at different times, or rather myself like the old philosopher, who upon being asked what country man he was, replied that he was a citizen of the world. (*The Spectator* 1711: May, No. 69)

Like Mahmut, Mr. Spectator of the Royal Exchange locates himself, into a position of observer. The experience of observation provides him with wisdom to see the vices and virtues of mankind. Mr. Spectator admits that he learns better about the "different walks and languages" by observing a Japanese merchant, a subject of the Great Mogul and a Muscovite interacting with Armenians, Danes, Frenchmen, Swedes, and Dutchmen. The concept of cosmopolitanism comes into play and Mr. Spectator becomes a citizen of the world in the Royal Exchange which is transformed into a little cosmos of the diversity and a liberal social sphere. Here "Mr. Spectator" realizes that "Mahometans" (merchants from the Middle East) dress in the British manner. But he also discovers that a single dress of a woman of quality is a product of a hundred climates. The fruits of one country are improved by the products of the other; the infusion of one plant is sweetened by the pith of the other. In the Royal Exchange, dissemination and mutual intercourse of mankind, cultures and products from the different regions of the world are a blessing for Mr. Spectator since the present conditions knit mankind together in a mutual intercourse of good offices and indicate how several parts of the world might be dependent upon one another and can be united by their common and different interests. He enjoys, as a citizen of the world, a "variety of solid and substantial entertainment". He becomes "a lover of mankind whose heart overflows with pleasure at the sight of prosperous and happy multitude" (4). But this privilege is peculiar to Mr. Spectator as an "observer" of mankind. His role as "a spectator of mankind" makes him competent in social affairs (5). He acts in all parts of life as a looker-on, and is resolved to preserve this character. Addison and Steele mediated satiric observers in *The Spectator* and *The Tatler*. Both Mr. Bickerstaff and Mr. Spectator are somewhat eccentric, self-mocking characters with a satiric, witty and urbane tone (Mackie 4).

Were the Ottomans Represented in Pseudo-oriental Letters?

The question must be "what is the relation of all this argument to the representation of the Ottoman Orient in 18th century English literature?" There are various answers to this question. We can use several different approaches to give possible answers. Firstly, we can answer the question by comparing the representation of the Ottomans to the traditional images of Turks in English texts such as poetic verse, drama and sermons. If we use this approach, we can make use of Edward Said's argument in *Orientalism* to show how Turks were re-presented as undeveloped, cruel, terrible, and primitive to reinforce Christian values and European civilization. It would not be difficult to find enough evidence in the works of different periods to justify the argument. As Aksan stated, there were forty seven plays written on Oriental society between 1579 and 1642. Thirty one of them are concerned with the Ottomans. Thomas Kyd's *Soliman and Perseda* (1588) and Marlowe's *Tamburlaine the Great* are among the most popular ones which sought and exemplified the strong reasons to confirm that the Ottomans were a threat and Turks were the enemy of the European civilization (Aksan 5). There are also indirect references to Turks in Elizabethan plays such as those by Shakespeare. In *Henry V*, for instance, the king warns his brothers against treachery with reference to the "despotic" Turkish court (qtd. in Aksan 75). It is possible to choose quotations from the pseudo-oriental letters to re-present a similar argument.

However, the main concern of my argument here is 18th century English literature; the above mentioned texts and Said's *Orientalism* cannot indicate the critical shift that took place in 18th century English literature.

Secondly, we can also find an answer in travel literature to the question stated at the beginning. The possible context of this answer to the question would survey the historical process that led up to the characterization of the oriental observer. Renaissance travel literature anticipates this critical perspective in the sense that European travellers in the seventeenth century went to the Ottoman Empire to observe the condition of Turks in their own context. The Ottoman order, sobriety, and military discipline attracted many Renaissance men. They were eager to travel and to learn about the military power of the Ottoman Empire. The Renaissance travellers who visited the Ottoman Orient praised the Ottomans for their integrity, the efficiency of their officials, the justice and ability to rule over the diverse ethnic and religious communities while they criticized European courts due to political conflicts and moral corruptions. For instance, Bartholomew Georgiewitz was a Hungarian adventurer who spent thirteen years as a slave in Turkey and achieved a considerable fame in Europe with the publication of his experiences in the seventeenth century (Almond 466). There are some other writers who achieved similar fame with the publications of their experiences in the Ottoman Empire. Busbecq, a Venetian ambassador, used the Ottoman state-order and Turkish moderation to attack the corruptions in the European courts. Some eminent Protestant writers and politicians went further to give the Ottomans a supernatural status as a future ally against the Roman Catholic Church; Queen Elizabeth I, Böhme, Kuhlmann and Comenius considered the Ottomans as a possible ally against Catholics. Comenius envisaged that Turks were fundamental for bringing down the House of Habsburg for which they would be rewarded with the light of the Gospel (Almond 466).

We can compare the pseudo-oriental letters to the Renaissance idea of Turks because it can be further argued that a similarly strategic and critical spirit re-appeared in the age of Enlightenment to re-evaluate contemporary European society. The Renaissance adventurer-observer was replaced by the critical Oriental observer in the 18th century to back up the enlightenment ideals. For instance, 18th century writers like Locke, Hume, and Rousseau used the Ottomans as anecdotal memory to reinforce intellectual views because it was safer and easier for them to criticize European governments on the basis of the Ottoman supremacy or corruptions. Ekhtiar states:

> In fact seventeenth and eighteenth-century Orientalism in all its forms was one of the major streams of the intellectual Enlightenment, though few literary historians acknowledged this. In a sense European Oriental Fiction can be viewed as [...] part of the European Orientalist vision. [...] Oriental societies were portrayed as hotbeds of cruelty, corruption, despotism, and perversion. (7)

"Turks and Persians were used as a vehicle for social comment and criticism of West" (Braude and Lewis 3). Rousseau argued that Turks were no better and no worse than Christians (4). As we have argued, Hume thought that a comparative study on the representation of different cultures provided evidence to convey the uniformity of human nature and similarity of human experience in all ages and places. Human nature was the same in all times and places and history informed us of nothing new and particular. The comparative study of different societies was a means to display the constant and universal principles of human nature (Ekhtiar 18). However, this perspective is as restrictive as the first and second ones we have referred to above in terms of expressing the aspects of the Ottomans illuminated through the pseudo-oriental letters.

The question of the representation of the Ottoman Orient in the pseudo-oriental letters, and the use of the Oriental observers can be transferred into a different context to maintain the priority of the moving spirit which inspired pseudo-oriental letters and the emergence of the observer. Bakhtin's idea of cultural interanimation is illuminating in that he states that the representation of the world changes from genre to genre and from era to era as literature develops (Bakhtin 849). There appears a "cultural interanimation" and an ideological interaction in the combination of a national monolithic world with the alien world. The native world comes near the alien world by means of dialogy between foreign and local characters (850-51). Bakhtin states that the Menippean satire was used by Xenophon, the ancient

Greek writer, in order to discuss the contemporary relations between the ancient Greeks and the Oriental world. According to Bakhtin, the epic genre dealt with the glory and depiction of the past; therefore, Xenophon could not express the immediate relations between the Greeks and Orientals through epic. Xenophon replaced the monolithic and historical discourse of the epic with the ironic discourse of the Menippean satire to renovate Greek political structure in a spirit close to Oriental autocracy. This transformation made it possible for Xenophon to unmask the Greek ideology and to create a flexible space in Greek discourse to integrate Eastern socio-political norms. This reconciliation of the Eastern and Greek contemporary world within the Menippean satire anticipated the power of novelistic discourse to "interanimate" different cultures (Bakhtin 28-9). The outside, alien, even hostile perspective maintained an essential frame to view and interpret the intersections, similarities and differences of the Greek and Oriental worlds.

Evincing Bakhtin's argument, it can be argued that pseudo-oriental letter-writing manifested a particular form of cultural interanimation between the Ottoman Orient and Europe. It was obvious that the relation between the Ottomans and Europe was not as antagonistic after the end of the 17th century as it was before. Once the physical threat of the Ottomans was withdrawn after the siege of Vienna, the hostility against the Ottomans was transformed in Europe into a more liberal ground which broke away from the traditional image of the Ottoman Orient in English literature. In particular, the pseudo-oriental letters, like the Menippean satire as handled by Bakhtin, transformed the dominant image of the Ottoman Empire as the enemy of European civilization. The Oriental visitors were transformed and accommodated into European space to enable counterarguments. The transformation laid the groundwork of the critical attitude and situated the narrative into a more interactive space. The Ottoman and the Oriental customs, previously seen as vulgar and threatening, became an essential correlating factor and powerful evidence in the verification or rejection of certain political, social and philosophical European propositions. The oriental gesture of the observer and the desire to alienate oneself from one's own community, to imagine Europe and European community through an Oriental point of view became an illuminating gesture which decentered the dominant concepts. This gesture took one's national identity as something detachable; as something one can step out of and view with foreign eyes. This transformation communicated a desire to negotiate with and acknowledge the usefulness of the Oriental perspective and culture. It was a movement from traditional stereotypes to the critical distance, which suggested a primacy of interactive, mutual and justifiable human experience.

The transformation of the perspective owed much to the historical interaction between the two continental cultures and to the familiarity of the European history with the Orient. It might have been more difficult or almost impossible for the 18th century writers to situate an all-knowing, critical oriental perspective without distorting familiar history. That is, the materials, style and perspective of the earlier travel writers and scholars were assimilated within the critical, contemporary discourse of the letters. We mean by the contemporariness of the letters commensurability of different social and political arguments within the context of 18th century literature. It is this aspect of the pseudo-oriental letters which reconciled Europe and the Ottoman Orient.

A critical foreign-oriental observer is given a central role in 18th century pseudo-oriental letters. This is important in terms of celebrating the facets of the cultural interanimation between the Ottomans and Europe. The foreign Oriental observer re-locates the Ottomans into a contemporary European social context; he renders and deciphers the familiar and unfamiliar aspects of the Oriental and European worlds by means of transformation. He represents the contemporary European thought from the perspective of the Oriental observer. This relocation and transformation helped the abstract ideas to become intelligible and recognizable. For instance, the Orient is used to experiment with and elevate the concept of "noble savage" in the story of the Troglodytes. The abstract utopian notion of Rousseau is tested, re-evaluated and made more intelligible by transforming it into the concrete Oriental space. Usbek, the oriental observer, introduces the history of the Troglodytes and he discusses natural justice, honesty, freedom and respect in the context of the Troglodytes society. The Troglodytes are a small tribe in

Arabia. It is known that they kill the rulers to get rid of governmental restrictions, and then they create a specific notion of justice and equality: "the natural savage instinct" determines "what is right and wrong" among the Troglodytes (*Persian Letters* 23). However, this change does not bring peace and justice. People become more selfish and begin thinking that "Why should I kill myself with works for those in whom I have no interest? [...] It is no concern of mine though all the other Troglodytes live in misery" (*Persian Letters* 23). In the agricultural lands the highlanders die of hunger during the season of draught; the lowlanders die of famine due to the rainy season. People do not pay attention to others' misery. In the end, there is no food and no government to rule, thus no security. People begin to kill one another: "a man killed his neighbor" because his neighbor had an affair with his wife. It becomes common in this tribe to kill one another for a piece of land: "the Troglodytes perished in their sins and became victims of their own righteousness" (*Persian Letters* 26). General welfare and security are forgotten. Usbek argues that men are not born with "natural wisdom" but with "natural wickedness" (28). When they are left without law and government, each person will be after his own interest and will kill the other. The story implies a necessity for the existence of a government which has to be stronger than any individual to prevent each citizen from attacking the other because liberty cannot exist without law, and property cannot be secured without a government. Natural instincts do not provide justice but cause natural wickedness. It is emphasized in the story that the noble instinct, which does not produce a better public morality for the Oriental Troglodytes, will not produce a better public morality for the Europeans. It is significant that the idea of "noble savage" is transformed into an experimental space as an Oriental practice. The theory and practice are brought together. The abstract notion is transformed into concrete experience; Europe is a spirit and Orient is a body in the story. Thus, Eastern and Western contexts are used interchangeably to provide further counterargument rather than to identify the East as the other or as anecdotal memory to support the theme[11]. Here the Oriental body mediates dialogy, and gives depth and intensity to the characters.

---

[11] During the Middle Ages the human body had a negative association. It was repressed and

Pseudo-oriental letters, in this respect, have a particular discourse which recognizes, allows, transforms and integrates the Oriental world. 18th century writers like Montesquieu use an eastern narrator to discuss the essential European philosophical notion. The Western idea of the "noble savage" expresses itself through an Eastern voice in the Oriental space.

The Oriental observers of the letters are introduced convincingly; Mahmut, Rica, and Usbek are introduced with a strong attachment to and feeling about the Orient. They have correspondents in Constantinople and Persia. They express deep sorrow due to the necessary displacement from the Orient. They have love for and loyalty to the East. Mahmut complains about his suffering in the letter IV of Book III to his friend. He says: "My resolution is to follow thee by suffering myself to be gradually abdicated from [my own] world and from my own will" (*Turkish Spy* 194). In the letter dated "fifteenth moon of Saphar 1711" (*Safer* in the Islamic calendar), Usbek writes to his friend Zachi in Ispahan: "Whatever part of the world I may be, you [are my] faithful friend" (*Persian Letters* 15). The Oriental context and background are made real by the use of the Oriental observers. Letters are also dated according to the Oriental Ottoman custom, and Oriental names are used to indicate months. There are references to actual Ottoman characters in the letters. Mahmut sends letters to the Grand Vizier "Achmet Cuprioglu" who was an eminent Ottoman Vizier known as Köprülü Ahmet Pasha; "Mufti," "Kaimacham" and "Dervish" are all Ottoman titles for different state offices. This attitude convinced the readers of the oriental voice in the letters.

Persistency of the Oriental voice and transformation of characters also indicate that the Orient is identifiable and familiar to the Europeans. The more the Persian observer participates in society, the more he realizes that he exists in every shop, on every mantelpiece: "one thing struck me: I found my portraits everywhere –in all the shops, on every mantelpiece. They were

---

represented as the undesirable part of existence. The soul was given a superior position to represent human existence. After the Renaissance and in the age of Enlightenment the body was given an essential position. Likewise, the Ottoman Orient, which was suppressed in the Middle Ages, was given an essential position in the 18th century.

fearful if they should not see enough of me" (*Persian Letters* 41). Weight states:

> In many respects, the Orient was known, identifiable, and coherent to Europeans, as evidenced by the rapid popularity and production of Oriental tales following the *Turkish Spy*: it should therefore come as no surprise that many authors could create the same Orient. (42)

However, Weight also admits that Europe's view of the Orient is "a view full of contradictions and ambivalence" (43). The ambivalence is an obvious aspect of the cultural interanimation which discloses itself through oriental observers in the pseudo-oriental letters. There is an on-going fluctuation between the Eastern and Western identity. This fluctuation becomes apparent in the characters' decisions to change their names, and dresses in the European manner. Mahmut hides his identity behind French manners. He says:

> I shall better conceal myself. Instead of my name, Mahmut the Arabian, I have taken on me that of Titus the Moldavian; and with a little cassock of black serge, which is the habit I have chosen, I make two figures, being at heart what I ought to be, but outwardly and in appearance what I never intend. (*Turkish Spy* 1)

Rica was more conservative at the beginning. He took great pleasure from the Parisian interest in his Persian manners. When he first introduced himself to the Parisian community, people were fascinated by his oriental dress and manners: "The inhabitants of Paris carry their curiosity almost to excess. When I arrived they looked at me as though I had been sent from Heaven [...] they all wanted to see me" (*Persian Letters* 83). They thought that he really looked Persian. But he soon decided to "free" himself "from all foreign adornments" to be exactly assessed (83). Mark Currie states that we are more likely to sympathize and be fascinated with people when we have a lot of information about their inner lives, motivations and fears; or we like people when they do not let us judge them incorrectly (Currie 19). Parisians were not unfamiliar with Persian qualities but Rica did not want to allow them to judge him by his appearance. Therefore, eventually he decided to change his Persian clothes to French ones, which created ambivalence. This transformation was taken as a challenge to the already established quintessential Oriental identity by Parisians. Whenever he introduced himself to a Frenchman or to a Parisian in his French manner, they asked him: "how can one be Persian?" (*Persian Letters* 20). The geographical connection to Persia and his physiognomic Persian identity did not convince the Parisian of his origin. This change of dress made his identity ambivalent: "The experiment" surprised Parisians. He began to hear a "buzz" around him: "Oh! Oh! Is he Persian? What a Most extraordinary thing! How can one be Persian?" (*Persian Letters* 21). The early response "he really looks Persian" was replaced by "how can one be Persian?" When cultural symbols, since they were replaceable, disappeared, it became impossible for Parisians to recognize the otherness of Orientals. The earlier assumption that he could be truly assessed by Parisians was challenged and his clothes became a signifier for and referent to the ambivalent identity; he was born as Persian and identified as Parisian. This transformation can also be considered as an attack on artificial marks which distinguish one's identity.

There is a continual fluctuation between Oriental and European cultures in the letters. While the oriental machinery dislocates the observers from the European social context, the articulate European voice relocates them in Europe. On the one hand, the characterization of the oriental observers illuminates the persistent Oriental machinery; on the other hand, the Oriental machinery cannot subjugate the rational and articulate European voice. This dichotomy is consistent throughout the works. The prefaces to the *Turkish Spy* and the *Persian Letters* reveal this fluctuation with respect to the contingency and correlation between the style of the letters and the author: "throughout the letters there is a quaintness of expression, peculiar to the Arabians" (qtd. in Weight 49). The letters are full of Oriental expressions, veracity and proverbs. But it is emphasized in the prefaces to the letters that the articulateness of the observers and the strength of thought have truly European traces. Mahmut and Rica retained oriental commodities, jewelleries and rarities but they also dressed in a Western manner (51). The European calendar was used together with the Oriental one. Oriental characters expressed themselves in the context of contradictions. This unstable and indeterminate position of the characters and the complexity of the style decentered the dominance of one world over the other.

The co-existence of the Oriental and European elements challenges radical distinctions between the East and West. The Oriental observers remain in the borderline of the two cultures and use this in-betweenness to direct the attention of the readers to the absurdities and contradictions of the two worlds. This in-betweenness becomes a kind of free zone to criticize ridiculous and irrational beliefs and customs and long held notions: "What are the conquests of Alexander compared with those of Zenghis Khan?" (*Persian Letters* 82). Mahmut writes: "European thinks that Turks do not travel in Europe. But Turks conformed to the fashions and manner of people in Europe and became the masters of Christians" (*Turkish Spy* 165). Mahmut considers the act of duelling as ridiculous. He states that duelling, which seems honorable to French, is ridiculous to Orientals. Mahmut criticizes the European notion of Oriental barbarism with reference to the act of duelling. He writes: "They call us Barbarians, when they are not the only people to teach us, and all other nations, the art of single combat, which is the most pernicious custom that can be introduced among men, who cut one another's throats oftentimes on slight occasions" (*Turkish Spy* 43).

According to Mahmut, duelling and wars between Christian kings are worse than Oriental barbarism and more primitive than any Oriental custom. Here there is a paradigm shift. The long-held European notion of superiority over the Orient is undermined and Oriental barbarism is tolerated by the observer. Mahmut also argues that the absolutism of Sultans is quintessential in terms of holding the diversities and mediating justice. In the lack of quick justice and absolute rule, the Empire would burst into several "signories". According to Mahmut, the same absolutism would be unnatural for European governments because kings in Europe do not rule over diversities. In the argument Mahmut questions and undermines the long-held parameters of the European superiority. He finds certain things, which render the paradigms of the civilization absurd. For instance, he argues that literacy and freedom of print culture, which seemed to provide a more civilized position to the Europeans, leads to corruption. He says: "the lowest sorts of people who can read have the privilege to become as knowing as their superiors" (*Turkish Spy* 87). But European scholars use books to abuse and to deliver lies. Polygamy and adultery are similarly used to compare and contrast the moral corruptions. Mahmut says:

> Although they 'accuse Mussulmans for having more wives than one [...] they lie with every wench that comes to their way. Adultery passes them as good breeding, and fornication is esteemed as innocent an action as eating and drinking'. (*Turkish Spy* 87)

Usbek, like Mahmut, also compares the French King Louis XIV to Ottoman Sultans in terms of the absolute power of the king. He writes that when Louis XIV was sixteen years old, nobles and courtiers related the Sultan's absolute power to him. He was so impressed by the Sultan's power that Louis XIV was often heard to say that of all existing governments, that of the Turks pleased him most (*Persian Letters* 46). Rica, the Persian observer, finds it ridiculous that the French king sells titles. He is "a great magician" and makes people think what he wishes; "so great is the power and influence he has over their minds" that although the king has "no mines of gold like his neighbor, the king of Spain; he is much wealthier than that prince; because his riches are drawn from a more inexhaustible source, the vanity of his subjects". This policy "fortified towns" and "equipped the troops" (*Persian Letters* 34-6).

There is also sarcasm in certain letters. The Oriental observers find Eastern and Western cultures similarly corrupted and absurd in certain aspects. Rica asks: "Must we be for ever blind to our own folly; is it blessing to find consolation in the absurdities of others?" (*Persian Letters* 59). "Like us also, they have appointed fasts, and times of mortification, by which they hope to move the divine clemency [...] They recognize, as we do, their own unworthiness, and the need they have for an intercessor with God" (*Persian Letters* 44). When a misfortune happens, the French public reads Seneca, but the Asians take infusion which cheers the heart and cleans the memory from its sufferings (*Persian Letters* 42). Women in France are not like women in the Orient. It seems as inevitable as fate for men in France to accept the infidelities of their wives (*Persian Letters* 62). While prohibition of divorce makes marriage intolerable for Christian countries, polygamy provides Mohammedans with an opportunity to increase their population and power (*Persian Letters* 122). Rica thinks that the caprices of the military class and lack of consent between the subject and the ruler has made the Ottomans weaker. As a result, towns have been dismantled, cities deserted, the country desolated, agriculture and commerce neglected; during this time the Europeans flourished in commerce and industry (*Persian Letters* 30-1).

When looked at from this perspective, it is useless to claim superiority for one culture over the other one. It is written in the *Persian Letters* that one's imagination inevitably adapts itself to the customs of the country. The regulations, justice, and equity are not better observed in Turkey, in Persia, or in the dominions of the Mogul, than in the Republics of Holland, and of Venice, and even in England: "it does not appear that fewer crimes are committed there, and that men, intimidated by the greatness of punishments, are more obedient to the laws" (*Persian Letters* 87). The absolute power of Sultans and the injustice of European princes produce similar monstrosities, and the princes of East and West bribe African chiefs and kings to depopulate their country and to sell their subjects as slaves. They similarly think of peopling large countries by means of colonies; they do not believe in divine justice, which destroys the destroyers (*Persian Letters* 125). Rica emphasizes that false notions and prejudice blind us to see our follies. For instance, he thinks that the intolerance of Christians, Jews, Muslims and ancient Egyptians creates hostility: "Proselytism, with its intolerance, its affliction of the consciences of the others, its wars and inquisitions, is an epidemic disease which the Jews caught from Egyptians, and which passed from them to the Christians and Mohammedans" (*Persian Letters* 90). According to Rica, it is not the multiplicity of religions which causes wars but it is the intolerant spirit of proselytism. The letters condemn the prejudice and challenge long-held false beliefs; Eastern and Western cultures are presented as interwoven, and inconsistent beliefs are parodied. It is emphasized that religion is intended for man's happiness and prejudice is a cultural invention, thus artificial. It is suggested that the long-held European prejudice and false notions of the Oriental world should be questioned. The critical distance unraveled, betrayed and reconciled the historical conflict and dialogy, harmony and dissonance between Europe and the Orient. Thus, the Eastern and Western idea of supremacy was eliminated and cultures were presented as equally corrupted and valuable in different ways.

The critical and interanimating spirit of the letters is dialogic in the sense that letters are presented as a cooperative work between the Persian visitors and the European editor. The editor emphasizes the trustworthiness and reliability of the Persians. Although the editor and the Persians are men of two different worlds, they do not conceal any secret from each other. The oriental visitors interpret society from a critical distance; the editor translates their comments into the European language by copying, refining the prejudice and re-appropriating the letters to the European taste. This cooperation becomes a metaphor for self-respect and virtue; they are sincere, men of moral dignity and learning. Readers are also made to rely on this cooperation. This argument also sheds light on the dialogic nature of the letters; the letters are a product of co-operation and interaction between Oriental and European points of view. The critical Oriental perspective and articulate European voice collide in the context of the letters to judge the two worlds. Richard argues that the "indigenous eye [native citizen] knows everything" but "sees nothing, whereas foreign eye sees everything, but knows nothing" (*Persian Letters* 222). If we can see with foreign and indigenous eyes, we can maintain an imperial view and render culture as a spectacle. The editor states that Persian observers were "communicative" and they comprehended European (French) customs and manner in a year. The editor also admits that he learnt from the observers the Persian customs. Thus, the letters brought together indigenous and foreign eyes, and this collaboration provided a particular critical vision and "intimate spectacle" to view culture in its "minutest particulars".

I esteem it crucial for the purpose of the study to emphasize the fact that the use of a critical oriental narrator provided an opportunity to look at the world in the 18th century from a more critical, global, sophisticated and universal perspective. This influence becomes apparent when we trace the transformation of the foreign observer into the local observer. That is, the critical relation between contemporary society and foreign observers was influential on the development of the periodical persona. We have already discussed how Ward, Addison and Steel transformed the foreign observer into the local observer. They also located the local observer in the coffeehouses and made it a critical voice of their periodicals. Habermas states that the modern public-sphere and public ideas developed in the coffee-houses[12]: "the physical site of the public sphere [...] was the coffee-houses in which aristocratic society and bourgeois intellectuals could meet on equal terms" (qtd. in Richetti 52). Keeping in mind the role of the coffeehouses for the circulation of the public ideas and the transformation of the foreign observer into the local observer to discuss contemporary public issues, it can be stated that the Orient was a consistent interanimating spirit in 18th century English literature. The critical spirit of the Oriental observer and coffeehouses comingled[13]. The observer inspired the development of public voice and the coffeehouses the development of a liberal public space. Characterizations of the oriental observers, periodical observers and the coffeehouses were similar in the sense that they had a critical role in 18th century England.

The critical distance of the Oriental observer is imminent and strategic; the critical distance of the periodical persona (observer) is intentional. The oriental observer is a foreign body in the European world. The Periodical persona is a local character. The union of the oriental observer and the distant local observer liberated the English perception of the world and led to the development of a cosmopolitan perspective. This new perception is celebrated by Mr. Spectator in the visit to the Royal Exchange. Mr. Spectator visits the Royal Exchange and he feels that he is a citizen of the world (*The Spectator*, 1710: No: 69). He symbolically moves in between the multi-layered world of the Exchange and the monolithic world of London with a cosmopoli-

---

[12] Usbek parodies coffee-houses as follows: "coffee is very much used in Paris; there are a great many public houses where it may be had. In some of these they meet to gossip, in others to play at chess. There is one where the coffee is prepared in such a way that it makes those who drink it witty: at least there is not a single soul who on quitting the house does not believe himself four times wittier than when he entered it" (Letter XXXVI).

[13] As I have discussed in the first chapter, coffeehouses were first introduced to English society by an Ottoman citizen.

tan spirit: "This grand scene [...] give[s] him a spectacle to observe infinite variety of solid and substantial entertainments" (3). Mr. Spectator re-introduces himself in the Royal Exchange as a great "lover of mankind" and takes great pleasure from the sight of the happy multitude. He says:

> Nature seems to have taken particular care to disseminate her blessings among the different regions of the world, with an eye to this mutual intercourse and traffic among mankind, that the natives of the several parts of the globe might have a kind of dependence upon one another and be united by their common interest. (4)

There is an interactive and interanimating relation between Mr. Spectator and the Royal Exchange. The commerce and the shared ground of material exchange between people create unions in the Exchange. Mr. Spectator re-introduces this interactive intercourse and traffic among mankind with an eye which similarly unites the different regions of the world. This cosmopolitan view implies the consistent interactions and co-existence of the world in a contact-zone where Oriental and Occidental cultures may preserve their unity but where long-held divisions appear rather unnecessary and artificial.

18th century English public was so fascinated with the Oriental observer that some individuals disguised themselves as such. Contrary to the oriental observers, European citizens were dressed in Oriental manners. Weight argues that George Psalmanazar disguised himself in an Oriental manner and introduced himself to London society as a native Formosan. He wrote about the history and language of his so-called native country, Formosa. It was fascinating for English people to read from Psalmanazar about cannibalism and polygamy in Formosa. What was even more interesting about him was that he was a light-haired, fair-skinned and well-educated man. Towards the end of his life, it was discovered that he was a Frenchman and confident of Samuel Johnson (Weight 2). Brown writes about the influence of the *Turkish Spy*. She discusses the influence on Defoe's political ambition to reform the English "Central Intelligence Agency". She writes that Defoe was arrested in May 1703 after he wrote *The Shortest Way with The Dissenters* (1702). He was suspected of conspiracy against the government. He had a difficult time in prison and appealed to Robert Harley who released him on condition that

Defoe serve him as a secret agent and pamphleteer. Defoe agreed and served Harley as a propagandist and journalist between 1704 and 1714. He started to publish the *Review* in 1704 in which he used the same critical distance of the observers to inform the government about public opinion and to defend the political projects of Harley. What is interesting is that he compared his mission to that of Mahmut in the *Turkish Spy*. Like Mahmut, Defoe travelled throughout Europe and especially in Scotland to write reports and give advice to Harley. He also published pamphlets about social and political issues to inform the central government. He admits that the *Turkish Spy* has assisted him in his political project. In his *Continuation of Letters Written by Turkish Spy* (1718) he emphasizes the component of the *Turkish Spy*. He outlines a plan for establishing a powerful English Intelligence Agency which will inform the central government on domestic and foreign events. Defoe suggests to Harley to use a spy in the English Intelligence Service in much the same way as done by Marana in the *Turkish Spy*. Defoe thinks that the implementation of the plan will allow Harley to know what is happening all over Europe. Defoe says: "The Secretary of State would be informed in advance of the political and social events" (qtd. in Brown 105). Defoe pursues his plan and begins to work as a spy. When he leaves England for Scotland as an agent for Harley, he closely observes the moral, political and social condition of Scotland and works on behalf of Harley to shape public opinion on matters such as the Spanish Succession and the Treaty of Union. According to Brown, Defoe considers this service as profitable for foreign and domestic affairs of the government. Brown states this as follows:

> Defoe's method for mending the 'Defect of Intelligence' in England recommends a rigorous assimilation of information through a network of correspondents and the preservation of secrecy about what is known. His plan for using agents to increase knowledge at home and abroad also involves maintaining the ignorance of agents who, like naïve empiricists, collect data without understanding who they are working for and what end they are serving. (108)

Agents in different places of Europe could strengthen the power of England in and abroad, thus the secret service would increase Harley's influence, popularity and power in the central government: "Defoe's success as an agent for Harley was, therefore, built upon his capacity to play roles and argue from a number of perspectives" (120).

The evidence discussed above indicates that the emergence, development and transformation of the oriental observer contradict Said's argument in *Orientalism* (1978). He argues that there is a coherent discourse of orientalism which treats everything as evidence to back up the division between East and West (Said 3). However, the letters indicate that "East and West" have no "advantage over one another except that which virtue gives" (*Persian Letters* 142). The letters also argue that the power of intellect arises from a variety of spiritual lights in Greek logic, and the scholastic theology of Avicenna and Averreos and Plotinus (*Persian Letters* 150). The oriental observers fixed their thoughts and concerns upon great changes which made the ages so different from one another, and the earth so unlike itself (*Persian Letters* 116). It is also argued that the Ottoman experience in the ancient territories of Babylon, Greece, Egypt, Persia and Constantinople is considered as significant for the developing European imperialism. Mahmut admits in the letters that one can find all ancient civilizations swallowed up in the universal empire of the Ottomans (qtd. in Aksan 210). Thus, the Oriental Ottoman history is presented in the letters as an implicit model for the expansion of European imperialism. 18th century Orientalism developed in this context of dialogy.

In many respects, the Orient is known, identifiable, and coherent to Europeans. It is not surprising that many authors could create the same historical narrative and emphasize racial ideas. It is crucial for the purpose of this study to indicate that the pseudo-oriental letters displayed how to transform the enormous backlog of information about the Ottoman Orient into liberal, critical and interactive fiction writing. It would be impossible for Marana to write the *Turkish Spy* without travelers' and scholars' information. Similarly, it would be more difficult for the 18th century writers to frame their oriental tales and travelogues without the interanimating spirit of the pseudo-oriental letters. This critical attitude anticipated the dialogic, interanimating and cosmopolitan worldview of the oriental tales and oriental travelogues. While the letters, tales and travelogues move between the East and West, they overthrow long-held beliefs, construct a particular intimacy between the values of Western and Eastern communities and create a further anxiety for the culture of the Ottoman Orient. In particular, the interconnectedness of the East and West is further celebrated in the Oriental tales. In such tales and travelogues the Orient or Occident are transformed into experimental human space where an outsider could learn about, have intimacy with, and adopt the world of the other. Oriental tales and travelogues made the Ottoman Orient closer and more familiar to the Europeans than ever before. Then, it can be argued that the pseudo-oriental genre is significant in terms of promoting a more comparative and reflective, less narrowly historical representation of the Ottoman Orient.

The Representation of the Ottoman Orient in 18th Century Oriental Tales in England

The popularity and influence of the pseudo-oriental letters, and the contribution of Jean Paulo Marana and Baron de Montesquieu to the development and popularity of interest in the Oriental cultures have already been discussed. It becomes apparent from the discussion that the use of the critical Oriental perspective and European knowledge of the Orient to compare and contrast ridiculous and serious aspects of the two worlds had a significant influence on 18th century English literature. The public's great interest in and demand for the continuation of the pseudo-oriental letters motivated 18th century English writers to produce Oriental fictions. Yet, the pseudo-oriental letters were not the only Oriental fictions which dealt with the representation of the Ottoman Orient; such letters reflected only comparative aspects of the European and the Oriental world. Another aspect of the European interest in the Ottoman Orient in the 18th century began with the translation of the *Arabian Nights* in 1713. The translation of the *Arabian Nights* started the second phase of the popularity of the representation of the Ottoman Orient in English literature. According to Martha Pike Conant, "the prelude was sounded by the first English translation of the *Turkish Spy*" but the period of Oriental fiction begins with the *Arabian Nights* which was "a book [very] different in character from any oriental fiction then known in England" (xvii).

Like the *Turkish Spy*, the *Arabian Nights* came from France;[1] and like the *Spy*, the *Nights* had a far reaching influence on the development of certain literary narratives in the 18th century. The literary influence of the *Nights* on the development of the Oriental fictions in England is binominal: oriental tales and pseudo-oriental tales. Oriental tales are literary works written or derived from those countries on Eastern Mediterranean and Asia; the pseudo-oriental tales are prose-works which appeared in England and were originally written by English writers in the English language. This chapter will shortly refer to the *Arabian Nights* and a few other oriental tales which were copied and translated from the original sources by Addison and Steele. Then, the two pseudo-oriental tales, *Rasselas, The Prince of Abyssinia* and *Vathek* will be discussed respectively. *Rasselas* was written by Samuel Johnson in 1759. *Vathek* was written by William Beckford in 1784. *Rasselas* has been chosen because it is one of the most typical imitations of the oriental tales in 18th English literature. *Vathek* was the last example of the pseudo-oriental tales written in 18th century English literature. This study will survey the unique positions of the Ottoman Orient in the pseudo-Oriental tales, *Rasselas* and *Vathek*.

The *Arabian Nights* and Pseudo-oriental Tales in 18th Century England

It is important for the purpose of our study to survey the introduction and popularity of the *Arabian Nights* (1712). The tales in the *Arabian Nights* were serialized in the *London News* for three years to teach and delight the readers. The collection of the tales contains love stories, travel tales, tales of criminals, pious tales, anecdotes about kings, queens and princes, and many entertaining and instructive fables. The narrative elements and topics are diverse; there are Indian, Egyptian, Arabic, Turkish and Greek elements in the tales. The text's several versions that have been created over centuries bear the marks of many authors, ages and settings, traces of pre-Islamic and Islamic and Christian worlds. The *Nights* "impels beyond the confines of any

---

[1] France had a colonial and commercial interest in the Ottoman Orient before England. French people considered such translations as significant to learn about the Oriental customs. They

single representation of its identity;" it is the only piece of literature which "inhabits the nexus of eastern history and western being" (Sallis 5). The tales are a composite of mosaics in which each different civilization has a constituent color and space to express itself. There are different myths, legends, stories, and beliefs from different cultures, nations, and religions. Each story in the *Nights* challenges the one that comes before and tries to outdo the predecessors by promising greater marvels next time. In most of the tales one surprising adventure succeeds another with kaleidoscopic rapidity; each story is unconnected except by the mere presence of the hero (Conant 8). To tell the most charming and marvellous tale is the central concern of the narrator. In this cycle the magical atmosphere, the rich variety of dramatic incidents, the adventurous spirit, together with princes, viziers, dervishes, cadis, sheiks, slaves, queens and beggars who exchange roles in time by means of disguising, make the thousand and one night tales of the oriental world truly carnivalesque. The *Arabian Nights* was evolved as a response or reaction to a social and spiritual structure generating carnival and carnivalesque inversions (Sallis 1). Therefore, to 18th century England, the *Arabian Nights* was a patchwork of marvels, enchantment and wonders. Conant expresses this as follows:

> One strange story follows another in bewildering profusion until the reader seems to be walking in a dream 'in the days of Haroun Alraschid,' when the unexpected always happens. In this land of wonder and enchantment any threatening cloud may assume the form of an enormous genie, white-bearded, terrific, with torch in hand and a voice like thunder, 'a Slave of the Lamp,' ready to carry a sleeping prince a thousand leagues through the air or to erect over night a palace of dazzling splendor; any serpent may be an enchanted fairy: any beautiful woman may be a disguised princess or a cruel sorceress with power to transform human beings into dogs or black stones: and at every turn one may meet African magicians who can pronounce the 'Open Sesame' to subterranean-caves. (3)

The stories take place in real settings like Baghdad, Cairo and China and marvels reflect the Eastern world in its own way. The *Nights* were read in

---

used the tales for folkloric investigation (Conant xxiii).

18th century England in a particular way which fostered reality and imagination. For instance, Lady Mary Wortley Montagu, having read the *Nights* before she travelled to the Ottoman Levant, wrote that Constantinople was very much like what she read in the *Arabian Nights*. She applied the exotic rubric to the real East as she perceived it and found that the tales and land matched: "She thought that Turkey was very much like the Orient as it existed in the *Arabian Nights* tales" (Sallis 72).

Despite all this mystery, atmosphere of wonder and magic, there is in the *Arabian Nights* a sense of reality, a "verisimilitude" which accounts in large part for "the steady popularity the book has engaged with the English people" (qtd. in Conant 7). Sallis states this as follows:

> The nights were for the 18th century Europe the indulgence of lawless imagination and immoderate improbability, the ultimate flights of fantastic unreality, and, with very little critical discussion, were also used [...] as an accurate picture of the manners and customs of the Other. The two readers, the armchair traveler and the reader in search of exotic and enchanting reality, existed side by side, even at times in one person. (6)

The tales mirrored the Orient: "The oriental tales, thus, became synonymous with the Orient" (Sampson 72). The fascination for the exotic and real Orient experienced in the Europe of the 18th century can be interpreted in two ways. European identity was preserved and assured by distance and by difference from its chosen other. According to Sallis, the diversity and narrative style of the *Nights* gave readers freedom to read it as they liked: "The European [readers read the] *Nights* as a text [which was] shorn of from its possible readers and displayed before strangers, a fact which left Europeans free to read as they liked" (65). But there was a strong drive to fit the *Nights* into some kind of context and make it real both textually and in interpretation. Many people were prejudiced and believed that Galland –who first translated the tales into French– had invented the tales. And many others strongly believed that the tales were about the real life experience of people in the countries where the events in the tale took place.

Ranelagh looks at the *Arabian Nights* from a different perspective. Although she does not reject Conant and Sallis' ideas, she argues that the tales were folkloric documents which were introduced into England before the 18th century. She compares a story in the *Nights* to a story written in English before the 18th century. The *Night*'s story "A Dream" is about a man in Baghdad who lost all his estates and saw a man in his dream. The man said to him to search for his fortune in Cairo. After he woke up, he went to Cairo, and decided to spend his first night in the mosque. A house near the mosque was robbed and he was arrested for the robbery. He spent the next day and the following ones in prison. He told his dream to another prisoner who first laughed, then told him about a person he saw in a dream. The person described to him a house in Baghdad and told him about the treasure at the lower end of the house's garden. The house in Baghdad which the prisoner saw in the dream belonged to the poor man who had come to Cairo to search for his fortune. Having been released from the prison, he returned to Baghdad, arrived at his home, dug the lower end of the garden and found the treasure. Ranelagh writes about the English version of the story which relates the tale of a pedlar named John Chapman[2]. He dreams of a treasure to be found on London Bridge. The pedlar goes to the bridge and meets a shopkeeper on the bridge. The shopkeeper relates his dream of a treasure located in the pedlar's own garden. Then, the pedlar goes home, digs his garden and finds the treasure. The story might have undergone "certain changes" in England but the philosophy behind the story is retained: "Levantine philosophy that man goes where the will of God sends him; what appears to be the wrong place is in fact a step to the right place" (Ranelagh 205). Ranelagh interprets the *Nights* with respect to the long historical interaction between the East and West. She argues that the Orient is one of the three significant cultural heritages[3] which contributed to the advancement of the European

---

[2] Tales in the *Nights* included certain stories which were already introduced to England before the translation of the *Arabian Nights*. Therefore, the readers did not find the *Nights* a completely unfamiliar text.
[3] The other two are ancient Greco-Roman and Judeo-Christian cultures.

civilization.[4] Europe has historical and intellectual links to Greco-Roman, Judeo-Christian and Arabic cultures: "Medieval culture was in fact Greek, Latin and Arab" (Ranelagh 3). Greek and Roman cultures were written and preserved in Latin manuscripts which were re-discovered and translated into many European languages during the Renaissance. A significant part of Greek knowledge was translated from the Greek into the Arabic language by Byzantines. Arab scholars like Averreos and Avicenna further developed Greek knowledge and re-introduced it into the European world when Spain and Sicily were the major bridges over which Arabic interpretation of Greek learning was transformed into Western Europe. Ranelagh says:

> What concerns us most because it is unfamiliar is our Arab heritage. It is not one simple thing. The people known in the Middle Ages as Saracens came from various ethnic groups, among them Greeks, Persians, Indians, Copts, Turks, Armenians and Jews. Their ancient rich civilizations had been assimilated into the Byzantine and Persian Empires, but the lightning spread of Islam in the seventh century imposed on them new culture, that of their conquerors, which expressed itself in a new Arabian way of life. (iii)

The "lightning spread of Islam" during the Middle Ages in the regions, which were once held by the Egyptian, Babylonian, Roman, Byzantium and Persian empires, created a diverse and complex cultural and intellectual history. This hybrid culture expressed itself in the language of the dominant religion. Major intellectual and local narratives recorded in Indian, Persian and

---

[4] Ranelagh re-locates her interpretation of the *Nights* into historical context of familiarity. She traces the ancient and medieval relations between the Middle East and Europe. She argues that the Greco-Roman Empires were in political, cultural and many times in hostile contacts with Egyptians and Persians. Eastern and Western civilizations claimed the right to occupy each other's territories for some time. In particular, Europe inherited and assimilated Eastern Judeo-Christian culture after the introduction of Christianity into Europe. Since Judaism, Christianity and Islam developed from the same ancient Hebrew tradition, there are a lot of common narratives in the Old Testament, Bible and Koran. Joseph and Potiphar's wife and Solomon and The Queen of Seba are only two common narratives which we can find in the three books. Byron once expressed to the publisher of his tale that Eastern and Western people were all acquainted with the stories in the Old Testament and Bible. There were also a lot of common European and Asian folk-tales. For instance, Boccaccio introduced a lot of Eastern tales in *Decameron* to European readers. Some of the tales in *Decameron* were re-written by Chaucer in the *Canterbury tales* (Ranelagh 1).

Roman languages were translated and developed by Arabs who later transmitted such narratives into the new countries they conquered. This hybrid Oriental culture was first introduced to the Medieval Europe from Andalusia, later by the Ottomans to the Modern Europe. Cross-cultural traffic continued at different levels in different ages, and Europe inherited and assimilated the Oriental culture to a significant extent. Ranelagh relocates the *Nights* in these cross-cultural interactions. She states that the *Nights* contributed in the 18th century to the growth of interest in Oriental studies, to the development of folklore and of narrative as fields of study, and to fiction in the rise of a whole school of pseudo-oriental novels and tales (Ranelagh 196).

It can be argued that there are three different modern interpretations about the perception of the Oriental tales in 18th century England. Firstly, the tales were read for the exotic experience. Because they came from the Orient, very little of them was seen as familiar with, or equivalent to, a European experience. Secondly, the interest in the fantastic Orient was transformed into real knowledge about the manners and customs of the people of the Middle East, and the tales became a textbook on the Middle Eastern Orient. The third represents the search for analogues and origins. In the first instance, the reading for the exotic amounted to no more than stating: "this is different," with some discussion of whether difference was good or bad. In the second it is clear that a story shows manners and customs. Lastly, a story can be satisfactorily described by discovering an analogous story.

It is significant to emphasize that the above mentioned three different perspectives illuminate certain aspects of the oriental tales. The popularity of the tales during the 18th century had something to do with the general atmosphere and moral tendency of the age. The tales also provided the contemporary writers with a moral setting to address ethical issues. Galland writes in the preface to the *Nights* that "readers may reap an advantage of profiting by the examples of virtues and vices in the tales" (qtd. in Sampson 72). 18th century English writers such as Samuel Johnson, Joseph Addison and Richard Steel identified the tales as very rich, fascinating and suitable for the instruction and entertainment of the public. They published translations from the *Nights* for moral and philosophical purposes. They also imitated the style and content to re-appropriate such tales to the contemporary public taste by giving them moral and philosophical perspectives. The moralizing tendency in the British oriental tales reflects a fundamental instinct of the British character of 18th century English literature. Sampson argues this as follows:

> Oriental tales [...] were used in Britain to evaluate and critique European political and moral codes from a safe distance under the guise of describing the Orient. This narrative 'veil' permitted writers to explore from a safe moral and cultural distance. Prominent writers such as Addison and Steele took the new, imaginative Oriental fiction [...] and attempted to mold it into something which conformed to their ideas of worthy literature. (79)

Oriental tales, then, also emerged as a cover up to teach and delight the contemporary readers. There are numerous oriental tales in the 18th century which have moral and philosophical characters. In particular, Joseph Addison and Richard Steel wrote oriental tales to reconcile wit and morality. For instance, in *The Spectator*, No. 512, Addison discusses justice with reference to a tale about a Vizier and a Bird. He admits that oriental tales may serve as moral fables in their natural simplicity. Addison refers to the Orient to criticize the English custom of marriage. In story No. 511 in *The Spectator*, the narrator Will Honeycomb tells how marriage confounds English women. Women in Persia are paid according to their beauty. But women in England come with a dowry. This is a satire on English society rather than on Persian customs. Comparing love for money and love for beauty, the narrator implies in the story that love of beauty has to be stronger than love of money for couples. In the same essay, the narrator also quotes from another oriental tale to criticize the role of money in marriage. In this story, we read about a man who buys a sack at a high price and discovers an old woman in it. He decides to throw the sack with the old woman into the river but the old woman promises wealth so he relents. She keeps her promise and they get married.

By arguing that he found the tale lately translated out of Arabic manuscripts, Addison gives an oriental turn to the story of Helim and Abdalla. Addison carefully works with oriental characters and settings and uses stock phrases like "a magnificent black marbled palace with five thousand lamps," "hundreds of ebony doors guarded by Negroes" and "the lovers escape in moonlight as white as the spirit". Although the stock phrases must be taken from the original oriental tale, the story ends with a neoclassical message: "virtue is rewarded and vice is thwarted" (Conant 85). The neoclassical message makes the story acceptable to British readers. According to Conant, Addison was of the opinion that the reading of the oriental tales should teach young people politeness, and a high sense of virtue together with geographical knowledge, the customs and manners of foreign countries. Conant quotes from Addison to illuminate the argument:

> By them they [readers] are led at once into Courts and into camps, are taught the language of toilette and drawing room, and are made acquainted with those superior Sentiments which inhabit only great souls, and distinguish true heroes from the Vulgar. [...] These are great advantages and very valuable Acquirements, even to Men; and many giddy young Fellows have been, by amusing themselves with such trifles, taught to conceive clearly, and to converse properly, in relation to things which otherwise they would have known nothing about. [That] 'True Virtue alone is capable of standing all trials and persisting therein is the only means of attaining solid happiness' is latent in the oriental tales. [...] From the perusal of these sheets [the reader] will have it in his Power to make a hundred Reflections, which may produce very happy Effects, if applied to the Regulation of his own Conduct. He will, for example, see how ridiculous it is for a Man in Years to hope for satisfaction from engaging new Amours. (88-9)

Addison's "The Vision of Mirza" is another invented oriental tale which deals with the pursuit of pleasure and death. In this story, Mirza is located on a pinnacle of the high hills of Baghdad. He beholds from the pinnacle of the hill people passing over the bridge of life. Everyone, sooner or later, falls from the bridge and is reborn again, either as cursed over the dark clouds or as blessed in the heavenly island. Conant states that Addison used the vision of Mirza to emphasize the vicissitudes of life, the certainty of death, consolation of faith, and the mystery enveloped in the existence of man (113). *The Story of a King and Dervish* is another story which Addison invented. This story is written in *The Spectator* No: 298. In the story, the dervish is invited to a palace. He mistakes the palace for an inn, which makes the King very angry. "Sir" says the dervish, "give me leave to ask your majesty a question or two. Who were the persons that lodged in this house when it was first built?" The king replies, "His ancestors". "And who," says the Dervish, "was the last person that lodged here?" The king replies, "His father". "And who is it," says the dervish that lodges here at present?" The king tells him that it is himself. "And who" says the dervish, "will be after you?" The king answers, the young prince, his son. "Ah, Sir," said the dervish, "a house that changes its inhabitants so often and receives perpetual succession of guests, is not a Palace, but a Caravansaray". It is clear from our discussion that oriental tales in the periodicals expressed spiritual and moral aspects of life with an Eastern spirit. The *Arabian Nights* was the source book to translate and sometimes to invent oriental tales for Addison and Steel. Although there are numerous pseudo-oriental tales invented or translated by Hawkesworth and some other 18th century writers, they will not be dealt with in this chapter. The two major pseudo-oriental novels, Ra*sselas; The Prince of Abyssinia,* and *Vathek* will be discussed in detail.

Rasselas: The Prince of Abyssinia (1759)

*Rasselas: The Prince of Abyssini*a [hereafter *Rasselas*] is a philosophical novel and consists of three parts. It is about a Prince and his friends. The prince is the son of the Abyssinian Emperor and lives in a Happy Valley an insulated existence. The novel is mainly about a choice of life. Rasselas, Nekayah, Pekuah and Imlac are confined in the happy valley. They realize that gratification of desire does not make them happy any more. The prince leaves the "Happy Valley" with his sister Nekayah, Imlac (his tutor) and Pekuah (Nekayah's servant). They escape from the fruitless meditation in the happy valley to seek for real happiness. They want to learn about real human experience and make a real life-choice in the outside world. They reach Egypt where their notions about human society are contradicted by the actual instances they encounter. They are hosted by a wealthy merchant, and by

Egyptian families, they visit a hermit and ancient Egyptian pyramids. Pekuah is kidnapped by primitive Arab tribes and kept in the desert for a while. In each of these instances, they discover a valuable lesson about the past and present conditions of human beings. Their discovery and learning affect their life-choice. In the end, they decide to return to the happy valley to think only about the choice of eternity.

Conant takes *Rasselas* as "the best type of the serious English Oriental tale" (140). Johnson is said to have written it in the evenings of a single week to pay for his mother's funeral (Ousby 766). In his letter [16 January 1759] to his step daughter Lucy Porter, he writes that he sent twelve guineas and hopes to send more[5]. He also writes to his mother in the same letter. He says: "Your weakness afflicts me beyond what I am willing to communicate to you. [...] I know not how to bear the thought of losing you". In his letter of Saturday, 20 January, to his printer William Strahan, he says: "When I was with you last night I told you of a thing which I was preparing for the press. The title will be 'The Choice of Life' or The History of Prince of Abyssinia. [...] I shall have occasion for thirty pounds on Monday night when I shall deliver the book which I must entreat you upon such delivery to procure me" (qtd. in Hardy 127). Therefore, the novel "expresses the substance of the author's somber philosophy of life" (Conant 140). But the novel touches the problems of government, causes of melancholy, mystery of good and evil, the glory of the ancient Egyptians and the corruptions of the contemporary Egypt under the Turkish dynasty.

Edward Tomorken in *Johnson, Rasselas and the Choice of Criticism* (1989) surveys the critical commentary on the theme and style of the novel. Tomorken discusses the formal and thematic significance of *Rasselas* in the history of English literature. Referring to Ernest Baker's *The History of the English Novel* (1934), and Joseph Wood Krutch's interpretation, Tomorken states that *Rasselas* is a scholarly masterpiece in terms of the careful treat-

---

[5] Johnson began to write *Rasselas* few weeks before his mother's death. He must have received some money from the publisher and sent it to his sister to spend it for their mother's health. However, their mother died just after the publication of the tale and the sum of money he received from the publisher was spent for the funeral.

ment of the oriental culture and it "was a singular kind of novel because of its use of the orient" (17). He agrees with Joseph Wood Krutch that *Rasselas* was a popular pseudo-oriental tale which had a neoclassical message. Like Krutch, he argues that by locating the theme of *Rasselas* in an Oriental context Johnson concerned himself in the inquiry of the ancient glory and present disaster of Egypt (18). Tomorken states that Krutch's interpretation went unrecognized for some time and his position was "at first inserted into the old religious controversy as if his secular reading was merely another attack on *Rasselas* for lack of religious resolution. But within a decade his influence began to be seen in the increasing interest in the formal properties of *Rasselas*" (19).

In *Rasselas*, Johnson imitates the structure and manner of the already popular *Arabian Nights*. Like the *Nights*, he uses dialogy and story within the story in the novel. But unlike the *Nights*, he treats his subject with irony and criticism. Joseph Addison's "Vision of Mirza" contributes most to the allegorical treatment of the theme in terms of expressing "the vanity of human wishes" (Hardy 128). More than any other work, the situation at the beginning of *Rasselas* is completely similar to the 18th pseudo-oriental letters. But like Marana and Montesquieu, Johnson creates an intelligent but inexperienced man about to view society and the condition of human life (Bond 156). Like the foreign observers of Montesquieu, Rasselas and the other characters decide to investigate both public and private life in contemporary society. This time they are located in Egypt; as foreigners they interact with the Egyptians and from the standpoint of the distant observers they confront and question the contemporary condition of Egypt. They comment on ridiculous and serious aspects of life in Egypt by meeting people from different social, intellectual, religious, ethnic and economic backgrounds; they also talk with the natives to learn about the ancient and present condition of the Egyptians. In the end, they attain self-discovery, they are illuminated about the contemporary Egyptians, and they return to the Happy Valley. In the following part, I am going to investigate Johnson's idea of the Orient and his specific treatment of the Oriental Egyptians in *Rasselas, The Prince of Abyssinia*.

Johnson's Idea of the Orient and the Source of *Rasselas*

Ghazi Nassir argues that Dr. Samuel Johnson was curious about the present and past condition of the Orient. Nassir begins his argument about Johnson's curiosity with a letter by Johnson to Warren Hasting. In the letter, Johnson writes:

> My knowledge of them [oriental societies] is too scanty to furnish me with proper topics of enquiry; I can only wish for information; and hope, that a mind comprehensive like yours will find leisure, amidst the cares of your important station, to enquire into many subjects of which the European world either thinks not at all, or thinks with deficient intelligence and uncertain conjecture. I shall hope, that he who once intended to increase the learning of this country by the introduction of the Persian language, will examine nicely the traditions and histories of the East. (qtd. in Nassir 2)

In the letter to Warren Hastings, Johnson argues that Europeans have either deficient thinking or uncertain conjecture about the region. Johnson believes that one first needs to learn an Eastern language to be able to read about the wonders of ancient history, to trace "the vestiges of its revived cities, know the arts and opinions of race of men" and the "splendor of wide extended empire" which supplied the rest of the world "with pride and luxury" (qtd. in Nassir 1-2). In another letter to Boswell, Johnson writes that the English public has an unusual interest in oriental countries and therefore such studies might be made part of the college curriculum (3). According to Nassir, Samuel Johnson did not know any oriental language and did not personally travel to the East, but he was an enthusiastic reader of oriental literature and could present accurate descriptions from his reading. As stated in the quotation above, Johnson encouraged Warren's keen investigation into Eastern history and culture. He admitted that he had too little information to conjecture on any topics of enquiry about the Orient. He once expressed his regret for not having visited Constantinople (12). Yet his study of eastern works began at an early age, so that when he wrote *Rasselas* and the eight tales in the *Rambler* and *Idler*, he was well acquainted with oriental life and culture (27). This acquaintance owed much to his two years' readings in his father's bookshop (29). Between the year 1726 and 1728, he worked in his father's bookshop. During those two years, Johnson became an active reader and found in his father's store a collection of books about the Orient (Clifford 30). As a businessman, Michael Johnson (Johnson's father) was aware of the popularity of oriental works and must have sold travel accounts about the Oriental society. Books like the *Arabian Nights*[6], *Persian Tales* and *Turkish Tales* must have been stored in Michael Johnson's bookstore. Johnson must have had a lot of time and opportunity to read as many books as possible about the traditions and histories of the East to increase his Oriental knowledge and understanding. Johnson, like Ranelagh, believed that Eastern civilization had a great influence on the advancement of European civilization. Johnson claimed that the East "had provided [...] almost all that sets [European society] above savages" (qtd. in Nassir 28). He told Boswell that "he read a great deal in a desultory manner from his father's stock to satisfy his curiosity about the Christian world and the Muhometan world" (31). He had more than forty books in his catalogue about the East written by European and Eastern scholars, which provided him with a wealth of references to and descriptions of the oriental world.

One of the oriental books Johnson kept in his library was Father Jerome Lobo's *A Voyage to Abyssinia*. John Hawkesworth also wrote an oriental tale upon the *Voyage to Abyssinia.* In the story of Hawkesworth, *Obadiah, the son of Abensina*, the prince "follows a pleasant but misleading path, is overtaken by a storm, and meets a Hermit who preaches to him about the journey of life and the necessity of following the right road" (Conant 93). Johnson translated Lobo's *A Voyage to Abyssinia* and wrote a preface to Hawkesworth's tale. In the preface, Dr. Johnson stated that he admires the actual author, Lobo, for his deep interest in the hardships and vicissitudes of human life and adventure. He appreciates Lobo for describing things as he sees them and copying nature from life. Johnson says: "there is no region cursed with bareness, or blessed with fecundity, no unceasing sunshine, nor nations devoid of a sense of humanity. The readers discover impartial enquiry, human nature,

---

[6] We know from the 4 November 1782 entry in his diary that Johnson enjoyed reading the *Arabian Nights* (qtd. in Nassir, 43).

vice and virtue, passion and reason" (qtd. in Nassir 32-3). Lobo's *Voyage* had an exotic setting which ensured the book a great success in England (Ousby 766). Dr. Johnson used this setting in *Rasselas*. Jenkins stated that the happy valley contained features from a number of Ethiopian travel books available in Johnson's day (qtd. in Tomorken 18). Although Johnson seems to have been well read and made use of Abyssinian materials from Hawkesworth's tale and Lobo's *Voyage* in *Rasselas*, he does not describe Ethiopians in detail. He is more concerned with Egyptians than Ethiopians. Such books are comparable in terms of the writers' specific treatment of the Oriental tales as a narrative device to discuss moral and philosophical issues.

Rasselas's decision to leave the valley and to learn about the world outside Happy Valley is closer in manner and spirit to the oriental observers of Marana and Montesquieu. The Prince decides to leave the Valley in order to search for knowledge. He has been living for a long time in ignorance in the peaceful condition of the Valley. He thinks that there must be no "difference between the beasts that stride in the Valley" and himself in terms of corporeal necessities (*Rasselas* 3). Yet, unlike the animals of the Valley, he is not at rest. He discovers within himself a desire for knowledge and experience that the Happy Valley cannot gratify, but which must be satisfied before he can be happy. He learns from Imlac, the tutor of the prince, that there is a struggle for good and evil between people (they have freedom to choose between good and evil) outside the Happy Valley. The prince, Imlac, Nekayah and Pakuah escaped from the valley to learn about good and evil and to make their own choice in life. Thus begins the quest of the prince.

The prince believes that a person is happier if he increases his knowledge: "we grow happier as our minds take a wider range" (216). The journey of Rasselas, Nekayah, Pakuah and Imlac is a search for truth and happiness in Oriental Egypt. During the journey, they "will see all the conditions of mankind" to increase their knowledge about the world (232). They will visit the pyramids to learn about the glorious history of the ancient Egyptians; they will see the progress of human mind, improvement of reason, advances of science, vicissitudes of learning, light and darkness, extinction and resurrection of art and revolutions of the intellectual world (280). *Rasselas* implies that in order to reap the advantages of the study of Oriental wisdom and good manners it is necessary to leave one's own social and cultural space. Abstract philosophical understanding cannot answer the moral problems of man. One needs to be able to compare and test one's own values. In the novel, the Abyssinian philosophy of the prince and the physical world of Egyptians are presented in a conflict. Thought and experience are not consistent; the same proposition may at the same time be true and false, and cogitation can be conferred on that which is created incapable of cogitation depending upon one's moral and philosophical perspective (Conant 345). The Abyssinian philosophy is represented by mystical and spiritual explanations. The Eastern experience is represented by the journey in Egypt. The prince's journey and spiritual quest are re-defined in relation to this image. Imlac thinks that a journey in search of truth is undertaken by self-will, not by another's command. The journey is part of life and it is necessary for the regulation of it; it is found where it is honestly sought and it brings happiness (*Rasselas* 215). If the prince wants to learn about life and be happy, he has to reconcile the conflict between Abyssinia and Egypt.

Both Imlac's characterization and his role are significant in this journey. He is Rasselas's intellectual and spiritual guide and he is the one who reconciles the abstract philosophy and concrete human experience. He has travelled before; therefore, he has enough knowledge and experience to guide the prince. Imlac resembles Rica and Mr. Spectator in certain aspects. Like them, he has visited very diverse, distant and unknown parts of the globe. He was born in the kingdom of Goiama near the Nile, traded in the inlands of Africa (*Rasselas* 10). He felt the pleasure of knowledge and was instructed in all matters; he exposed himself to travel (11). He visited Agra, the capital of the great Mogul Empire and learnt their native language in a few months. He was recommended to the emperor and became a vice-counsel in the court (12-3). Since there was nothing left for him to learn from the emperor of Agra (the wisest man Imlac had met till then), he went to Persia where he saw many remains of ancient magnificence and human nature through all its variations before he passed into Arabia where he witnessed a warlike and pastoral life of human beings; he was able to repeat from his memory all the volumes of

Persian and Arabian literature that were suspended in the mosque of Mecca (13). Imlac made a significant decision in Palestine, the birth-place and spiritual centre of Christianity. He met Eastern and Western scholars there and learnt about universal human conduct. This meeting was a turning point in Imlac's life. After speaking to the "great men" from the northern and western nations of Europe in Palestine, Imlac decided to be a poet because only a poet could be acquainted with all the modes of life. As a poet, Imlac began to have "a new purpose" (14).

His new purpose is to teach transcendental truths to the prince. It is apparent from the presentation of Imlac that he has reconciled Eastern and Western worlds and become a "citizen of the world". Imlac's decision to be a poet moves the line of the argument in the story from a moral dimension into a philosophical one. The perspective also changes; the oriental perspective is replaced by 18th century neo-classical one. Imlac, like the Dr. Johnson of the neo-classical age, finds truth in the study of nature and man. Imlac's eastern wisdom, his learning, travels and experiences begin to appear as a vehicle that may contribute to his poetical skills. Nature is to be the subject and men his auditors since he cannot feel the delight and misery of men whose interests he does not understand. After he becomes a poet, Imlac begins to see everything with "a new purpose" (14). Imlac's argument on the poet and poetry indicates this relation:

> The business of a poet [...] is to examine, not the individual, but the species; to remark general properties and large appearances: he does not number the streaks of the tulips, or describe the different shades in the verdure of the forest. He is to exhibit in his portraits of nature such prominent and striking features, as recall the original to every mind; and must neglect the minute discriminations, which one may have remarked, another have neglected [...] Knowledge of nature is [...] a task of a poet. He must be acquainted likewise with all the modes of life [...]. He must divest himself of the prejudice of his age and country, he must consider right and wrong in their abstracted and invariable state; he must disregard present laws and opinions, and rise to general transcendental truths, which will always be the same: he must therefore content himself with the slow progress of his name; condemn the applause of his on time, and commit his

claims to the justice of posterity. His labor is not yet at an end: he must know many languages and many sciences: and, that his stile may be worthy of his thoughts, must, by incessant practice, familiarize to himself every delicacy of speech and grace of harmony. (14)

Imlac argues that only poets could reconcile the conflicts between thought and experience. These statements upon the character and responsibility of the poet display a critical stance which could reconcile East and West. In this argument, we see Johnson's idea of oriental scholarship. As we have quoted from Johnson's letter to Warren Hasting, Johnson encourages Oriental learning and inquiry of "the wonders of ancient edifices, the vestiges of revived cities, the arts and opinions of race of men" and the "splendor of wide extended empire" (qtd. in Nassir 1-2). Here, Imlac believes that a poet "must know many languages and many sciences [...] and by incessant practice, familiarize to himself every delicacy of speech" (*Rasselas* 14). The poet discovers excellence and enduring models in nature, acquires skills, and perfects his talents by a long study and practice. He reconciles abstract thoughts and concrete moral experience. Conant argues that the moralistic oriental tales represent the opinions of 18th century British scholars. The tales produced in England emphasize the negotiation of philosophical ideas and moral codes. The primary aim of the tales is "to reconcile wit and morality, to entertain and to preach, to hold the mirror of kindly ridicule up to society, to smile away the follies or vices of the world, and to present serene, temperate, and beautiful ideals of thought and of conduct" (79-80). Then, Imlac, as a poet, is transformed into a position where to reconcile new and universal human experience in different parts of the world. The reconciliation of the particular and the universal also reflects the typical and most extensive neoclassical idea of 18th century English literature. Based on this argument, it can be claimed that the Abyssinian philosophy (here also Western thoughts) and Egyptian journey (the Oriental experience) are reconciled in the oriental fiction, *Rasselas*.

The Prince's journey through Egypt is consistent with Imlac's earlier journey. Like Imlac, the Prince travels in the oriental world to reconcile his thought with a real experience. The prince begins to learn about life in Cairo.

The city is full of strangers who come from all over the world for commerce. The first experience of the prince is also in commerce. He observes the prosperity and marketing in the despotic government of Egypt. He is curious about the benefits and nature of money. After he is admitted to the Egyptian community in Cairo, he observes the vicissitudes, frankness and courtesy of the young people. In this process, he luckily meets a man who teaches the prince what is "necessary to be known" about money and government:

> He shewed, with great strength of sentiment, and variety of illustration, that human nature is degraded and debased, when the lower faculties predominate over the higher; that when fancy, the parent of passion, usurps the dominion of the mind, nothing ensues but the natural effect of unlawful government, perturbation and confusion. (24)

They together visit the market place to observe merchants; discuss with men of learning and enter into assemblies. They discover in the end that gold and silver are the "necessaries of life" (22). But the prince learns from a wealthy man how gold and silver can be a disaster for a person. The wealthy man who welcomes him and Imlac with eastern hospitality relates his experience in Egypt, whose governor is a despot. The Prince learns from the conversation with this wise man that human nature is degraded and lower faculties predominate over the higher ones in the despotic government of the Bassa. The wealthy man admits that his prosperity puts his life in jeopardy:

> The Bassa of Egypt is my enemy, [he is] incensed only by my wealth and popularity. I have been hitherto protected against him by the princes of the country: but, as the favor of the great is uncertain, I know not how soon my defenders may be persuaded to share the plunder with the Bassa. I have sent my treasures into a distant country, and, upon the first alarm, am prepared to follow them. Then will my enemies riot in my mansion, and enjoy the gardens which I have planted. They all joined in lamenting his danger, and deprecating his exile. (26)

The debate is transformed from an economic sphere into a political one. The court of the Bassa represents oriental tyranny, persecution and despotism. Not only the prosperous merchants but also the rulers and all the members of government hate each other. The oppressive situation leaves the subjects in a continual succession of "defection, escapes and treachery" (30). Because of the Bassa, "every tongue" is censured, every eye is in search for the "faulty," the result of which is the persecution of the Bassa by the Sultan. The situation does not get better since there is no wise administration in the Ottoman Empire. After the first ruler of the town, the second Bassa is deposed because the Sultan that advanced him is murdered by the Janissaries (32). The prince, thus, learns that the Ottomans do not rule wisely according to the rules of nature[7]. People are unhappy with the despotic administration. The Sultan's authority is supported by fear, force, and a deficient system. The tyranny of the Ottoman Empire at Constantinople makes life miserable for Egyptians in Cairo. The prince discovers in the first quest that what is true of others is true for him (23). The absolute power of the king needs to be controlled by the rational system of law and democracy which is a universal and unalterable law with which every heart is originally impressed (28). It is implied in the novel that tyranny causes disaster.

After the debate about money and government with the wise merchant, the prince thinks that seclusion from society is better than wealth. He discusses this choice with a hermit who knows the difference between wealth and seclusion better than the Prince. Here, it has to be stated, Johnson has transformed the original anecdote in *Rasselas*, since there is a difference between the original one and the one used by Johnson. The original anecdote in the Turkish Tale deals with a Tunisian sheik who retired into a cave of a small village near the royal town. He used to come out of the cave once a week, on Fridays. People used to visit the sheik from different towns. Once he was visited by the prince. The prince asked him about his choice of life. He wondered whether it was right or wrong to live in a state of wealth and pleasure. The sheik did not answer the prince's question. When the prince

---

[7] As I have discussed in the earlier chapter, the same argument was made by Rica in the *Persian Letter*.

insisted, the sheik compared the prince to a dog. He said: "Think about a dog which eats the corps and lifts his leg to avoid the dirt while urinating. There is no difference between you and this dog". The prince was shocked for a while and could not say anything. The Sheik went to his cave. The prince ran after the Sheik and did not come back. In the original tale, seclusion was presented as a right choice. However, in *Rasselas* the hermit does not suggest such a choice. The hermit is not happy to live in seclusion. He hides the treasure among the rocks and tries to remove apparent evil from his life. The hermit instructs the prince about the true choice. He says: "the rule of a choice is to remove all apparent evil" (27). The prince likes the idea and resolves to retire into seclusion to remove all the apparent evil from his life. However, the hermit does not suggest this choice to the prince since it is miserable to retire into seclusion from society. After fifteen years in seclusion, the hermit calls his occupation "irksome and tasteless" and he feels "distracted and unsettled" (27-8). In the story, it is the hermit, not the prince, who changes his situation after the discussion.

The conflict of thought and experience is an on-going theme in the novel. This conflict is consistent with the perspective of innocence vs. experience. The journey of the Prince and theme of the tale are constructed upon this disparity. Such a distance between the idea of the prince and experience of the people he meets is applied to the question of reconciliation. The scientists' failure to reconcile theory and practice is another question which creates distance between theory and practice. The criticism of a science begins with the introduction of the artist skilled in mechanics and continues through the tales of the astronomer and philosopher. When the prince decides to leave the Valley, the man who is skilled in mechanical arts tells him that it is possible for men to swim through the air as the fish swim through the water. The artist makes artificial wings but he falls down into the lake right after he leaps (9). It is implied in this instance that the mechanic confines himself to what he has created. It is more apparent in the story of the astronomer. The astronomer regrets that he spent his time with experiments. He prefers comforts in life to marriage. Thus, he misses "enduring female friendship" and "domestic tenderness". At the end, he discovers that his scientific experiments have ended in error and he has "suffered much in vain" (58). Rasselas hears similar regrets from the two philosophers. He once meets a philosopher who espouses a philosophy which he claims will enable a human being to deal with the vicissitudes of life; when the philosopher is tested by the death of his daughter, his philosophy turns into failure. In each case, the correct and right choice becomes unattainable (25). He meets another man of learning who says that man has to live according to nature. When the prince asks him to define what he means by "living according to nature," the philosopher says:

> to live according to nature is to act always with due regard to the fitness arising from the relations [...] of cause and effects; to concur with the great [...] scheme of universal felicity; to cooperate with the general dispositions and tendency of present system of things. (28)

However, the philosopher's statement is more abstract than his definition and less applicable to real life; therefore, the prince thinks that he is one of the sages whom one understands less as one hears more. The silence of the prince makes the philosopher think that the prince is satisfied with the argument. The same complexity between knowledge and experience goes on in interactions between different characters. Wherever they travel, they fail to see anyone who is able to turn his knowledge and talent to experience. The mechanist discourses upon the art of flying but his flying machine refuses to fly. The wise man wisely instructs how to live according to nature but he is unable to sustain the loss of his daughter. There is disillusionment in the end. The prince is hindered by a fatal obstacle in the quest.

The conflict between theory and practice is a significant device which metaphorically illuminates the difference between the Orient and Europe. We have already argued that the European inquisitive spirit, articulate voice and philosophy are represented by Imlac and the Prince. While they travel throughout Egypt, they compare and contrast Europe and the Orient. Imlac re-places contemporary European civilization and the Oriental Ottomans into different orders of being. He claims that Europe has many advantages over the East. He says:

> I conversed with great numbers of the northern and western nations of Europe, the nations which are now in possession of all power and all knowledge, whose armies are irresistible and whose fleets command the remotest parts of the globe. When I compared these men with the natives of our own kingdom and those that surround us, they appeared almost another order of beings. In their countries it is difficult to wish for anything that may not be obtained. A thousand arts, of which we never heard, are continually laboring for their convenience and pleasure, and whatever their own climate has denied them is supplied by their commerce. (15)

Imlac lives in Palestine for three years. There he meets people from Western nations. His spiritual links to the centre of Christian religion (Palestine) and his worldly contact with the glorious western civilization are central to the representation of the Orient in the tale. Imlac's attitude and the distinctions he makes are significant because he is presented as a philosopher-poet and as the only character that is able to reconcile his knowledge with his experience. He admits that he has saved himself from the prejudice of the age and achieved transcendental truth. In spite of his knowledge of oriental learning and experience, Imlac cannot help admiring the Western civilization upon meeting some people from the northern and western Europe, though he has not visited Europe. Imlac identifies western superiority with what he hears from the speech of some men he met in Palestine. He hears that the Western nations possess all the power and knowledge, are rewarded with a thousand arts and pleasure; they enumerate the particular comforts of life, cure the diseases the Easterners perish from, obviate the inclemency of weather, dispatch laborious works with machines, are in communication with distant places, have roads cut through mountains, and live in security (14-5). Here, Imlac identifies "freedom, justice, wealth, science and knowledge" as the highest perfections of civilization, which together set the order of the progress of the Europeans. The lack of these "perfections" in addition to oriental ignorance and the corruptions of oriental countries under tyrants (the Bassa of Egypt) make the oriental world different from Europe.

The difference between Oriental society and European civilization is emphasized by savages who kidnap Pakuah. In their visit to the Egyptian pyramids, Imlac, Rasselas and Nekayah enter into the Pyramid but Pakuah cannot pass through the narrow gate. She feels safer outside. Although she escapes from the "unquiet souls" of the pyramid, she cannot escape from the unquiet savages of the desert. The Arabs kidnap Pakuah. The Bassa and Turkish armies cannot save the lady. Imlac thinks that it is not possible for Pakuah to escape without being harmed; he thinks that the Arabs will first keep her in the Seraglio due to her distinguishing quality among the savages (51). Here, the tribal Arabs and the Ottomans are referred to as invaders and low-born tyrants (47). The Arabs are presented as natural and hereditary lords of the desert; they are a warlike pastoral society and descendants of Ishmael, the illegitimate son of Abraham, whose mother was an Egyptian. He is not, unlike Isaac, promised blessing and salvation. He is a wild man whose hand is against every man (Genesis 16:12). Nassir argues this as follows:

> As descendants of Ishmael, Muslims (Arabs) are usually given wild, destructive and inferior roles in order to confirm the righteousness and supremacy of Christianity. Thus in *Rasselas* the fact that the chief of the Arabs is a son of Ishmael brings him closer to those who have been categorized under that name for centuries. It is not a compliment: his 'occupation is war.' Though he is 'not one of the lawless and cruel rovers of the desert' because he knows 'the rules of civil life,' his motive for kidnapping Pakuah is purely monetary: to increase [his] riches or more properly, to gather tribute. It is not even political struggle against the Turks, those 'invaders and low- born tyrants'. In making this distinction, Johnson perhaps forgot that the Turks are Ishmaelite, too. This picture of the chief of the Arabs fits perfectly the description of Ishmael in the Bible. He is wild, uncivilized and destructive. Definitely his hand is 'against every man and everyman's hand against him'. (141)

In the story the present image is reiterated. Oriental Arab people are presented as descendants of Ishmael, and given a minor place in the advancement of human civilization. It is implied that oriental people have through the ages been in a hereditary war with all mankind. They have been savages and robbers (*Rasselas* 34). The kidnapping becomes a metaphor to illustrate this idea. But it is also surprising for Imlac and Prince to hear that the chief of the savages would restore her for two hundred ounces of gold. The chief says:

> The purpose of my incursion is to increase my riches, or more properly to gather tribute. The sons of Ishmael are natural and hereditary lords of this part of the continent, which is usurped by late invaders, and low-born tyrants, from whom we are compelled to take by the sword what is denied to justice. The violence of war admits no distinction. (47)

The chief of the tribe is an illiterate man who is able to travel by the stars and marks in his erratic expeditions to such places in which passengers take a rest. He is not a man of the lawless and cruel rovers of the desert. He knows the rules of civil life and he promises to free Pakuah after he gets the ransom. When the Prince pays the ransom, she is released.

Johnson must be using "kidnapping" as a metaphor to attack Rousseau's idea of the noble savage and to emphasize the difference between Oriental and European society. This is made clear by Pekuah's observation on the condition of women. The representation of Oriental women in *Rasselas* is not dissimilar from the representation of women in the *Persian Letters* and the *Turkish Spy*. Pakuah observes among the tribal Arab society the condition of oriental women. She agrees that they are beautiful, but she claims that they are not intelligent or witty. Oriental "women are of low intellect and understanding" (40). For instance, the chief of the tribe looks at women as flowers casually plucked and carelessly thrown away, and to be sometimes turned away from with disgust. The Arab chief and the women in his seraglio belong to the oriental world order. In this world, women are considered inferior; there are no loves or feelings of a natural relationship between men and women. Men are not exalted by the smile of women, they are never sure of the sincerity of women who do not see any men other than their husbands (50). Pakuah describes the life of the tribal women as follows:

> They run from room to room as a bird hops from wire to wire in his cage. They danced for the sake of motion, as lambs frolic in a meadow. One sometimes pretended to be hurt that the rest might be alarmed or hid herself that another might seek her. […] They had

> lived in that narrow spot. Of what they had not seen, they could have no knowledge, for they could not read. [...] They hardly had names for anything but their clothes and their food. (48-9)

Here, once more oriental people, this time oriental women, are compared to animals. They are caged and they are denied access to knowledge. They cannot read, learn or know about anything. They know only about their clothes and their food (which may represent the animal instinct necessary for survival). The general image of oriental women enslaved in the Harem is represented in *Rasselas* with the two animal similes of "birds" and "frolicking lambs". Nekayah visits many families and observes the same condition of women. She discovers that oriental women have narrow thoughts, low expectations and artificial happiness:

> Their pleasures, poor as they are, could not be preserved pure, but were embittered by petty competitions and worthless emulation. They were always jealous of the beauty of each other, of a quality to which solicitude can add nothing and from which detraction can nothing away. Many were in love with trifles like themselves, and many fancied that they were in love when in truth they were only idle. (30)

Egyptian women do not have a sense of virtue; they do not have a sense of joy and grief. They are lascivious and led by their desire; therefore, they do not have a past or a future (31). They belong to a different civilization, therefore "it is impossible for them to pass independent judgment. Whatever they say, they say it to emphasize the order of difference between Eastern and Western civilizations" (qtd. in Nassir 145).

The depiction of the Oriental Egyptians as savages and the re-placement of the Orient as a different civilization by Imlac seem to contradict Johnson's admiration of the East as the origin of all good ancient things in Western civilization. However, there is a difference in *Rasselas* between the Ancient Orient and contemporary Orient. Johnson states that "among all these good eastern things Christianity is the highest perfection of humanity". He admires the ancient Egyptians and the spiritual Christian heritage of the Orient in *Rasselas*. There is a desire to search for the origin and traces of the ancient

Oriental civilizations; a search for new and lost knowledge, which has to be distinguished from the representation of the Oriental Islamic civilization. Mohan argues that 18th century Enlightenment writers admitted the contribution of the ancient Eastern civilization to the body of European knowledge. They attempted to trace the diffusion of knowledge from the ancient world to the modern. He says:

> The Enlightenment represented a search for new and lost knowledge, an understanding of other cultures and people, and an attempt to trace the diffusion of knowledge from the ancient world to the modern. In a sense, the Enlightenment actually saw the glimmerings of what can be termed 'world history'. (Mohan 173)

Imlac first distinguishes the position of contemporary European and Oriental civilizations. He identifies the Orient as a different civilization and admires the position of European nations in the birth place of Christianity. Then, he attempts to contextualize the position of the ancient Egyptians and the lessons that he anticipates pyramids would teach the world in terms of morality. Imlac considers the pyramids as the second greatest work of man and decides to stay among them until he glimpses the mystery of the great monument (39-40). Imlac explains to the prince and Nekayah the principles of the great works:

> When they came to the Great Pyramid they were astonished at the extent of the base, and the height of the top. Imlac explained to them the principles upon which the pyramidal form was chosen for a fabrick intended to co-extend its duration with that of the world: he showed that its gradual diminution gave it such stability, as defeated all the common attacks of the elements, and could scarcely be overthrown by earthquakes themselves, the least resistible of natural violence. A concussion that should shatter the pyramid would threaten the dissolution of the continent. (39)

Imlac views the Ancient Egypt as a superior culture worthy of notice. He focuses on this aspect of the Egyptian culture and tries to anticipate what kinds of lessons the Egyptian pyramids can teach him. Imlac, Rasselas, Pakuah and Nekayah visit the distant rooms of the pyramid and they measure all the dimensions of its structure. When they come to the narrow entrance, Pakuah trembles and she refuses to go in. Imlac thinks that the great wall of China "secured a wealthy and timorous nation from the incursion of Barbarians," but "for the pyramids" he cannot give any adequate reason. He interprets the structure; the chambers are narrow so that the treasure of the king might be securely protected (40). The close-up view of these great works of men provides Imlac with a moral lesson. Having visited the pyramids and failed to understand the motives for the construction of these monuments, he considers this mighty structure as a monument of the insufficiency of human enjoyments:

> A king, whose power is unlimited, and whose treasures surmount all real and imaginary wants, is compelled to solace, by the erection of a pyramid, the satiety of dominion and tastelessness of pleasures, and to amuse the tediousness of declining life, by seeing thousands laboring without end, and one stone, for no purpose, laid upon another. Whoever thou art, that not content with a moderate condition, imagines happiness in royal magnificence, and dreams that command or riches can feed the appetite of novelty with perpetual gratifications, survey the pyramids, and confess thy folly! (40)

In describing the greatness and magnificent achievement of the ancient Egypt, he regrets the lost knowledge of this great civilization. He implies that Arab savagery and Ottoman tyranny were probably responsible for the corruption of Egypt. The ancient pyramids do not anticipate the contribution of ancient Egypt to the human progress. They remain as "the piles of stones and mounds of earth" (41).

Representation of the Middle Eastern Orient in *Vathek* (1786)

There are two arguments about Beckford's tale. Conant treats *Vathek* as one of the typical imaginative pseudo-oriental tales of the 18th century (36) while Robert Gemmet argues that *Vathek* presents a different image of the East because of Beckford's researches about the Orient (117). We have to state that Beckford's *Vathek* is more important than Johnson's *Rasselas* for the present study for two reasons. Firstly, *Rasselas* is a moral tale and deals with the glory of the ancient Oriental Egyptian civilization. In *Rasselas*, the Christian Orient is valued differently by Imlac (Johnson's mouthpiece) who bestows a lower cultural status on the Ottoman Orient. *Vathek*, on the other hand, is about the medieval Islamic Orient. Secondly, *Rasselas* is a moral and philosophical tale which does not have a dominant Oriental context. *Vathek*, on the other hand, includes a lot of Oriental references, and it is closer in spirit to the *Arabian Nights* than *Rasselas*. Thus, *Vathek*, as a pseudo-oriental tale, has to be given a particular place in the 18th century tradition of the Oriental tales in English literature. My aim here is to illuminate these three aspects: first to explain the special relation between Beckford's biography and *Vathek*; secondly, to review Beckford's research and idea of the Orient; and lastly, to discuss the difference of *Vathek* from any other 18th century pseudo-oriental tale.

William Beckford's Biography and *Vathek* (1786)

There are two different accounts of the birth of William Beckford. Ousby says that he was born in 1759, the year before the accession of King George III, at Fonthill, Wiltshire as a son of a wealthy Alderman, who became twice Lord Mayor of London (70). Tinker thinks that William Beckford was born into a wealthy and politically prominent family on September 28, 1760. However, it is certain that his father represented London in Parliament and became twice a Mayor of London. After his father's death, he became one of the wealthiest son of England. Lord Chatham and Lord Chancellor Thurlow shared guardianship of Beckford. He was educated privately in political and liberal sciences. His passions were the cause of his ruin. One of the passions that proved to be Beckford's ruin was his lifelong attraction to pre-adolescent boys. In 1779 he fell in love with Lord Courtenay of Powderham's cousin William which ended his political career with Lord Loughborough's rumor that Beckford was seen through a keyhole at Powderham Castle in sodomy with his nephew, William Courtenay. After this incident, he was excluded from political life and polite society (Tinker 1-2). Beckford was not a man who cared about a political career. He was a compulsive collector and builder. He purchased and collected rarities. He says: "I am determined to enjoy my dreams, my phantasies and all my singularity [...] however irksome and discordant they are to the worldlings round me. In spite of them, I will be happy" (qtd. in James 71). To realize his dream, he first bought the old family mansion at Fonthill Abbey and spent most of his fortune to reconstruct an elaborate gothic mansion as "the most astonishing private house ever to be built in England" (73). Yet, he abandoned the mansion after the fall of its immense tower. Beckford married Lady Margaret Gordon in 1783; they together traveled for one year in Europe. After the death of his wife, Beckford went into bitter depression and spent most of the next ten years of his life in exile (74).

It is possible to find parallels between Caliph Vathek and William Beckford. The rumor secluded Beckford from the social world of London after which he developed sympathy for the dissenter: "when Beckford was accused by political rivals of sodomizing Lord Loughborough's fifteen-year old nephew, he excluded himself from political life" (Tinker 2). Then, he traveled to Grand Chartreuse in Switzerland where he wrote *Excursion to Grand Chartreuse* (1779). His reflections in the *Excursion to Grand Chartreuse*, display the profound effect of this retreat upon the sensitive mind of young Beckford (Fothergill 33). He writes: "The Grand Chartreuse has exceeded my imagination, it is wonderfully wilder than I can describe or even you can imagine" ("Thoughts and Incidents" 263). The Grand Chartreuse, where he compared himself to Moses who received his revelation in the desert, stimulated Beckford's spirit. He finds a vast forest, "frowning on the brows of a mountain in which there were broken pines, pointed rocks and stakes of iron" ("Thoughts and Incidents" 267). Here, he feels seized by the genius of the place and with its religious gloom. According to Beckford, the sublimity of this place would alone be "sufficient to impress the idea" which forms the foundation of creative work (268).

He falls so much under the influence of this place that he can neither think nor speak. The excursion to the Chartreuse becomes a pilgrimage and journey for revelation. During his residence at the Chartreuse, he goes through the cleft, cavern, valley and cataract, listens to the mingling murmurs of nature and hears "the strangest sound that ever reached his ear"

("Thoughts and Incidents" 264). He re-imagines the despair of Saint Bruno, who entered the valley and did not return from the Desert of the Charthusians. Beckford also compares himself to St. Bruno, who was like Beckford possessed considerable wealth. He was talented in science and was remarkable in the qualities of the mind. Yet, "being always poetical, singular and visionary, he soon grew disgusted with the world and in early life went into retirement" ("Thoughts and Incidents" 274)[8]. According to Beckford, St. Bruno's retirement to this holy place enabled the Saint to have spiritual wisdom. He thinks that the Saint's retirement to the desert was rewarded by good fathers "with admirable dish of miracle, well-seasoned with the devil, and prettily garnished with angels and moon-beams". Beckford expresses this as follows:

> This venerable prelate imparted him a vision. [...] Whilst he was ardently gazing at this wonder; a still voice was heard, declaring it, the future abode of Bruno; by him to be consecrated, as a retirement for holy man, desirous of holding converse with their God. No shepherd's pipe was to be heard within these precincts: no huntsman's prophane feet to tread these silent regions, which were to be dedicated, solely, to their Creator. ("Thoughts and Incidents" 274)

In the Chartreuse, Beckford sits down before the works of St. Bruno during the nights to read the allegory of the birds, beasts, fishes, paradise, the glory of Solomon's temple, the New Jerusalem and numberless other subjects full of superstitions. Beckford writes: "Saint Bruno was certainly a mighty genius: I admire the motives which drew him to this desert" ("Thoughts and Incidents" 274). This distant desert and the Saint inspire extravagant feelings in Beckford. This is apparent in Beckford's description of the Saint's portrait with his pupils. He is captured by the painting of the Saint in the Chartreuse and reflects his revelation upon this portrait:

---

[8] St. Bruno became the head chancellor at the age of twenty-one. He protested against the misdoings of the Archbishop, disposed of all his offices and flew to seclusion in 1076. He founded the Charthusian Order near Grenoble. Later, he refused to be Archbishop and all ecclesiastical offices. He spent the rest of his life in the desert in Calabria in a monastery. This monastery was an asylum for anyone who was disgusted with the world (for further information visit www.vikipedia.com).

> Were I, after walking along the dim cloisters, and passing through the anti-chapel, faintly illuminated by a solitary lamp, suddenly to enter this solitary hall at midnight, when the convocation is assembled, and the synod of the venerable fathers, all in solemn order, surrounding the successor of Bruno; it would be a long while, I believe, before I could recover from the surprise of so august a spectacle. [...] For my own part, I must confess, that the hall, though divested of all this accompaniment, filled me with veneration I scarcely knew how to account for; [...] the form of Bruno was almost lost in the splendors of stars which hovered above him. (271)

Beckford fancies himself capable of plunging into the horrors of the desert by forgoing all the vanities and delights of the world for the sake of this sublime consecration. He is much tempted by the wonders and miraculous nature of St. Bruno and his seclusion in the desert near Grand Chartreuse. In this excursion, Beckford is contented enough to relate his own inspirations, apparitions and mystery. The tranquillity of the region fills him with the most pleasing and sublime sensations (277). He follows the impulse which drives him to the summit of mountains, he "casts a look upon the whole extent of wild woods and romantic precipices," contemplates on every rock "that might have met" the Saint's eyes. He runs to every "withered pine" whose appearance bespeaks the antiquity or witnesses the repose of Bruno to feel the sacred spirit of his institutions. During "this wild excursion" he thinks of the days of St. Bruno but cannot "unfold the strange things" in prose (279). Beckford's feelings and extraordinary sensations continue until he leaves the valley.

Beckford's residence in and reflections at the Grand Chartreuse are significant because his experience of seclusion from society as represented in the story of St. Bruno anticipates the content and structure of *Vathek*. The idea of excursion to the desert is further developed in the story of Vathek. Caliph Vathek curses the religious and traditional codes in favor of power and knowledge and consistently pursues his own destiny. Traditional orthodox Islam suggests rationality as a condition for happiness. Caliph Vathek, however, abandons moral discipline and bravely attacks orthodox beliefs and morality with his excessive appetites and vices. He establishes his own heaven in the Hall of Eblis where he can gratify all his forbidden desires. As noted by Brian Fothergill, the visit to the Grande Chartreuse provides visual properties and atmospheric effects that are to reappear in a sinister form in *Vathek* (39). When Beckford began to write *Vathek* he recreated the same atmosphere. He worked on the mountains, valleys, dark forests, good fathers, and the vast desert of Grenoble. He made the Caliph's palace as attractive as Grenoble. It is similarly one of the rarities of the world. The Caliph has omitted nothing in his palace that might gratify the curiosity of those who resort to it (*Vathek* 2). As Tinker stated, Beckford must have developed the idea of an unorthodox caliph upon his visit to Grenoble (70). Vathek, very much like the Saint and visitor of Grenoble, curses the social restrains and chooses ways of his own. In addition, there is obvious similarity between the description of Grande Chartreuse and the ruins of Isthakar; they are both described as secluded like the desert of Calabria. Caliph Vathek, like Beckford of the Grande Chartreuse, is led and inspired by the spiritual guidance of the devil and the spirits of the valley.

It was not only Grand Chartreuse which influenced Beckford's imagination. He admits that the residence in Fonthill Abbey provided him with some necessary images for the description of the Hall of Eblis. In the letter to Louisa and in the Chapman edition of Beckford's biography, the following description of the Hall of Eblis is recalled from Beckford's home at Fonthill:

> The solid Egyptian Hall looked as if hewn out of a living rock. The line of apartments and apparently endless passages extending from it on either side were all vaulted, an interminable staircase, which when you looked down it, appeared as deep as the well in the pyramid, and when you looked up, was lost in vapour. [...] [T]he vastness, the intimacy of this vaulted labyrinth occasioned so bewildering an effect that it became almost impossible for any one to define – at the moment – where he stood, where he had been, or to whither he was wandering. [...] No wonder such scenery inspired the description of the Halls of Eblis. (qtd. in Garret 21)

After the publication of *Vathek,* Beckford wrote to Clarke, the book seller. He stated that he was very young when he committed *Vathek* to paper. He stated that the scenes which preceded and followed the magnificent celebration of his twenty-first birthday –the Egyptian halls and vaulted chambers of Fonthill, peopled with the prototypes of Gulchenrouz and Nouronihar, solely visible for three consecutive days and nights by the glow of lamps and fires – suggested his first ideas of the Palace of Eblis (qtd. in Marzick vi). He worked with this vision to create an Eastern atmosphere.

William Beckford's Source of the Oriental Perspective in *Vathek*

Vathek (1786) is a story of an extraordinary Arabian caliph. Caliph Vathek is introduced as the ninth caliph of the Abbasids. He is the grandson of Haroun Al-Rachid and the son of Motassam. In the story, Beckford deals with Vathek's pursuit of power and knowledge. He builds a tower to study stars and he is fond of debating with the learned. He is visited by an extraordinary man who gives him a saber which has magical inscriptions. Vathek receives help from a stranger to learn about the inscription. Later, we understand that the stranger who gave the saber and the stranger who translated the inscription are the same person, Giaour. Giaour promises Caliph Vathek access to the secret world of darkness and the treasure of Pre-Adamite Sultans on condition that Vathek abjures Mohammed. The Caliph agrees and follows Giaour's commandments to get the promise. He sacrifices fifty children; burns his subjects in the tower and curses Heaven. On his way to the subterranean palace and to the Hall of the Eblis, he visits the sacred valley of Fakreddin. Here, Vathek is given one more chance by Heaven and he is re-invited to repent by a Genii. He rejects and curses Heaven again. He also falls in love with Nouronihar, Fakreddin's daughter who is engaged to Gulchenrouz. She joins Vathek on the journey and they together go to the Hall of Eblis. Vathek's mother, Carathis, helps Vathek throughout the journey. They arrive at the Hall but they realize that the promise of the Devil is permanent fire.

Although there is a cloud over Beckford's own experience, Beckford's ability to reconcile his life-experience with his extensive reading about the Orient locates *Vathek* in a peculiar place in terms of the representation of the Ottoman Orient in 18th century English literature. *Vathek*'s difference from Johnson's *Rasselas* and other pseudo-oriental tales can be illuminated with respect to its process of creation and to its extensive Oriental references. It is significant to explain the process, which created the story of Vathek for the purpose of this study. Beckford wrote in a letter to Samuel Henley, his tutor, that he set to work so horridly that he trembled to relate it and called *Vathek* a "wild and terrible story of unbridled passion" (qtd. in Gemmett 21). But this "wild" story was not a production of "the unbridled passion alone;" the story was written in collaboration and in constant communication with Henley (Beckford's tutor). The exchange of letters between Beckford and Henley indicates the significance of this interaction. In Beckford's letter of April 23, 1782, this influence is apparent:

> I have given my attention for several days past to 'Vathek', and have made several little alterations which you will not perhaps disapprove. The 'Arabian Nights' will furnish some illustrations, particularly as to Goules, &c.; but much more may be learned from Herbelot's 'Bibliotheque Orientale' and Richardson's 'Dissertations.' I know not how to make the damnations you advise. I have always thought Nouronihar too severely punished, and if I knew how conveniently, would add a crime or two to her share. What say you? Let me know. (qtd. in Garnett x)

Henley's assistance was the moving spirit of the process from the beginning. As Beckford admits: "I shut up myself in my apartment as you advised (the spirit has moved me) I have given way to fancies and imagination" (qtd. in Marzik vi). Beckford frequently wrote to Henley to inform him about the process. On April of 1783, he wrote to Henley that his "Arabian Tale" went on prodigiously; on May 1 he wrote that *Vathek* went on surprisingly (iv). On April 9 he wrote to Henley again: "You make me proud of *Vathek*. [...] I should run wild amongst my rocks, forests, telling stones and trees and laborers how gloriously I succeeded" (ix). He wrote another letter to Henley on February 9 in 1786 to inform him that *Vathek* was almost finished and he wanted to see it in print (xi). He also expressed in this letter that he enjoyed Henley's notes and "preliminary dissertation" about the Orient. He informed Henley about the sources of certain motifs in the story of Caliph *Vathek*. Beckford wrote: "the nine pillars are his own erection;" "the Cocknos is a bird much esteemed in Persia," and "the butterflies of Cachemire are taken from Meschi's poem" (xiii).

Beckford's interest in the Orient and his readings about Oriental history, culture and society are the other important aspects which will illuminate our argument. The Orient was one of the Beckford's dreams which he was determined to enjoy. From a very early age he obsessively occupied himself with reading Oriental literature. He used to go to his bed with Oriental tales in his hand and fall asleep reading them; once his tutor suggested to his aunt that little Beckford should be prevented from reading the *Arabian Nights*, which would influence his character badly: "From boyhood, he was fascinated by Asia" (qtd. in James 71). When his tutor forced him to burn "a splendid heap of oriental drawings," Beckford had one of the greatest traumas of his childhood (72). Nobody could convince him to abandon his oriental fantasies. After he built the great mansion at the Fonthill Abbey, Beckford bought the library of the great English orientalist, Edward Gibbon. He says: "I shut off myself for six weeks, from early in the morning until night, only now and then taking a ride. The People thought me mad. I read myself nearly blind" (qtd. in James 74). He read extensively from eastern writers and travellers who described the Eastern manners, countries and people (Marzick xvi). He wrote about his fascination for the Orient to his sister. He stated in one letter to her that he delighted in reading about the spice trees and strange animals of the East:

> Don't fancy, my Dear Sister, I am enraptured with Orientals themselves. It is the country they inhabit which claims all the admiration I bestow on that quarter of the Globe. It is their woods of Spice trees, their strange animals, and their vast rivers I delight in. The East must be better known than it is sufficiently liked or disliked. If you would form a tolerable judgment upon it in a single relation, not one voyage or volume of travels must be neglected. (qtd. in Hayward 121)

Beckford must have been determined to know the Oriental world sufficiently in order to improve his judgment and knowledge. In particular, his enthusiasm and love for the Orient was encouraged by his tutor Samuel Henley who was also an enthusiastic student of Persian and Arabian literature. Beckford studied with Henley after the return from his journey in 1781: "he nourished his imagination with oriental lore from Henley" (Marzik vi). William Beckford possessed a broad and deep knowledge of the Orient which he filed away in his memory. In addition to the books in the library of Edward Gibbon, he got in his library the works of William Jones, Rycaut's *The Present State of the Turkish Empire*, D'Herbelot's *Bibliotheque Orientale*, Montagu's *The Turkish Embassy Letters*, Galland's *Arabian Nights*, the *Mogul Tales,* and the *Turkish Tales*, and Sale's translation of the *Koran* (Hayward 120). The *Story of Caliph Vathek* is an embodiment of Beckford's extensive reading about the Middle Eastern Orient. There are quotations and notes from the above mentioned and also other books on the Orient. These notes create a belief that *Vathek* is a novel about the customs, culture and religion of the Orient: "they create a sense of reality [;] [...] they ask the reader to believe in the basic truth of Beckford's character" (Hayward 121). Sampson also states:

> The last notable Oriental tale of the eighteenth century, *Vathek* was considered a watershed in that it displayed the author's in depth understanding of Eastern languages, customs, history and religion. Beckford attempted to authenticate his narrative with the use of notation and references to actual places, personages, and words. [...] Beckford's acquired knowledge of the East grew to become a scholarly, literary, and personal obsession. (101)

Vathek holds a unique place among the eighteenth century Oriental tales for creating a shift toward and anticipating the more informed Orientalism of the nineteenth century. Beckford made use of significant sources to write Vathek from the informed Oriental point of view. Hayward states that D'Herbelot's *Bibliotheque Orientale* (1778) was one of the sources Beckford relied on to create *Vathek* (120). In the *Bibliotheque Orientale*, D'Herbelot refers to Vathek Billah as the ninth caliph of the Abbasids and the grandson of Haron al-Rachid from his son's (Motassam) Greek wife. Beckford also introduced Vathek in the novel as the ninth Caliph of the race of the Abbasids, the son of Motassam and the grandson of Haroun Al Rachid (*Vathek* 17). Beckford's use of D'Herbelot's notes is illuminating but incomplete. As Beckford wrote, Vathek was the 3rd son of Motassam. After the death of Mutassam, Vasık (Vathek must be Beckford's or D'Herbelot's translation, the original Arabic name of the Mutassam's 3rd son was Vasık) became the ninth Sultan of the Abbasid[9]. As written by Beckford, Vathek was different from his father to a certain extent. When his father (Mutassam) became the 8th caliph of the Abbasids, he declared *Mutezile* as the formal religion of the state and had the scholars, who rejected Mutezile, severely whipped. Vasık, like his father, resolved to have reason on his side. But unlike his father, he was fond of engaging in disputes with the learned, but liked them not to push their opposition with warmth; he stopped the mouths of those with presents whose mouths could be stopped, while others, whom his liberty was unable to subdue, "he sent to prison to cool their blood" (*Vathek* 18). Quotations and notes from the Oriental literature and religion are noteworthy. For instance, the reference to Monker and Nakir, to the animals admitted to the Paradise and the story of Leileh and Megnoun indicate Beckford's extensive readings. Fakreddin and Sutlememe, in order to save Nouronihar and Gulchenrouz from Vathek, decide to give them a magical powder, which will temporarily make them dead. This trick will save Nouronihar and Gulchenrouz from the Caliph. They drink the sherbet and sleep. When they awake, Gulchenrouz asks: "Where are we? Do you not see those specters that are stirring the burning coals? Are they Monker and Nakir?" (46). "The ass of Balaam," "dogs of seven sleepers" and other animals admitted into the paradise of Mahomet are referred to on page 31. Gulchenrouz is introduced as the most delicate and lovely creature in the world who can recite the love story of Leila and Megnoun: "When he sang the loves of Megnoun and Leileh, tears insensibly overflowed the checks of his auditors" (41).

---

[9] Beckford introduces Vathek as the son of Motassam, which is consistent with the Islamic historical sources. Vasik (Vathek) was the ninth caliph and son of Motassam, but Beckford later writes about a fight between Vathek and his brother Mutevekkil (48). In the Islamic historical source, Motavakel [Mutevekkil] is introduced as one of the three sons of Vasik who fought against his two brothers to become Sultan. The fight was actually between the sons of Vasik (www.kitapmollacami.com). It is also written that Caliph Vasik (Vathek in Beckford's tale) made Mutezile a formal religion of the state. Mutezile relies on reason and rejects the spiritual aspects of Islam. Beckford also uses the struggle between Vathek and Mutevekkil in the tale. This conflict actually took place between Vasik's three sons, one of whose name was Mutevekkil. The Abbasid State was divided into three different states after Vasik's death. Detailed information about this issue can also be found in Macid Fahri's book, *Islam Felsefe Tarihi* (1987).

William Beckford also works with actual historical Oriental texts and characters in *Vathek*. Vasık was a historical character; Haroun Al Rachid, Omar Ben Abdalaziz, Motassam, Mutevekkil, Bababalouk, Nimrod, Suleiman and Princess of Saba, dwarves, mutes and eunuchs are all Oriental characters he uses in *Vathek*. Haroun Al Rachid[10] appears as one of the righteous rulers in the *Arabian Nights*. He was one of the common Sultan characters of the *Nights*. As in the story of Beckford, Haroun Al Rachid appears in several cycles of anecdotes in the *Nights* (Ranelagh 196). Omar Ben Abdalaziz is presented in *Vathek* as a caliph who believes that "it was necessary to make hell of this world to enjoy Paradise in the next" (*Vathek* 18). Historically it is evidenced that Omar Ben Abdalaziz was a wealthy man before he became caliph; and after he became caliph, he devoted all his wealth and the jewellery of his wife to the government budget and lived a simple life during his reign, believing that he would be rewarded by God hereafter.[11] Beckford made use of this historical information to create a contrast between caliph Vathek and Omar Ben Abdalaziz. Beckford introduces Vathek as follows: "Being much addicted to women and the pleasures of table, he sought by his affability to procure agreeable companions [...] nor he thinks with the Caliph Omar Ben Abdalaziz that it was necessary to make hell of this world to enjoy Paradise in the next" (18). Vathek resembles Nimrod and Pharaoh more than any other characters in the tale. Nimrod of the *Genesis*, the *Koran* and the *Arabian Nights* built a high tower to reach Heaven. Then, "in order to attack God, [he] lifted himself to heaven in a chest flown by four young eagles" (Ranelagh 77). Vathek spends his nights on the summit of his tower to become an adept in the mysteries of astrology (*Vathek* 19). The sacrifice of fifty children must have been taken from the story of the Pharaoh in the *Old Testament* and *Koran*. In the scripture, the Pharaoh orders the slaughter of every new-born male-child of the Jews in Egypt in order to save his kingdom. It is believed that Moses was supplied with all the strength of the children slaughtered by the Pharaoh. Likewise, Vathek's mother believed that the sacrifice of the most beautiful children of the preeminent family in Isthakar would give the

---

[10] The word Rachid means honest and just. This title was said to have been given to Caliph Haroun for his justice and righteousness.
[11] www.4fakulte.com (Istanbul University, Faculty of Theology)

Caliph the strength and privilege to get the key to the Subterranean fire and treasure of Soliman (18). The description is as follows:

> Suspecting nothing, they went forward towards the plain full of childish pranks. Some chased butterflies, others picked flowers or gathered up shining pebbles, and a few rambled away for the greater pleasure it gave them to overtake their companions again and salute them with kisses. (20)

Vathek prepares the victims for the sacrifice. He undresses with them to encourage the children. He hurls them down into the hand of the insatiable Giaour. The Caliph completes his mission and comes closer to the subterranean fire.

The reference to the story of Suleiman and The Queen of Sheba on page 51 was also taken from an Islamic source. Beckford must have taken this reference from Sali's *Koran* since the story of Solomon and The Queen of Sheba is recorded in Sura XXVII in the Koran (Ranelagh 25). Flat characters like Bababalouk, dwarves, mutes and eunuchs must have been taken from Rycaut's *The Present State of the Turkish Empire* (1668). Rycaut gives detailed descriptions of the dwarves, mutes, eunuchs and black eunuchs at the Ottoman court. He says that there are sorts of Attendants at the Ottoman court called Eunuchs, Mutes and dwarves. They are lodged among the Pages at the inner palace. They have a special language to express themselves. They protect the harem and serve the Grand Signior in the palace (Rycaut 34-5). They have a similar role in *Vathek*. Mutes, blinds and female Negroes are presented as "vigilant guards" (33), submissive servants and permanent waiters of the tower. They never allow anyone except for the chief eunuch to go through the door of the tower (28-9). Bababalouk is first introduced as the chief eunuch who protects the most precious Circassian of Caliph Vathek (23); he and eunuchs in the harem take care of the Circassian (31). Fakreddin[12] has dwarves in his harem. They direct Bababalouk to the secret apartment of the women in Fakreddin's harem. There is a special sign language which Bababalouk speaks with the Vizier (28).

---

[12] Fakreddin is Gulchenrouz's father and Nouronihar's uncle.

Vathek's relation to the oriental tales is consistent. Beckford, as mentioned before, had in his library the *Mogul Tales* and *Turkish Tales*. The first *Turkish Tales* was translated in 1707 by Petis de La Croix, a French orientalist. Petis's *Tales* was translated into English by Ambrose Philips in 1707 for "half a-crown" for each section. Pope made fun of this payment: "The Bard who pilfer'd Pastorals renown / Who turns a Persian tale for a half-a-crown" (qtd. in Nassir 19). The translations of the *Turkish Tales* and the *Persian Tales* were published and had made six editions by 1750. The tales were read by and influenced Johnson, Addison, Steel and Beckford. According to Conant, the *Turkish Tales* became the source of William Beckford's *Vathek*. Beckford "reconstructs *Vathek* upon the story of 'The History of Santon Barsisa' and 'Adventures of Abdalla'" (Conant 26). The story of Barsisa consists of a dialogue between the devil and the saint. The Saint is determined to get rid of all worldly pleasures. A woman comes to visit him. She asks the Saint to make a choice: the Saint has to choose between drinking wine, committing adultery or killing the little child. He chooses to drink the wine. But he becomes drunk after which he commits adultery and murders the child. In the end, he is sentenced to death. On the scaffold, the saint hears the whisper of the devil: "Saint, if you will worship me, I will extricate you out of this difficulty and transport you two thousand leagues from here, into a country where you shall be reverenced by men as much as you were before this adventure" (qtd. in Conant 27). Saint Barsisa consents to the Devil and agrees to worship him on condition that he is delivered. Having the bowl as a sign of adoration, the Devil is satisfied and disappears after spitting in the saint's face (28). William Beckford in *Vathek* changes the direction of the tale with further additions; Vathek's fate is re-written with respect to the Saint's destiny. The two are true men at the beginning. The saint is protected by the Holy Spirit before he drinks the wine. Caliph Vathek is given a chance until he completely absconds with the Devil. The dialogues between the Devil and the two characters are also similar. The Devil knows and cunningly uses their weaknesses. Yet, Vathek is closer in spirit to Faustus than to the Saint in that "he wishes to know everything, even sciences that do not exist" (*Vathek* 5).

There are also some obvious points of similarity between the "Story of Abdalla" and *Vathek* in terms of description. The "Story of Abdalla" was first written in England by Addison in the *Guardian* No. 167. There is a correspondence between Vathek and Alnareschin, Fakreddin and Selim, Balsora and Nouronihar. For instance, Balsora's accidental meeting with his brother Abdalla in the "Story of Abdalla" is very similar to Vathek's meeting of Nouronihar (Svilpis 59). But, Beckford's imagination adds more vividness and diversity to the destiny of the character compared to the original story of Abdalla (Conant 36). Conant quotes from the *Mogul Tales* and *Vathek* to indicate the similarities and differences. The description in the *Mogul Tales* is as follows:

> Aboul-Assam tells how he saw "flambeau [...] carried by little man [...] entering a subterranean passage. [...] We went down together [...] into the mountain; at last we traversed a long alley of black marble; but so finely polished, that it had appearance of a looking-glass; [...] we reached a large hall, where we found three man standing mute, and in postures of sorrow. They were looking earnestly on a triangular table, whereon lay a book with clasp of gold; on its back was this inscription: 'Let no man touch this divine treatise that is not perfectly pure' [...]. I wish said I [...] that this peace may continue always among you. Peace is banished from these sad places, replied the eldest of three, with an air of sternness [...]. We, wait, said the second in this sepulcher, for the just judgment of God. You are then, continued I, great sinners. Alas, cried the third, we are continually tortured for our evil actions. [...] They unbuttoned their waistcoats, and through their skin, which appeared like crystal, I saw their hearts compassed with fire, by which, though burnt without ceasing, yet (they were) [...] never consumed; I then was at no loss for the reason of their looking so ghastly and affrighted. (37-8)

In the "History of the Blind Man of Chitor," in the *Mogul Tales*, the description of the "flaming hearts of sinners" in the ghastly subterranean passage is similar to the description of men in the hall of Eblis. The scene reminds Aboul-Assam of his past sins. Due to his sins, he was condemned to blindness for seven years. Vathek has the same destiny. He is similarly punished for his sins, but Vathek's fate is more dramatic and tragic. Beckford emphasizes the catastrophe of the character rather than what prepares the catastrophe. According to Conant, the catastrophe in the Hall of Eblis indicates the greatness of *Vathek*. She argues this as follows:

> the catastrophe in the Hall of Eblis –in which the author, having laid aside the mockery, the coarseness, and the flippancy that reduce the first part of the book to the level of a mere jeu d'sprit, shows himself capable of conceiving and depicting an impressive catastrophe. From the moment when Vathek and Nouronihar approach the dark mountains guarding the infernal regions until they meet their doom, the note of horror is sustained. 'A deathlike stillness reigned over the mountain and through the air; the moon dilated on a vast platform the shade of the lofty columns which reached from the terrace almost to the clouds; the gloomy watch-towers were veiled by no roof, and their capitals, of an architecture unknown in the records of the earth, served as an asylum for the birth of darkness, which alarmed at the approach of such visitants, fled away croaking'. They proceeded, and ascending the steps of a vast staircase, reached the terrace which was flagged with squares of marble, and resembled a smooth expanse of water, upon whose surface not a leaf even dared to vegetate; on the right rose the watch-towers, ranged before the ruin of an immense palace. (62-3)

The similarities between the "History of the Blind Man of Chitor" and *Vathek* clearly indicate Beckford's indebtedness to the *Mogul Tale*. Both Caliph Vathek and Aboul-Assam pass through the halls and "behold the multitudes of dead figures, their hands in their hearts". However, the objects described in *Vathek* have the liveliness of imagination. Vathek's attention is directed to the magnificent structure and design of the Hall. He peers at the terrace reared on the mountain with excitement rather than horror, secretly admires the whiteness of marbles standing at the abyss, which indicates the end of the journey; he trembles while watching the rocks yawning and the staircase disclosing behind him, which are all together not different from what "Nouronihar had seen in her vision". Like Milton's Satan, Giaour is a protagonist of the journey and leads Vathek all through the way to his catastrophe. Giaour, as in the Faustus saga and in the story of Saint Barsisa, appears whenever Vathek's hopes begin to shake, and tempts him again to the magnificent hall.

***Vathek*'s Difference from Other 18th Century Pseudo-oriental Tales**

Edward Said discusses William Beckford's idea of the Orient in the historical context of Western Orientalism. As we know, Said's argument emphasizes the European tendency to look at the Orient as images rather than as an actual entity. He writes that writers like Beckford, Byron and Goethe were provoked by certain Oriental images, rhythms and motifs. The actual Orient rarely guided them. In *Orientalism* Said states this as follows:

> William Beckford, Byron, Goethe and Hugo restructured the Orient by their art and made its colors, lights, and people visible through their images, rhythms, and motifs. At most, the real Orient provoked a writer to his vision; it very rarely guided him. (22)

Said's argument makes the imaginary European perception of the Orient vs. actual social and geographical existence of the Orient a central debate in *Orientalism*. The argument, though it criticizes this perspective, makes the imaginary vs. actual division a central phenomenon. It is argued, however, that Beckford, Byron and Goethe employ certain Oriental images to express their vision of the Orient. It is significant that these writers do not have a strong claim to represent the actual Orient. It is made clear by such writers that the Orient they write about consists of their own visions, which are various. In particular, William Beckford's idea and vision of the Orient presents a rich and complex vision of the East because of the research and Oriental references he used in *Vathek* (1786). The Orient is more comprehensive in *Vathek* than in other contemporary pseudo-oriental tales. The oriental setting, evocation and exotic Arabic tone in *Vathek* were beyond the simple references of any other 18th century oriental tales (Gill 137). For instance, Byron argued that the correctness of costumes, the beauty of description, and the power of imagination in *Vathek* surpassed the difference between the real East and the tale (qtd. in Sampson 102).

Like Johnson, Beckford admired Oriental culture and wrote a tale about the Orient. But unlike Johnson's *Rasselas*, *Vathek* indicates a radical shift from the conventional structure of 18th century oriental tales: "Previous eighteenth century Oriental tales had an eastern setting but were centered culturally in the West. They were in marked contrast to the fantastic, but informed the Oriental fiction of *Vathek*" (Sampson 102). The contrast is great between a mainstream 18th century pseudo-oriental tale like *Rasselas* and the unconventional *Vathek*, which has a more sensual and informed perspective. Beckford was deeply interested in the oriental world and knowledge, and in *Vathek* he attempted to display his understanding of oriental languages, history, culture, and religion by means of notations, references to actual places, words and people. In the first French edition of *Vathek* (1784), the notes and references took as many pages as the original story. Unlike the traditional writers like Samuel Johnson and Oliver Goldsmith who emphasize the distinction between the Christian West and Muslim Orient, Beckford reconciles the Faustus saga with the spirit of the *Arabian Nights* to deal with the fantastic aspects of the Arabian society, life and culture. The narrative structure has some oriental motifs, like the interpolation of new stories to defer the anticipated climax. In the arrival at the Hall of Eblis, for instance, the hero meets four men each of whom tells his own story. In the original episode of *Vathek*, each character tells in detail how he found the way to the hall and the subsequent loss of souls (*Vathek* 20). This kind of interpolation is a common motif of the oriental tale to defer the predicaments.

In the conventional form of the Oriental tale, the hero is like a puppet in the hands of fate. Vathek, on the other hand, is a self-confident villain who challenges Heaven. Like Marlow's Faustus, Vathek is motivated by an insatiable curiosity, and abjures Prophet Mohammed for immortal knowledge (22). He curses the Orthodox mullah and imams of Shiraz. Vathek says that they were "seated backwards on their mules" (102). Like the Helen of Faustus, Nouronihar appears to him as the object that enthralls his soul and arouses desire for illicit intercourse. The Caliph wants to "respire her sweet breadth" but her "course was as difficult to follow as the flight of one of those beautiful butterflies of Cashmere" (63). Like the old wise man of Faustus, the Genie tells the Caliph to "abandon" his "atrocious purpose" (105), the Caliph denounces what is sacred and wants to get the treasure of Pre-Adamite kings. At the end, like Faustus, Vathek cannot repent on the brink of damnation. As Garret writes, within the timeless frame of the Arabian setting of *Vathek* a highly-conscious drama of Faustus is re-enacted (15). Yet, what makes Vathek different from Faustus is that the Caliph's life-span begins after he dies. It is a Christian tale in content but typically oriental in closure by ending in infinity (Garret 16). Then, Vathek is at once "very Oriental and very European, very frivolous and very tragic, very shallow and very profound" (Garnett xxvi). Thus, the Oriental tale (*Vathek*) and the European myth (Faustus) interanimated each other in *Vathek*.

Then, there are two questions concerning the significance of the Oriental tales and pseudo-oriental tales for the representation of the Ottoman Orient in 18th century English literature. Firstly, it is apparent from the argument that the Ottoman Orient had a specific treatment in *Rasselas*. The oriental tales take as their model the *Arabian Nights* which "inaugurated and initiated" the interest in oriental literature in England and "determined the lines of thought" about oriental studies (Sampson 25). Most of the oriental tales written during the 18th century in England employ the narrative-format of the original tales; the frame-tale and other separate tales in the work are conflated within the context and for the moral purpose of the main story. The form provides a coherent and effective narrative for the message (Sampson 76). As emphasized, the foreign observer enters into new relations with a Western world. He is illuminated during this process of interactions. This transformation was significant for our study to illustrate the representation of the Ottoman Empire in the letters because it became a metaphor to evaluate Eastern and Western cultures from a critical point of view. The motif of transformation and the idea of a new relation between East and West also constituted the backbone of *Rasselas* and *Vathek*. This time it was not the *narrator* (foreign-observer) who was transformed to the West. The narrative (oriental tales) was transformed to discuss Eastern and Western customs, moral messages and world views. The transformation of the narrative was more significant than the transformation of the narrator. In the case of the narrator, the readers were made aware of the articulate European voice; in the case of the narrative there was a dominant eastern voice and narrator. The Orient expressed itself with its own voice and perspective to European readers. The characters of the oriental tales in the works of English writers had an Eastern identity. This time it was an Eastern voice which commented on the social and moral issues of English society. Due to faithfulness to actual oriental manners and customs in the oriental tales, the Orient created a distinctive space in the life and imagination of 18th century people.

Secondly, 18th century writers and readers established a unique and critical cultural and spiritual position with respect to the Orient. As Sambrook argued, 18th century scholars pronounced a common belief that "the most ancient poetry, wisdom and religion came from the Near East" (216). Thomas Blackwell wrote that Thales and Homer had studied in Egypt at a time when Greece "had scarcely emerged from barbarism and when Egyptians were living in peace and splendor" (217). As we have stated before, 18th century writers recognized and appreciated the ancient and Christian heritage of the Orient. As such, the ancient and Christian past of the Eastern civilizations was emphasized in the Oriental tales. The past glory and store of the Oriental civilizations were reflected and the tales rephrased the life, the color and the glamour of the Ottoman Orient. However, it is significant to state that the Orient which was admired and given a significant position in *Rasselas* had mostly the ancient and Christian character of the Orient. Johnson carefully distinguished the Ottoman Orient from the ancient and Christian Orient. Beckford, on the other hand, conflated a Christian myth with a typical oriental tale.

The Representation of the Ottoman World in 18th Century Travel-Writing in England

It can be argued that there was a critical and inquisitive perspective in 18th century pseudo-oriental letters and Oriental tales. This perspective was a significant aspect of the representation of the Ottoman Orient for two main reasons. Firstly, it is apparent that the distant oriental observer of the letters was a literary device that developed in a certain historical and cultural context and relied on extensive knowledge about oriental countries: "contemporary writers and scholars like Marana, Montesquieu, and Addison had access to and knew well the travel literature of many nations" (Adams 76). 18th century writers in England and France made use of this literary device to re-evaluate Europe and the Oriental world with a more critical and inquisitive spirit than ever before; the observer challenged the conventional European notion that the Orientals and the Ottomans were the enemy of European civilization. They interpreted the Ottoman-Europe relations from an open-minded, secular perspective that negotiated the political, cultural and social aspects of European and Oriental countries. Secondly, pseudo-oriental letters were the earlier popular model for the oriental tales. They anticipated and pre-conditioned a new perspective which recognized and illuminated the historical and cultural aspects of the ancient and contemporary Orient. The critical spirit of the letters was taken further by the inquisitive and negotiating perspective of the Oriental tales. The translation of the *Arabian Nights*, *Turkish Tales* and *Mogul Tales* stimulated a desire to explore and learn about the past and present conditions of the Oriental countries. Samuel Johnson's

Rasselas was based on historical documents; William Beckford made use of extensive Oriental documents to write a tale closer in spirit to the *Arabian Nights*. The critical perspective of the foreign observers and the inquisitive ethnographic spirit of the tales changed and to a certain extent challenged the conventional image of the Ottoman Orient.

In addition to the pseudo-oriental letters and Oriental tales, we have to take the representation of the Ottomans in 18th century travel-writing into account. As stated, behind the critical and inquisitive perspective of the letters and tales, there was a long tradition of travellers' documents which were discussed to a certain extent in the first chapter of our study. But the travel-writing in England before the 18th century was written from a less peaceful perspective. Such travel accounts emphasized the fact that the Ottomans were the enemy of European civilization. Thus, they reflected a conflict between Europe and the Ottomans rather than negotiation. Although the eighteenth century image of the Ottomans in the letters and tales was mostly taken from travellers' reports and historical documents, the hostility against the Ottoman Empire was replaced by a critical point of view in the eighteenth century. This critical perspective is significant because 18th century travel-writing centralized and took the critical-inquisitive perspective further to represent the Ottoman world. Therefore, it is necessary for the purpose of this study to investigate the representation of the Ottoman Empire in 18th century English travel literature.

Percy G. Adams has illuminated the history of travel literature in *Travel Literature and the Evolution of the Novel* (1983). There were basically two types of travel-writing: actual and imaginary. Actual travel-writings dealt with the observation and experience of actual people in foreign countries. Adams states that travellers between 1600 and 1800 worked for missionary orders, trading companies, and political alliance. European ambassadors, traders, merchants, medical doctors, missioners and members of other occupations went to foreign countries and wrote about their travels: "Perhaps without exception each embassy included at least one person who wrote the journey" (Adams 62). There were many who went to the Ottoman Empire. For instance, Lady Mary Wortley Montagu accompanied her diplomat husband to Turkey in 1716-18. Elizabeth Craven travelled to Turkey for three months to flee from the persecution due to her illegitimate affair with a nobleman. We learn from the Sherley brothers that they fought in Asia and Robert Sherley married the niece of the Emperor of Persia. Alexander de Bonneval got a good position and later became a secretary of state in the Ottoman Empire (qtd. in Adams 62). It is apparent from Adams' discussion that actual travel accounts indicated active interactions between Europe and the Ottomans in almost every aspect of life and great variety. There were also accounts of imaginary voyages in prose fiction in the eighteenth century which fabricated realistic and extraordinary experiences. Adams states that the uses of shipwreck, of slavery and of castaways are three main traditions of the sea fiction in the seventeenth and eighteenth centuries that provide romance and realism. Captivity in the Ottoman Mediterranean was a serious social and political problem which eighteenth century imaginary voyage fictions dealt with (Adams 123-25). We know that Cervantes was captivated by the Ottomans and escaped; and he wrote about the Mediterranean captivity in *Don Quixote*. Penelope Aubin's *Strange Adventure of Count de Vinevil* (1735) is an imaginary voyage on Barbary captivity.

It is beyond the limit of this study to scrutinize all eighteenth century travellers' observations and to discuss every imaginary voyage to the Ottoman Empire. I have selected three texts to discussin this chapter: Penelope Aubin's *Strange Adventure of Count de Vinevil*, Lady Mary Wortley Montagu's *Turkish Embassy Letters* and Elizabeth Craven's *Journey Through Crimea to Constantinople*. The reason for this choice is that in the earlier chapters I selected texts written by male writers and tried to illuminate their perspectives. Eighteenth century English travellers' accounts of the Ottoman Empire do not show much difference from the ones we have discussed. But we know that female travellers wrote against the male tradition; i.e. Penelope Aubin fabricated Barbary captivity to attack male adventurers who were tempted by the Ottoman world. Lady Montagu claimed that those male travellers' perception and representation of the Ottoman world were erroneous. She thought that she had an advantage as a woman over the male travellers and could give a more complete and rightful image of the Ottoman world (Bowen

25). Lady Craven, however, challenged Lady Mary's idea of the Ottomans in the *Journey Through Crimea to Constantinople*. This chapter, then, aims to illuminate the critical perspectives and perceptions of the Ottoman world by these three 18th century women writers.

Barbary Captivity and Penelope Aubin's *Strange Adventure of Count de Vinevil*

Corsairs, pirates and slavery in the sea were common incidents in seventeenth and eighteenth centuries Europe. Every European nation and the Ottomans too, had problems with corsairs but also benefited from slave trades in different ways. It was very common for a European adventurer to be captured by a corsair, sold in the Mediterranean slave market, to serve the Ottoman master, and being converted to Islam and, if possible, return home. One of the significant reasons for such incidents was the fact that the Ottoman Empire, as a wealthy nation and powerful military power until the end of the 18th century, provided many Europeans with a lot of worldly advantages and an opportunity to earn and increase wealth. During the seventeenth century, European travellers to the Ottoman territories were very much struck by the numbers of Christians converted to Islam. Mattar also states that the commercial power of the Ottomans was tempting for many travellers and adventurers. After the sixteenth century, Christians of low social and financial rank "willingly renounced their faith in pursuit of wealth, power and position in the Ottoman Empire" (Mattar 489). The poet Samuel Rowland wrote a short poem on Ward for being an apostate. He identified Ward as a renegade and attacked him with a warning that God would punish his renouncement soon. Rowland in the poem tried to show that renegades were the evil within Christian English community. In particular, the renegade's adaptation of the Turk's manner and costumes was attacked by the contemporary writers. For instance, "turban" was associated with Turks and wearing it signified renegades; and it was interpreted as a sign of undermining the national identity. Writers in the 17th and 18th centuries dealt with this issue and treated the renegade as a villain, traitor and corrupted figure, but in "the Restoration renegade was a familiar figure in the English imagination" (Mattar, "Renegade" 497). Greeks, Albanians, Italians, Spaniards, and Frenchmen renounced Christianity for Islam and took service in the Ottoman administration. The rising power of the Ottoman army was also frightening for many travellers and Europeans. On one occasion Muslim pirates landed in Baltimore, on another they penetrated the Thames and in 1640 came near Cornwall. They captured men, women and children, and hauled them in the slave markets of Algiers and Constantinople (Mattar, "Captivity" 489).

For many European adventurers the Ottoman religion served as a means to get material prosperity and social rank. They were most probably from a low social class and went to the Ottoman Empire to obtain wealth and fame. We have already discussed the adventure of T. S., a seventeenth century English traveller who worked for the Ottoman state as a tax collector in North Africa and willingly fought against the rebellious tribes with Ben Osman Butcher, the governor. We learn from T. S. that it was common in the seventeenth century for a European to look for wealth and prosperity in the Ottoman Empire. There were many in numbers who achieved wealth, prosperity and fame as renegades. Many of them willingly adjusted themselves to the new way of life in the Levant and remained among the Turks in the Ottoman Empire being happy and prosperous. For instance, Captain Hamilton was sent to the Levant to ransom the enslaved English. He found many of them converted into Islam. He was disappointed to see them "tempted to forsake their God for the love of Turkish women who are generally very beautiful" (Mattar, "Renegade" 491). In an anonymous letter from the Turkish Sultan Ahmet I to the Pope, the Sultan says: "many [...] Christians [who] attend our artillery ordinance, [...] are founders of our artillery and other instruments. [...] [A]ll Renegades fight in defense of our law, and with us to conquer your country" (qtd. in Windet 7).

Authors, playwrights and poets developed strategies to deal in their works with the renegades. They were sometimes represented as an internal evil in society that would bring about the collapse of Christendom. At other times, they were described as being in a spiritual turmoil; punished for their apostasy, they could only gain peace when converted to true Christian faith.

Robert Daborn's *Christian Turned Turk* (1612) deals with the English renegade John Ward who undergoes a conversion rite and circumcision in order to win the love of the Muslim woman Voada. Mattar argues that Daborn reappropriated the Faustus image as a model to denigrate the renegade; renegades, like Faustus, sell their souls to the Devil. The play was performed in London and Ward became famous for the wealth and power he gained after he "turned into Turk". The rumors of Ward's wealth were "so attractive that they captured the imagination of adventurers" (Mattar, "Renegade" 493).

The public also learnt about the renegades from the accounts written by Barbary captives. During the 17th century there appeared numbers of captivity accounts in England. The general purpose of the accounts was to warn the travellers about the possible danger they might face in their contacts with the Ottomans. Mattar argues in the *English Account of Captivity* (2001) that the captives were treated as heroes and their escape was interpreted as a demonstration of the power of God over the infidel Turks ("Captivity" 556). In the narratives of the captives, the public was introduced to the living-conditions, food, humiliation, violence and pressure under which the captives were converted into Islam. Before Aubin, Anthony Munday had published a captivity story, where he described the naval battle between the English and Turks in which the Christians were captivated. They were brought to Alexandria, where they were saved by three English men (563).

The captivity accounts also present the ideology and propaganda of the nation, which ironically display the "barbarian" and "civil" binary. Mattar refers to Rawlin's story. He writes that English sailors, who saved the Christian slaves and who heroically killed the Muslims either "by cutting with axes or by throwing overboard in their chains," were depicted as "national heroes" ("Captivity" 565). Mattar argues that between 1577 and 1625 ten English men dictated their accounts of captivity among the Muslims (566). They were also encouraged by the government to write captivity accounts in order to alienate their readers from the temptation of the Ottoman world.[1] In addi-

---

[1] In certain cases the actions in North Africa were prompted by the destructive attacks of Christian soldiers, traders and pirates who burned the towns, which were not included in the captivity accounts. Therefore, the piracy and captivity need to be looked at from both angles.

tion, there were captives who wrote and submitted accounts for personal benefit and to seek employment in governmental positions (O'Connor 106). Yet, the anti-Turk propaganda was a general tendency of the accounts for two reasons. Firstly, it was a reflection of fear and hatred against the powerful enemy which had been threatening the Christendom for ages. Secondly, the captives did not want to imply any collusion with Turks. The accounts were part of the captives' CV in the application for an employment.

The "captives" and "renegades" began to appear as a social and political problem in England and other European states, as a result of which many writers engaged themselves with this issue. Percy G. Adams also states that in the eighteenth century such episodes were to become routine for novels of adventure. Adams states:

> narratives of Barbary escapes as told by English men or their editors point out favorite narrative formula and close affinity to the dramatic incidents, tormented characters, the epic, moral and the providential design of contemporary fiction-writing; both forms of writing mixing the realistic and the marvelously exotic with drama, suspense, intrigue, misery and the clash of religion. (126)

Adams further states that captivity in the open seas inspired fiction writers like Daniel Defoe and Penelope Aubin. Penelope Aubin wrote three adventure novels on captivity in the open sea. *Strange Adventure of Count de Vinevil* (1721) is the first one which deals with "captives" and "renegades" and is based on captivity on the Ottoman Mediterranean coasts. The story begins with Count de Vinevil's decision to leave France for the Ottoman Empire. He thinks that he can earn a fortune in the Ottoman Empire and can return to France as a prosperous man. On his way to Constantinople, he is attacked by pirates and has a difficult time due to a storm. The attacks are thwarted and he arrives safely at Constantinople. However, misfortunes do not leave him in the new land. He is forced to engage his only sister to the Ottoman governor; he earns money but Turks claim to have a right on his fortune. In addition, he has to fight against merchants to protect his wealth and life. In the end, he secretly escapes from Constantinople and returns home with wealth and prosperity. Aubin presents the adventures of Count de Vinevil in this structure. She bases the tale upon a conflict between the family of Count de Vinevil and the Ottoman soldiers; she works with comparison by means of which she attacks the "renegades" who were tempted by the worldly opportunities of the Ottoman world by means of a female character who resists and rejects such temptations. She reveals the moral of the tale in the preface to the *Strange Adventure*:

> I present this Book to the Publick, in which you will find a Story where Divine Providence manifests itself in every transaction, where Virtue is tried with Misfortunes and rewarded with Blessing: In fine Men behave themselves as Christians, and Women are really Virtuous, and such as we ought to imitate. (1)

Aubin refers to Robinson Crusoe in the same preface and argues that the adventures of Count de Vinevil are more probable than Crusoe's tale with an emphasis on moral values such as virtue, nobility, faith, divine providence and bravery. Here Aubin must have used the preface to create in her reader faith in Vinevil's story.

Travel literature was a popular form to compare and contrast moral values of people in different countries. Adams quotes this tendency from Steel's *Tatler* No. 254, 1710: "There are no books which I delight in more than Travels, especially those that describe remote countries and give the writer an Opportunity of showing his part" (101). The traveller's tale could express the pirates' adventure as a moral example, since pirates were regarded as powerful, aggressive, brave and in control of their fate. Likewise, Aubin's purpose must have been to persuade female readers to be brave and virtuous; therefore, she used a traveller tale. Moreover, in the 18th century women were not thought to posses physical qualities like bravery, courage and strength. She could also express through the tale that women have such physical qualities which were denied to women. She depicted how Ardelisa (the heroine of the tale) achieved economic prosperity and individual freedom by resisting the temptation of the Ottoman lieutenant. Aubin stated that the readers would be sure to hear about female courage (*Vinevil* 2).

As stated earlier, the Ottoman Levant presented commercial and political opportunities to the Europeans between the 16th and 18th centuries. Merchants and adventurers from Europe benefited from these opportunities. Count de Vinevil, father of the heroine in Aubin's story, was presented as one of the merchants who made a "plentiful estate" in the Levant. He was at Constantinople with his uncle for ten years and had enough knowledge of the Ottoman world. When he resolved to dispose of his estate and save it from impoverishment due to the high taxation in his home country, France, he decided to sail for Turkey (*Vinevil* 2). He was a widower and had no child but the "beautiful Ardelisa" who was humble, generous, unaffected, wise, modest and prudent. Aubin describes her as the "most charming Maid of fourteen Nature ever formed" (2). Count De Vinevil loaded all his goods, and purchased a ship *Bon-Avanturer* and set sail for Constantinople. He trusted his estate to Count Longueville, a brave, generous, affable, constant, honest young gentleman of seventeen whom De Vinevil looked upon as a son and be pleased to see that Ardelisa and this virtuous young man "grew together in Affection" (2). According to the narrator, the young man and lady "seemed only born for one another" (3).

Since Count de Vinevil would be sailing in the "faithless sea," to the country of "faithless Muhometans," he had to consider the possible dangers he might face; it was probable that he might be attacked by Muslim pirates and die. He decided to negotiate with the Count of Longueville about his daughter. The "virtuous" young man insisted on his wish "to live and die" with De Vinevil and Ardelisa. Together they left France for Constantinople with the "Rising-sun" (3). It was the 12th day of March in the year 1702 when they left France. They planned to reach Constantinople on May 1st.

Their first impression of Constantinople is hostile. The young Longueville depicts the Ottoman Constantinople as "a strange Country," where they can "no more see Christian Churches, where religion is not in splendor and God is not worshipped with harmony" (*Vinevil* 4). He thinks that the Mosques echo the "Imposter's name," and that the "cursed Mahometans profane sacred piles". In addition, Turks are merciless and lustful; they are "mighty in Slave and Power". Once they see the "lovely face" of the beautiful Ardelisa, they will take her. Therefore, the young man tells the young lady not to show herself in public: "Let the House conceal you till the Divine Providence delivers us from here" (4). She is frightened. She fears that in the absence of the young man and her father there will be no one to protect her from the Infidels' Insolence.

It is emphasized in the story that Turks are "lustful, merciless and despotic". This attitude is once more depicted in the story of the passionate love of the Captain of the Port's son, Mohamet; in the commercial traffic between Turks and De Vinevil, in which the young man and Count De Vinevil manage all the affairs with merchants who come to purchase the European goods, Mohamet sees and falls in love with Ardelisa. He sends a letter to her and a lot of expensive gifts. After he falls in love with Ardelisa he realizes that her father would never consent to her being his. Therefore, he decides to take her by force (5). This is terrifying for Ardelisa, her father and her lover. Now that the young man's earlier "prophetic Fears are verified," and since Christianity forbids a noble Death, they have to run away before the Turkish Bassa seizes their Ship (5). Ardelisa, the young man and the Count are in jeopardy. They decide that the young man will go first, and then Ardelisa and her father will leave the town. She is strong and virtuous, thus she promises her lover never to permit any Infidel to dishonor her while alive. He sets sail but the Providence sends a storm; he is shipwrecked and spends 14 days where he is shipwrecked (6).

The Count and his daughter are still among the Infidels. The merciless Turks break the gate and enter the house right after Ardelisa and Nannetta, her nurse, leave the house. Enraged by not encountering Ardelisa, Mohamet says "show me to your Daughter's bed, Insolent Lord, make me happy in her Arms and glut my self in her Embraces" (7). The lord answers "My Daughter [...] will prefer a noble Death to such Dishonor" (8). The answer arouses the Turk's anger and "At these Words the cruel Mohamet plunged his Dagger into his breast" (8). The Count is mercilessly murdered by the Turk. He was the only man to protect Ardelisa and Nannetta from the strange and violent condition of the foreign country of the "cruel Turks". The women are by themselves now. Ardelisa and Nannetta have to rely on female intelligence, instinct and courage to survive among the infidels.

The two women make a plan and decide to deliver a report of their death to Count De Vinevil's only friend in Constantinople. When Mohamet "who has done this hellish Deed" learns of the death of Ardelisa and her father, he will be disappointed. Meanwhile Nannetta and Ardelisa could secretly be "delivered to some distant Port" from where they may "safely get off" (8). The Count's friend's wife decides to hide them in their country house which is "thirty Miles from the City [...] till a fit Opportunity presents to get off" (9). The secret and clever plan of the women safely delivers them to the country house in Domez-Dure. The Turkish troops look for Ardelisa everywhere. Joseph, their slave, mediates the news during this time. He discovers a safe retreat among the woods which might have been used by a Christian slave before he escaped. They decide to move there when they feel any sign of pursuit.

Joseph meets on his way to the country house a Turkish slave and learns that the slave, who knows about their hiding place, is going to inform his master. Joseph first make the Turk drink wine,[2] and then, stabs the Turk in the heart: "Go, Dog, said he, bear thy Message to the Prince of Hell" (10). Before he passes away, he repents and warns Joseph that they are not safe at Domez-Dure. They move to the cottage in the wood. They are befriended by a hermit who was once a missionary in Japan and whose ship was driven by a cruel storm to this coast. The hermit and his brother were enslaved by Turks. His brother died of maltreatment under the Turk's rule. Joseph learns that the Hermit is also from Picardy; he knew and loved Count de Vinevil. He tells their story to the old man who in return says that God has preserved him in this cruel place to "assist the others in Distress" (11). The old man and Joseph assist the ladies in the cottage until they can safely return to France.

Ardelisa and her friends learn that the young count is alive and has safely returned to France; luckily, by this time Mohamet, their enemy, has

---

[2] It was usual in imaginative travel writings to find Turks who drank wine, though drinking wine was not allowed in the Turkish religion.

been taken to the Army by the Grand Vizier and sent to a battle field. A French ship arrives at the harbor in Constantinople to take Ardelisa and her friends to France. "But nothing is to be depended on in this world" (13). On the way to the harbour, the Turkish general Osman suspects that they are "Slaves run away from their owners," thus decides to take them to Constantinople to investigate the case (14). Once more they are prevented by the Devil's cohorts. Once more a Turk, Osman, is enchanted with Ardelisa's charm of face and eloquence of tongue and resolves to secure her for himself. He takes them to his pavilion and says to Ardelisa:

> renounce your faith, adore our prophet and my Great Emperor, and I will give you Honors and Wealth exceeding your imagination; if you are a woman, here are the Apartments where Painting, Downy Beds, and Habits fit for to cover that soft frame. [...] I will feast each Sense and make you happy as Mortality can. (14)

Here, it is obvious that Aubin presents an image of a woman who can resist temptation in the Levant and can be as brave as a man. Ardelisa, as a representative of this image, resolves to perish rather than "yield to lustful Infidels" (14). Osman visits the Grand Seignior when he is in an angry mood. The Sultan, in accordance with the barbarous Customs of his Nation, "wracked his rage upon the luckless Osman" and imprisoned him "in the Seven Towers" (15). Rejecting Osman and the prosperity he offered, Ardelisa escapes. She meets another Christian woman, Violetta, a beautiful Venetian woman, who helps her.[3] Violetta was of a noble and ancient Venetian family before she was made slave "to the Lust of cruel Infidels" and given to Osman. Since she was captured and made a slave, Violetta had no freedom to resist. But she had secretly baptized her son and prayed to God to be saved (15-6). Her prayers not to end her life among the infidels are answered by Providence with the help of Ardelisa. They together escape and return to France.

The story attacks European men who are tempted by the Levant. Ardelisa and her friends are presented as stronger than men in terms of resisting

---

[3] Violetta is another image of strong and virtuous women in the story. Although she was enslaved and became Osman's wife by force, she does not accept the Captain's proposal until she learns that Osman died (26).

temptation. This is made clear with the story of a Spanish courtier who was tempted by the wealth and prosperity of life in the Levant. Don Fernando De Cardiole was by birth a noble Spaniard and was a commander in the Army. He fell in love with a beautiful girl in Spain. Due to her disloyalty, he killed her and escaped from Spain. He decided to travel to Constantinople and reveal to the Sultan the secrets of Christian princes. He was welcomed, circumcised and rewarded with a pension and lived in full enjoyment of all earthly delights among beautiful women until "his conscience was awakened and he was afflicted with bitter pain in the soul" (17). Since he could not return to Spain, he "determined to leave all his fortune," escaped to a secret cottage in the forest and spent the rest of his life repenting of his deeds (18). He met another captive who had escaped to the secret cottage in the wilderness. The captive was a hermit. They lived together for a while but Don Fernando died. Fortunately, he was re-baptized by the hermit before death. The story of Don Fernando indicates the weakness of European men to resist the temptation of the Ottoman Levant.

Ardelisa, Nannetta, Violetta and Joseph learn about the story of Don Fernando. Since they do not want to regret like Don Fernando, they set Osman's Seraglio on fire. Everyone in the Seraglio is in distraction which provides Ardelisa and her friends with the opportunity to escape and take shelter. They find a cottage inside the wood where they are once more re-united. They secretly apply to the French Ambassador in Constantinople who prepares the *St. Francis*, a ship, for their safe departure. They set off on the 20th of August, 1705 (19). But they are struck by a terrible storm at sea and have to land on the Island Delos[4] (21). They consider themselves safe on this desolate island where "there is no inhuman Turk to murder or enslave" them (21). They are happily fed by the fruits and goats of the Island and comforted by their faith in God until one day they discover that Violetta's father, Don Manuel, is on the shore on a ship (22). They set sail for Venice on the 2nd of February, 1705.

---

[4] Although the story emphasized resistance against wealth and prosperity on the Barbary coasts, Ardelisa and her friends were rewarded by treasure in the desolate Mediterranean island, another place on the Barbary coasts.

The story must have been designed to indicate that captives have power to resist the Ottoman world. Aubin creates female characters who are virtuous, brave, loyal and intelligent. They can be stronger than men in terms of resisting the temptations of the Ottoman world and still be rewarded with wealth and happiness (30). Addressing the curiosity of the public about the temptation of the Ottoman Orient, the *Strange Adventure of Count de Vinevil* incorporates shipwreck, pirate attacks and slavery with themes such as sexual violation, marriage, rape and the resistance of Christian women to temptation (Zagrodnik 24). The story of Count de Vinevil has textual and contextual parts. The textual context consists of the story. What is important in the textual context is the characters' travel and arrival in an Ottoman territory where they meet extra-ordinary incidents. Meeting the Turks, fighting against them and resisting temptation are significant aspects of the verbal context. However, the context displays the actual social and political background of the tale which is rather different from the textual one, as is apparent from our earlier discussion, where it was pointed out that the Ottoman Empire was a land of opportunity for many Europeans until the end of the eighteenth century. Young men from England, France and Spain travelled to Turkey with a desire to earn wealth and fame. They served in the army, fought against Europeans for the Sultan, and worked as tax collectors along with many other occupations. It must not have been difficult for European adventurers to negotiate with the Ottomans although there was a radical cultural difference between Europe and the Ottoman world. *The Strange Adventure of Count de Vinevil* indicated the resistance of virtuous female characters to the temptation of the Ottoman world. The context challenged such a notion and indicated that such a temptation was irresistible for many European men, as shown by the anecdote of Don Fernando in *The Adventure*.

Lady Mary Wortley Montagu: *Turkish Embassy Letters* (1769)

While Penelope Aubin in *The Strange Adventure of Count de Vinevil* rejects the prosperity and fame of the Ottoman Levant, Lady Mary in the *Turkish Embassy Letters* admires such prosperity. Unlike Aubin, she was an actual traveller to the Ottoman Levant. Lady Mary Wortley Montagu was not only an actual traveller but she claimed the role of an inquisitive female ethnographer who visited and observed the Ottoman Empire in its most alluring period. Harold Bowen admits this and states that it is fortunate that "the most delightful of all English writers on Turkey should have visited that country and recorded her observations in the most charming period of Ottoman history: *Lale Devri* –'the Age of Tulips'" (24). Lady Mary Pierrepont (Montagu's maiden surname) was witty, well educated and unprejudiced. She was known in England's literary circles. Her intellectual distinction was recognized by Alexander Pope, Samuel Johnson, Joseph Addison, William Congreve and other contemporaries. She married Edward Wortley Montagu who had been appointed the British ambassador of the Levant Company in Ottoman Turkey, in 1712, and went with her husband to Constantinople in 1716. She lived in Turkey for two years; during this time she gave birth to her son, learnt Turkish, entered a close interaction with Ottoman people and had intimate female friends. As a witty and well educated woman, she made use of any opportunity to learn and write about the mysterious world of the Turks, in particular of Turkish women. In a letter (April 1, 1717), she wrote to Alexander Pope that she had undergone a journey not undertaken by any traveller of some hundred years. She argues in the same letter that most of the ideas current in England and Europe about Turks were "laughable". She writes this as follows:

> It is certain we have but very imperfect accounts of the manners and religion of these people, this part of the world being but seldom visited by merchants, who mind little but their own affairs; or travelers, who make too short a stay to be able to report exactly of their own knowledge. The Turks are too proud to converse familiarly with merchants etc. who can only pick up some confused information, which are generally false, and give no better account of the ways here than a French refugee lodging in a garret in Greek Street , could write of the court of England. (60)

Lady Mary, during her stay in Turkey saw Crimea, Adrianople and Constantinople. She made use of opportunities to converse closely with Turks. She observed the Ottoman world through a keen and intimate female perspective. Relying on her own observations she "set about correcting the[se] erroneous notions to the best of her power" (Bowen 25).

Lady Mary has to be given a special place due to her claim that as a woman she had intimate acquaintance with the Ottoman way of life. Lisa Lowe states that Lady Mary created an individual tradition of representation of the Ottoman Turkey as a woman traveller (3). Among all 18th century texts about Ottoman Turkey the most path-breaking and influential one is Lady Mary's *Turkish Embassy Letters;* she seems to enjoy writing about the mistakes of the preceding male travellers. It is necessary, then, to review the observations of the male travellers whose accounts seemed erroneous to Lady Mary. We know from her letters that she was familiar with and carefully read the travel literature accounts of male travellers. Among the ones she refers to are Robert Withers's *A Description of Grand Seignior's Seraglio* (1650), George Sandys' *Sandys Travailes* (1658); John Covel's *Early Voyages and Travel in the Levant* (1670); Jean Dumont's *A New Voyage to the Levant* (1696) and Aaron Hill's *A Full and Just Account of the Present State of Ottoman Empire* (1709). She must have read them just before her journey to Turkey.

Robert Withers in his *A Description of Grand Seignior's Seraglio*, to make the narrative credible, claims that he was given admittance to the Seraglio where he "perfect[ed] his observation" (110). In the next pages, however, he states that no white man could go into the Seraglio.[5] Sometimes, he imagined what was not true. For example, he claimed that the Sultan selected his mistress for the evening by dropping a handkerchief into her hand. This claim is contradicted in Lady Mary's *Letters*. She states that "The Sultana [...] assured me that the story of the Sultan's throwing a Handkerchief is altogether fabulous" (E. L. 383). The lust and brutality of Turkish women, the inhuman treatment of eunuchs, and ugliness of girls were all stated by Withers who treated women's veiling, like many male travellers, as a sign of the enslavement of women, thus an uncivilized, inferior and barbaric aspect of the

---

[5] It is certain that Withers had no direct access to the Harem. It is argued that he took the description of the Harem from Otto Ben's work *Seraglio of the Grand Segnior*. There is a great similarity between the descriptions of the two writers.

Ottoman civilization. But he also argued that veiled women were not free from sexual attraction: "the Turkish women are the most charming creatures in the world. They seem to be made for love. Their actions, gestures, discourse and looks are all amorous" (Whithers 273). Like Sandy and Dumont, Withers described Turkish women as sexual objects of the male desire. Lady Mary contradicted these stereotypes with her own acquaintances with Turkish women in the Ottoman world.

Jean Dumont similarly claims admittance to the Seraglio: "We went to the great Seignior's seraglio which I cannot describe exactly since I was not suffered to go further than the Second Court" (qtd. in Bowen 165). However, he says he was allowed to know where the Sultan's wives were "lodged," and how they were guarded by the black eunuchs. Like Withers, he colors the narrative with exotic rituals which display the brutality of Turkish customs. For instance, he depicts Turkish men as contended with "their Lot," "they sit whole Days on Sopha, without any other occupation than drinking coffee, smoking Tobacco, or caressing their wives". Life of Turkish people is a "continual revolution of eating, drinking, sleeping, intermixed with some dull recreations" (166). According to Dumont, Turkish people are insensible and weak for inexcusable reasons.

Dr. John Covel, another male visitor whose reports Lady Mary considers erroneous, was a man of learning and served in Constantinople from 1670 to 1677 as a chaplain to the ambassador. Sir George Wheeler says that Covel wrote about many curiosities of the Turkish society. For instance, he set some Turkish songs to music (Bent xxvii). His description of Sultan Mustapha and his circumcision ceremony must have created much curiosity in the readers. The English public read from Covel's diary about the costumes, manners and life of the Turks at Constantinople, the great celebration in honor of Prince Mustapha, and the marriage of the Sultan's daughter. He was a careful observer of daily life. His account of people who came together for the celebration of the Sultan's birthday is notable. Covel describes this as follows:

> Among so many people it was most wonderful to see order and strange silence, not the least rudeness in boys or men; yet to keep the crowd of people of and in good order there are men on purpose in all these public meetings appointed, called Tooloonjes. [...] The Turks run from these people as from the Devil. [...] [T]here were about 200 of these Raga-muffins [...] in the midst of great multitude of Turkes, and yet I assure you I never met the least affront in the world, but rather extraordinary kindness, as shall be hinted particularly afterwards; and amongst these vast multitudes all are as hush and orderly as we were at sermon. I could not possibly believe it till I found it always so, and from me you may believe this wonder. (204-205)

To see the Ottomans in everyday life and to get into their world as an observer seem to have created a sense of wonder in Dr Covel. He paid attention to whatever he witnessed and relied on his observation. He realized that the Ottomans were multicultural and ethnically diversified society, in which Christian and Muslim values, beliefs, and life-styles were mixed. Fortunately, he benefited from this diversity and wrote also on his observations about the Eastern Christians. His work *Some Account of the Present Greek Church* [...] is a work of long observation and careful scholarship which Dr. Covel wrote while he was in Constantinople. He observed and wrote about the dervishes, marriage ceremonies, superstitions and entertainments like rope-walking which were most probably written to please contemporary English readers.

Aaron Hill's *Present State of the Ottoman Empire*[6] (1709) is considered to be one of the most amusing and informative surveys of Turkish manners by Bowen (26). Hill worked for five years in Constantinople in the household of the ambassador Lord Paget of Beaudesert. He must have learnt Turkish during this time. He observes Turks from a remote distance. Bowen thinks that his book is written with much elaboration but has no wit. This is obvious from the following description:

> [One] can travel half a day in the Turkish Territories but shall see a grave long-bearded Mussulman sitting cross-legg'd, under some Oak, or shady Cypress, pleasing his conceit with melancholy Ditties, to the

---

[6] Bowen also states that Aaron Hill professed to be ashamed of his book on Turkey (26).

Strum-Strum Musick of his thrum'd Ghittar, while his poor horse is turned to graze about the Field, and seeks the pleasure of a more substantial Entertainment. (qtd. in Bowen 27)

Lady Mary achieves a certain degree of wit, fame and originality with her ambition to represent the Ottoman world from an intimate female perspective. She carefully traces what has been cited by male travellers before her and refutes such observations by her own intimate female experience. According to her, things are not what they seem in Turkey. She does not completely reject the ideas that women are naked in the bath, go veiled in public and are guarded by servants; or that the Greek and Jewish populations deal with trade and are very much alike Turks in ignorance and infidelity. However, Lady Mary has two major claims in her *Turkish Embassy Letters*; the first claim is that she has gone on a journey not undertaken by any male traveller for some 100 years. A claim that is contradicted by Lady Mary herself when she refers to several male travellers who visited the Ottoman Empire a short time before her. Her second claim is that as a woman she has an advantage over the male traveller in that she can enter and have intimate friendships with Ottoman women who can explain to her strange and mysterious aspects of the Ottoman world. The second claim seems more appealing, thus needs further investigation because it is apparent that, rather than being contented with what the predecessors stated Lady Mary construed the Ottoman world from a particular female perspective.

Whether there is a specific, privileged female perspective in Lady Mary's letters which is significantly different from that of the male travellers necessitates the close analysis of her letters. Lady Mary Wortley Montagu begins her letter with a desire to write a reflection from a new world in which the readers will find charm and novelty. Although she faced a certain amount of conflict and trouble during the journey,[7] she did her best to record what she thought as remarkable in this new world. For instance, the diversity of the Pera[8] was charming to Lady Mary. She considered this as one of

---

[7] Lady Mary is angry about the ruthlessness of Janissary (25).
[8] Taksim used to be a Christian district of Constantinople. European ambassadors were located here.

the most curious things. She observed that people had very different customs and habits at Pera. For instance, women did not veil, if they "ever veiled" they did it to "show their beauty". All the "foreign ambassadors" were located in Pera and they were "lodged very near to each other". It was possible in Pera to see the "jarring of different atoms in one child whose mother might be Greek and father Dutch; the Greek perfidiousness, Italian difference, the French loquacity, and English thoughtfulness inherited in a family at Pera" (E. L. 111). Pera represented the "Tower of Babel" in that people spoke "'Turkish, Greek, Hebrew, Armenian, Wallachian, German, Dutch, French, English, Italian, Hungarian, Slovenian, Albanian, Russian" etc. She wrote: "I live in a perpetual medley of sounds, which produces a very extraordinary effect upon the people that are born here" (112). Her grooms were Arabs, her footmen were French, English and German, her nurse was Armenian, her housemaids were Russian, her servants were Greek, her steward was Italian, and janissaries were Turks (114).

Lady Mary wrote, in particular, about the condition of women whose friendship she admired most while she was in Turkey. In her visits to Turkish houses, she was welcomed by beautiful female servants, taken to the guestroom where she was introduced to the owners of the house (86-7). She seems to be pleased with the hospitality of Ottoman women and admits that she liked the habit that servants served the handkerchief and bowed the guest in courtesy to show their pleasure. She dined with ladies and drank coffee after dinner. The girls in the house played music and danced to entertain her; she was given a perfumed handkerchief. Lady Montagu wrote in the letters about this happy atmosphere of the Ottoman house and the condition of the upper class Ottoman women with pleasure.

The first remarkable thing to Lady Montagu, was a "bathhouse" or what she calls the Turkish bagnio resorted to by women for diversion and health. After visiting a bath in Athens, Lady Mary described it in a letter to her friend. She begins the description from structures and designs. She writes that the bathhouse has five domes, each for a separate room. Two of them are for hot baths, two for normal baths and there is a big hole in the middle of the building. It has hot and cold streams in it. The inside is so hot that it is not possible to stay with clothes on. She distinguishes her position by rejecting the preceding male travellers who wrote that the Turkish bath was an incestuous sphere. In the male travellers' texts, the space was given a special significance for the gathering of eastern women (who have very restricted freedom) for collective sexual affairs. Men were also said to come together in baths for homosexual affairs. Yet, Lady Montagu has a somewhat realistic observation and experience of the Turkish bath. She writes that male travellers cannot visit women in the bath. In addition, Ottoman Muslims and Christians in the Empire are allowed to bathe on different days of the week. Therefore, it is not possible for male travellers to observe the inside of a Turkish bath. She writes of her observation as follows:

> All women being in the state of nature, that is, in plain English, stark naked, without any beauty or defect concealed,[9] yet there was not the least wanton smile or immodest gesture among them. They walked and moved with the same majestic grace which Milton describes of our 'general mother'. There were many amongst them as exactly proportioned as ever any goddess was drawn by the pencil of Guido or Titian, and most of their skins shiningly white, only adorned by their beautiful hair divided into many tresses hanging on their shoulders, braided either with pearl or rib and, perfectly representing the figures of the Graces. (134)

According to Lady Mary, the bath was women's coffee-house in Turkey where all the news of the town was told and scandals were invented: "Baths were also a social sphere where women used to meet for diversion" (D'ohsson 197). Lady Montagu noticed that Ottoman women come together in a bath at least once a week for health and diversion. They converse, work, drink coffee and sherbet, lie on the sofa, and exchange all the recent news and take diversion for five hours once a week in baths. She "was charmed with civility and beauty and should have been glad to pass more time with them". To see "so many fine women in the state of nature," shining white,

---

[9] Since a boy and a girl could not see one another before marriage, boys' mothers saw and studied the physical condition of girls not to cause any excuse for divorce by the son due to physical deformity. Thomas More in *Utopia* also discusses this issue and argues that boys and girls should see one another naked in a separate room not to use physical deformity as an excuse for divorce afterwards (*Utopia* 58-9).

"with beautifully divided hairs as figures of graces" would improve the art of any artist. This place seemed more interesting and charming to Lady Mary than the Justinian's church,[10] one of the greatest monuments of Christianity (E. L. 135-36). The baths, in a sense, were not only female meeting places but had a social significance. Firstly, there was no separate bagnio in houses, and baths were the only community cleaning centers. Secondly, marriages were arranged at baths where would-be mothers-in-law could see the girls. Unlike the male travellers, Lady Mary described the Turkish bath and the social function of the baths in Turkey from a specific perspective which recognizes and respects the value of the other culture.

The way Turkish women dressed was another controversial issue about the Ottoman society in England. It was a popular fashion among English women during the 17th century to wear a Turkish dress. Queen Elizabeth I ordered her ambassador to buy a Turkish dress for her from Turkey. In one of the 17th century anonymous papers "Man's Answer to the Petition," it was written that portraits of Turkish women were particularly exhibited in the coffeehouses to sexually provoke English men. It was argued that "the little houses [coffeehouse] with the *Turkish Woman* on their Signs are nurseries to promote and stock hopeful Plants for the future service of the Republique" (In the *Old English Coffee Houses* 57). In Defoe's *Roxana,* the heroine wears a Turkish dress to tease the Dutch merchant. But, Lady Mary aims to present a different image of the Turkish woman's dress. In a letter to the Countess, she says: "I am careful [...] to amuse you by [...] What I see that I think you care to hear". This is a common attitude in almost all the letters of Lady Mary Wortley Montagu. When she decides to say something new and interesting, she emphasizes that she aims to "amuse" the reader by saying something interesting and different. She describes the Turkish dress with a particular emphasis on its practicality and cultural significance. She finds herself closer to the Turkish way of dressing and can identify herself with a Turkish woman. She is anxious to wear an "entari". She writes to Lady Mar while she has an "entari" on herself. She describes it as follows:

---

[10] Hagia Sophia.

> The entary is a waistcoat made close to the shape, of white and gold damask, with very long sleeves falling back and fringed with deep gold fringe, and should have diamond and gold buttons. [...] The *curdele* is a loose robe they throw off or put on according to the weather, being in rich brocade either lined with ermine or sables. The headdress is composed of a cap called talpock [kalpak], which is in winter of fine velvet embroidered with pearls or diamonds and in summer a light of shining silver stuff [...] [This masquerade gives them entire liberty, 2577]. It is surprising not to see a young woman that is not very handsome. They have naturally the most beautiful complexion in the world and generally black eyes. As for the morality or conduct [...] It is just as it is with you. [...] The Turkish women do not commit one sin the less for not being Christian. (69-70)

According to Lady Mary, "entari" does not have any sexual significance. Turkish women do not put on such a dress to tease their husbands or to repress their desire. They put on entari because it is a state regulation.[11] In the Ottoman society, women had to dress in this way. Recognizing the cultural and social significance of the way women dressed in the Ottoman Empire, she describes the design and practicality of entari. She thinks that the way women dress in the Ottoman Empire does not stand for the slavery of the Turkish woman; rather it may signify a liberty to a certain extent because veiling provides Turkish women with liberty which unveiled English women cannot enjoy at home. She says:

> This perpetual masquerade gives them entire liberty of following their inclinations without danger of discovery. [...] The great ladies seldom let their gallants know who they are. [...] You may easily imagine [the] number of faithful wives [is] very small in a country where they have nothing to fear from their lovers' indiscretion, since we see so many that have the courage to expose themselves to that in this

---

[11] A loose-fitting shirt made of silk or cotton and *entari* made of velvet and silk were typical ornaments of women from a high rank of society in Constantinople. Embroidered veils might be fastened to a fez with a brooch to make the headdress elaborate. When women went outside, they had to put on *ferace* which made them almost invisible to others' eyes. The state sometimes declared items concerning the type and material of the clothes. There were a number of decrees which restricted the jewelry, embroidery and textile. Minority and Christian women were also subject to these restrictions; but as an exception they did not veil their faces, though women in Athens and Armenian women in Anatolia wore veils like Muslim women (Faroqhi "Subjects of Sultan" 112).

world, and all the threatened punishment of the next, which is never preached to the Turkish damsels. [...] Upon the whole, I look upon the Turkish women as the only free people in the empire. (Letter, 71-2)

According to Lady Mary, veiling provided women with sexual, economic and social freedom in 18th century Ottoman society. She did not mind veiling herself while visiting public places. She also rejected the male travel-writers' arguments that Turks had many wives. "It is true that their law permits them 4 wives; but there is no instance of a man of quality that makes use of this liberty, or of a woman of rank that would suffer it". When a husband commits adultery or decides to get married, he keeps his mistress in a separate house. The only instance she witnessed "amongst all the great men" was "the treasurer" that kept a number of slave women for his own use. And his wife never sees him, though "she continues to live in his house" (72). According to Lady Mary Wortley Montagu, young boys and girls in the Ottoman society invented a particular form of exchange to communicate. Letters and certain symbols were exchanged between men and women to escape restrictions. The young people kept a collection of certain objects in their purses to express their feelings to the beloved. Each object represented different feelings. A small pearl was given to a girl to signify that she was a pearl among the fairest; a symbol of clove or a small clove given to the beloved symbolized the secret and long lasting love of a man. When given to a woman, the clove meant that the beloved was a clove which does not fade, and a rosebud which could not be tended. Girls expressed their feelings with different objects and symbols. A young Turkish girl gave a boy her hair to express that he was a crown on her head. Grapes signified the eyes of love through which she saw the world. A gold wire represented the pain and desperate feelings of the beloved who wanted to be united; a postscript of little pepper in the letter expressed hesitation and desire for a true message (72-5).

Lady Mary also rejected the male travellers' conviction that Turks are terrible. She thought of Turks as a civil and kind people. She discusses this with reference to the way Turks treated their slaves. According to Lady Mary, Turks treat their slaves in a humane manner. Although she considers slavery as the worst servitude all over the world, she admires the fact that Turks gave their slaves "yearly clothes to a higher value than our salaries" and "never ill used" them; slaves were happy in the Ottoman Empire (125-26). She writes about a Christian Lady who was enslaved as a galley slave. She was a Spaniard and enslaved by Turks in the attack on a Spanish ship. The Admiral of the ship was charmed by her beauty; he freed her brothers and parents who made haste to Spain to collect the necessary amount of money to save her. The Admiral took the money and presented it to her and gave her liberty. He asked her to marry him. She agreed to be his "legal wife rather than confine herself to a nunnery" in Spain. She never repented the choice she made (123).

When her friend Lady Mar asked Lady Montagu to buy her a Greek slave, Lady Montagu wrote:

> I really could not forbear heartily laughing at your letter and the commissions you are pleased to honor me with. You desire me to buy you a Greek slave who is to be mistress of a thousand qualities. The Greeks are subjects not slaves. Those who are to be bought in that manner are either such as are taken in war or stole by the Tartars from Russia, Circassia or Georgia and are such miserable, awkward, poor, wretches you would not think any of them worthy to be your housemaid. The fine slaves that wait upon the great ladies or serve the pleasure of the great men are all bought at the age of eight or nine year old and educated with great care to accomplish them in singing, dancing, embroidery etc. They are commonly Circassian and their patron never sells them except it is as a punishment for some very great fault. If they ever grow weary of them, they either present them to a friend or give them their freedoms. (103-04)

In another letter, Lady Mary writes about the condition of slave-servants in the Ottoman Empire. She was invited to dinner by a wealthy Ottoman woman and she witnessed that the noble Lady who invited Lady Mary had a very moderate dress and furniture but her slaves were great in number and their dresses were expensive. The noble Lady told Lady Mary that "the whole expense was in charity like the slaves she keeps" (88-9).

Observing the Ottoman world through a female perspective, she felt a particular form of nearness to Turks. The female nearness made it easier for Lady Montagu to identify herself with the Ottoman female culture. She did not consider gender-based cultural and social differences between England and Turkey as incompatible. She believed that the distance between Turkish and English culture should not create a fundamental difference. She wrote: "Thus you see, dear sister, the manners of mankind does not so widely differ as our voyage Writers would make us believe" (72). Lady Montagu's description and analysis exhibit her familiarity with and knowledge of the Turkish female style and the uses of possessives in her letter indicate Lady Mary's peculiar attitude towards Turkish women. Lowe states this as follows:

> The juxtaposition of the description of the 'Turkish Ladies' with Montagu's description of herself in Turkish dress creates a structural equivalence between her position and that of Turkish women that reiterates Montagu's initial gesture of identification. This gesture implies not only an equivalence of gender but also equivalence between the two [...] societies [...] between these women's social rank and her own. (42)

She admits, like Dumont and Withers, that the Turkish woman is the fairest thing in the whole world because they are surprisingly beautiful. Lady Mary Montagu agrees that women in Turkey are beautiful and virtuous. She describes them with intimacy and sympathy unlike the previous male travellers who constructed rhetoric of otherness to describe Turkish women. She is critical of this stance and builds up her rhetoric on the similarities between Turkish and English women rather than differences. Lowe also agrees with this idea and discusses this with reference to Lady Mary Wortley Montagu's as follows:

> Thus, when Montagu repeatedly likens English and Turkish women, her rhetoric of similitude directly contradicts the logic of difference that characterizes the observations of the male travel writers. At the same time to a certain degree, the rhetoric of identification through which Montagu displays her knowledge of Turkish women's culture inevitably restates an Orientalist topos of differentiation in order to

target it, ironically recalling the established separation of Occident and Orient. (45)

In this sense, her "competing and fluctuating logic of similarity" separates her from the common male rhetoric, and her rhetoric of identification marks the critical distance indicating a "heterogeneous, divergent and dissenting" narrative position (46). Lowe also argues that this dichotomy between the rhetoric of stereotypical Orientalism and emphatic identification pervades Montagu's narrative. Lowe compares the harem in the male narratives with Montagu's and says:

> In Orientalism, the female harem, forbidden to male spectators and travelers, is invented as the site of limitless possibilities for sexual practices among women. But the harem is not merely an Orientalist voyeur's fantasy of imagined female sexuality; it is also the possibility of an erotic universe in which there are no men, a site of social and sexual practices that are not organized around the phallus or a central male authority. (48)

Lowe thinks that Lady Montagu's letters can also be compared to that of the male travellers in the sense that she continually schematizes the female-context and invokes the Orientalist topos of female harem by means of her own homoeroticism as a powerful intervention in the male discourse of Orientalism (48). Lowe thinks that Lady Montagu is able to "reconcile her affection for Fatima"[12] with a female image of courtly love poetry. Lowe states:

> Following this literary convention, Montagu takes up a posture towards Fatima that still expresses love by means of aesthetics and anatomizing gaze. This view is taken by 'exact proportion of Body,' and proceeds to praise the beloved skin, mouth, eyes, as Petrarch would evoke the unsurpassable beauty of Laura's features. [...] [Then], Montagu frames the praise of Turkish women's beauty, independence, and manner as an intervention and challenge to the male voyage writers' subordination of Turkish women. [...] Montagu articulates these interventions of praise by means of male literary and rhetorical, models such as courtly love poetry. (48)

---

[12] Fatima is an Ottoman woman Lady Montagu met in Adrianople. Lady Mary was fascinated with her beauty.

Looking at Lady Mary's description one should not think that she presents the Ottoman women as the happiest people of the world. She also writes of the rules and customs which cause misfortunes and tragedy for women in Turkey. The story of Sultan Hafise, the favourite of Sultan Mustafa, is an instance of a strange custom which causes despair and tragedy. Lady Montagu writes that Hafise Sultan was once the favourite of the Sultan, but after his death, she was ordered to leave the Seraglio and find a husband from the eminent officers of the port. She considered liberty outside the harem as a disgrace and asked the new Sultan to free her from the general practice. She was refused and she married an old man, Bekir Efendi, the Secretary of State. She chose the old man —who was also the person who had presented her to the Sultan— not to suffer from the agony of a young and active husband (113-16).

Considering the strange custom of marriage which forces a widow to marry again and the absolute power of the soldiers,[13] Lady Montagu is critical about the patriarchal aspects of the Ottoman society. She had nearness, intimacy and identification with the female society. However, her close acquaintance was with the educated and upper class women in the Ottoman society that had a culture of their own.[14] The unprejudiced female perspective is disrupted in certain cases and she underestimates certain aspects of Turkish culture like the male travellers. Her letter to Anne Thistlethwayte explicitly discriminates London and the Ottoman Turkey. Turkish life is like a theatrical entertainment and has "nothing extraordinary in it which would be as great a disappointment as my visitors will receive at London if I return thither without any rarity" (E. L. 108). In particular, Lady Mary changes her attitudes when writing about subjects like animals. She thinks that camels,

---

[13] Lady Mary is also critical about the ruthlessness of the Ottoman soldiers and weakness of the Sultan. She says: "I could not look without horror on such numbers of mangled human bodies, and reflect on the injustice of war that makes murder not only necessary but meritorious [...] janissaries have an absolute authority here. [...] I cannot be very easy in a town which is really under the government of insolent soldiery" (E. L. 52-3).

[14] Lady Mary Wortley Montagu had a direct acquaintance only with one man from the Ottoman society. This man, Achmet Bey, was also from the upper class of society. She talked about Turkish religion and poetry with Achmet Bey. Except for Achmet Bey, she does not mention any male Ottoman Turk whom she met.

asses, buffalos, are very ugly creatures whose heads are ill-formed and bodies are badly proportioned. Asses have little white eyes that make them look like Devils (E. L. 83). She despises these animals and compares them to the "fine" spirited and elegant horses in Britain. She curses camels, asses, and buffalos, and locates horses at a superior position by distinguishing them from the kinds of labor horses and other animals employed at work. Horses are not physically suited for difficult labor. She writes of her experience on a horse, and her attitude towards other animals:

> I will assure you I never rid a horse in my life so much at my command. My side-saddle is the first was ever seen in this part of the world and gazed at with as much wonder as the ship of Columbus was in America. Here are some birds held in a sort of religious reverence and for that reason multiply prodigiously: Turtles on the account of the innocence, storks because they are supposed to make every winter pilgrimage to Mecha. To say the truth, they are the happiest Subjects under the Turkish government, and are so sensible of their privileges they walk streets without fear and generally build in the low parts of houses. Happy are those that are so distinguished: the vulgar Turks are perfectly persuaded that they will not be that year either attacked by fire or pestilence. (82-4)

In this letter we clearly observe the 18th century idea about the order in the universe. She begins her description with what she considers to be the lowest animals; asses, camels and buffalos. She compares these beasts to a more refined and superior animal, the horse. She deliberately scales the horse as superior to other animals in the Ottoman world. Montagu, here, is not free from the prejudice that Turks are superstitious about their ugly and strange animals. It can be deduced from her argument that English people have a more refined and rational taste. She also implies this in her letter when she talks with a Turkish scholar about religion. She states that the Turkish religion is comparable to the plain deism of England.

As Lisa Lowe admits, Lady Mary's ride on the side-saddle is an emblem of British command and control over and domestication of animals in contradiction to vulgar Turks who honor turtledoves, and storks, granting them religious significance (50). Her scaling of the animals and evaluating British and Turkish attitudes towards animals are a general reflection of 18th century British rationalism and belief in the great chain of being, in which she may unconsciously be reflecting male gaze. In particular, she locates herself as an object of wonder when she claims that Turks are ignorant observers who look at her with as much wonder as at the ship of Columbus. Here, maybe unintentionally, but certainly erroneously Turks are equated with American Indians who, as distinct from the norm of European civilization, gave the Ship of Columbus a magical and divine significance. Lady Mary equates herself with Columbus when she arrives at the Ottoman territory and, like Columbus, she naturally feels herself superior with a right to command and rule over the Ottoman world. Then, as Lowe argues, this metaphor locates Turks in a similar social position to the native Indians before the British lady on the side-saddle. Furthermore, the happiness of Turkish people and birds and animals in Turkey is given a similar value.

Then, Lady Mary's apparent claim that she observed the Ottoman society from a particular female perspective is true but incomplete. Her letters have a special rhetoric which reflects a less prejudiced female point of view. Yet, the nearness and identification with the Ottoman world take place in the moments when her texts refute the constructed topos of the enslavement of Turkish women (Lowe 51). Her perception and description are infected with prejudice and distance whenever she talks about the issues she was not intimately acquainted with. In this case, she reiterates the established traditional, cultural and national British attitudes of the male travellers towards the Ottomans before she introduces her own arguments that distinguish her letters from the previous travellers' descriptions. Being a woman, besides having a greater access to female society, she can identify with Turkish women and can speak of what is common among the women of British and Ottoman society. What makes Lady Mary's *Turkish Embassy Letters* a peculiarly female narrative is her sympathy for and identification with the female society of the Ottoman Turkey. This is how she frames her narrative. Lady Mary explicitly challenges the representation of the Turkish society furnished by these male travel writers. Like them, she writes her accounts in letters, yet she distinctly sets herself apart from the tradition by criticizing the representations of women, marriage, sexuality and certain aspects of the Ottoman culture. In redressing many of what she insisted on as misconceptions and inaccurate representations of Turkish women propagated by these male travel writers, Lady Mary reports how as a woman she was permitted a greater access to Turkish female society.

Elizabeth Craven: *A Journey Through Crimea to Constantinople* (1789)

Adams states that there were other female travellers who, unlike Lady Mary Wortley Montagu, "'fled litigation, family problems, persecution, or unhealthy climates and sought safer, happier or healthier countries" (67). The object of Lady Craven in publishing the letters "appears to be an effort to wipe out unfavorable imputations at home and to manifest respect shown to the writer abroad" (Turner 117). Lady Craven must have fled to Turkey after her scandalous affair with a noble man following her divorce in 1781. She must have thought that escape from England for a tour to exotic locations may remove the shame her affairs with Margrave created. She admits that it was very difficult for her to be left alone by her husband after she gave birth to six children. She needed escape and she chose to travel through Crimea to Constantinople. She "casts herself in the role of restless exile, happy neither at home nor abroad, whose journeying is less a violation than a proof of propriety" ("Crimea" 118). The journey to the Ottoman Empire may as well be an opportunity to enjoy the Oriental way of life.

Elizabeth Craven writes in the preface to the letters that she had to travel through Crimea to Constantinople between 1785 and 1786. She began the journey from Paris in 1785, and visited Italy, Switzerland, Venice, Austria, Poland, Russia and Turkey in one year. Her travel began right after her divorce, following her affair with Margrave. Bowen states that Elizabeth Lady Craven was in Turkey for three months in the summer of 1786. She stayed in Constantinople with the French ambassador. She visited Smyrna and Bursa. Bowen also argues that Lady Craven was struck by and disliked Turkish culture; for instance, she admired liberty of the Ottoman women but disliked Turkish music and coffee (27). The questions like "Are you married? Have you

Children?" (296) irritated her. She was also unhappy with the obstructive behavior of the *çokadar* (dragoman) who was ordered to accompany her to the frontier.

In the preface to the letters, Lady Craven admits that she wrote her travel observation after she returned to England. Upon her arrival, her friends curiously asked her about the countries and people she had observed during her journey. Then, she decided to give her friends information about the long and extraordinary journey. She admits:

> The best I could give, and in the most agreeable manner to myself, was [...] my letters [...] in which, though in a cursory manner, I have given you a faithful picture of what I have seen. Besides curiosity my friends in these letters see at least for some time where the real Elizabeth Craven has been and where she is to be found. (5)

Lady Craven thinks that she will be appreciated by readers for reporting such a difficult and almost impossible journey. According to Lady Craven, the documentation of her letters in epistolary form is the most agreeable manner –besides satisfying curiosity– to give a faithful picture of what the "real" Craven saw. The narrative voice of the preface makes it apparent that there is a "distance" in time and space between her journey and her letters. Unlike Lady Mary, she does not depict as an observer or describe as a writer but reports her observations to inform curious readers. Thus, her documentation, not observation, is made central. That she writes about what happened to her rather than what she observed also betrays the priority of remembrance. But her memory must have deceived her in certain cases. She seems to be ignorant of the Ottoman calendar because she has incomplete accounts of certain significant dates. For instance, she states that Ramadan lasts (the fasting season) six weeks in Constantinople (356), which is normally four and a half weeks. She also implies in the preface that her aim is not to give information about the foreign Ottoman culture; she writes the letters to answer the curious questions of her friends. The incomplete information and contradictions indicate that there is an uncertain correspondence between the letters and the writer's real experience. Then, the letters in the *Journey through*

Crimea to Constantinople reflect a limited point of the writer's actual experience.

Lady Craven, like Aubin, aims to display in this highly adventurous journey that women have the courage and moral integrity to survive in foreign countries and can resist the temptations of the alien world. But, like Lady Montagu, she finds things to admire in the foreign Ottoman world. According to Lady Craven, Turks have very simple and good habits. She likes the way they salute one another: "I wish the Turkish salute was in fashion instead of ridiculous bow and curtesy we have" (363). She admits Turks are interesting but they are nevertheless inferior in civilization to the British society. She says: "the elegance, the order and the cleanliness English people have is found nowhere in Turkey" (171). This contradictory feeling dominates her perception of the Ottoman world.

There are parallels and differences between Lady Mary's *Embassy Letters* and Lady Craven's *A Journey Through Crimea to Constantinople*. As Turner states, Montagu's impressions of Turkish women are Craven's chief targets (114). Lady Craven worked together with Montagu's daughter Lady Bute. They both argued that *Embassy Letters* were composed by men. She read Lady Montagu's *Embassy Letters*, and tried to benefit from the pubic interest in Turkish customs, the harem and society which were very powerful in the British readers' imagination (Turner 115). Although Constantinople is the climax of the story, only 70 pages of the 327 pages of Craven's *Journey* deal with Turkey. She particularly worked to contradict *Embassy Letters*. Turner quotes from *Gentlemans' Magazine*, 1789: Issue 59, 237: "What Lady C. here offers to the publick in a costly quarto might certainly have been very well compressed to the size of Lady Montagu's *Letters*" (117).

Lady Mary Wortley Montagu was fascinated with the diversity of the Ottoman world. Her letter about Pera indicated this. Lady Craven also met different races from different religious communities. But it was a matter of confusion to her. She witnessed that the coast in Varna was inhabited by Turks, Greeks and Armenians beyond the control of the port. They cultivated vines and corn (Craven 375). She realized that there is peace and wealth for Greek populations. She writes:

> And now, Sir, we will turn to the Greek, which are as numerous as the Turks here. [...] They retire with great fortunes, which they lay out in houses and gardens in the neighborhood of Constantinople, where they are pretty sure they shall not be suffered to die in peace, but are generally beheaded. [...] Greeks are prisoners in their own houses. (311)

It was surprising for her to see that the ancient customs of the Greeks were preserved: "The lyre of the ancient is often to be seen in the hands of the Greeks; but I suppose in ancient days, as in these, whatever harmony possessed their souls, it affected only their eyes" (312). She was surprised to see a Greek riding around the courtyard with twenty horsemen and "too proud to appear in public without his attendants" (313). She argues that "the idleness of Turks means peace for other religious communities, produces a happy opportunity for Hungarians to be wealthiest people of the globe" (412), and enables the Greeks to achieve their freedom from vengeful Turks. She says:

> Turkish idleness, which probably ever remain the same, gives a fine opportunity for the inhabitants of Hungary to become richest and happiest people in the world –if fate had made me mistress of that particular spot [...] how I would encourage Asiatic splendor, superstitions, and laziness, and never do anything that would weaken such a barrier. (413)

Craven's interpretation of the Turkish idleness betrays the difference between her observation and her convictions. She admits that the diversity lived in comparable peace and security, but she later argues that Greeks and other non-Muslim communities lived in the Ottoman Empire "at the risk of their lives" (354). She thinks that the Christian community of the Ottoman Empire does not feel like a subject of the empire. Therefore, the Christian community in the Ottoman Empire consists of "a nation of strangers who are forced to remain in it" (318). She identifies the general condition of the minorities like the Greeks, Armenians and Wallachian with a metaphor "Statues of strangers". She also explains this by referring to the Venetian Ambassador at Constantinople. She thinks that the ambassador is like the Prince in the *Arabian Nights* "who landed in a country where all the inhabitants were turned into stone" (317).

The transcendental line that divided people and labeled identity in the Ottoman Empire was religion. The Ottoman Empire consisted of diversities. It was more than necessary for the central government to be tolerant, and to recognize the rights and relative autonomy of the minorities in order to preserve the balance and peace between the subjects of the Empire from different religions and ethnic backgrounds. Therefore, rather than ruling over the minority as a conqueror the Ottoman state recognized autonomy and freedom to minority: "The Ottomans allowed the [minority] to maintain its physical existence, language, sense of history, cultural traditions and religious integrity over several centuries" (Lewis and Braude 16). Lady Mary noticed this but Lady Craven did not.

Lady Craven admits that it was very difficult and dangerous to travel from Crimea to Constantinople. Unlike Lady Mary, she does not think that as a woman she has a certain privilege to access the mystery of the Ottoman world. She is very careful to make a distinction between herself and Turkish women. In certain aspects Lady Mary's accounts of the Ottoman elite women are contradicted and challenged by Craven's image of the ordinary middle class Ottoman women. We have argued that the way women dressed and the way they walked in the streets were restricted by state rules and regulations in the 18th century Ottoman world. A young and single lady was recognized by the color of her dress. She was expected to wear red and green clothes. Middle aged and married women put on less colorful clothes, and old ladies were almost always in black. The types of dresses also changed in different communities of the Empire. The Greek Orthodox, the ambassadors' and merchants' wives from Venice, France, and England; the Armenians and Turkish women of different ranks were all recognized by the way they dressed. The clothes, then, were social symbols; and they indicated how gender, class, rank, religion and ethnicity were recognized in 18th century Ottoman society. Lady Mary wrote about the cultural significance and practicality of *entary* and *yeşmak*. They were fascinating female emblems to Lady Mary; Craven, on the other hand, finds the yeşmak and veil that ordinary Turkish women wear banal and disgusting ("Crimea" 85). She thinks that "entari" covers women from the neck to the ground, wraps the shoulders and the arms. She says: "judge, Sir, if all these coverings do not confound all shapes or air so much, that men or women, princes and slaves, may be concealed among them" (87).

She found women's habits of going bath in Constantinople absurd: "The Turkish women pass most of their time in the bath or upon their dress; [...] the first spoils their persons and the last disfigure them" (296). Lady Craven's description of the bath has interesting contrast to Lady Montagu's view of Turkish bath:

> I saw here Turkish and Greek nature, through every degree of concealment, in her primitive state –for the women sitting in their inner room were absolutely so many Eves– and as they came out their flesh looked boiled. [...] These baths are the great amusement of the women, they stay generally five hours in them; that is in the water and at their toilet together –but I think I never saw so many fat women at once together nor fat ones as fat as these. [...] [F]ew of these women had fair skins or fine forms –hardly any– and Madame Gaspari tells me, that the encomiums and flatteries a fine young woman would meet with in these baths, would be astonishing. (341-42)

In another letter, she admits that though the frequent use of the bath makes women look older, it is healthy: "Baths are beneficial for rheumatism" (341). Lady Montagu thought that Turkish women had a natural and most beautiful complexion, and large black eyes. Lady Craven also challenged this view. She argued that Turkish women have "white and red ill applied eyebrows hid under the two black lines which make them uglier; their teeth are black by smoking which show them disgusting rather than handsome" (226).

Craven's strategy is to de-aestheticise Turkish women and furthermore render them as indolent. This is obvious in the following description: "As to the women, as many, if not more than men are to be seen in the streets –but they look like walking mummies" (270). The mummy is lifeless and spiritless flesh. It is not possible to have any interaction with a mummy. Lady Craven's positioning of Turkish women as "walking mummies" betrays her unwillingness to interact with Turkish women. On the one hand, she considers them as dead bodies, which creates a sense of hatred and fear. On the other hand, she identifies the dead body with the action of walking. The metaphor, which is employed to depict Turkish women, makes them unrecognizable, thus, may also imply that Turkish women were unintelligible to her. She does not want to see the living spirit of the Ottoman women. She first compares veiled Turkish women to walking mummies, and then she states:

> I think I have never seen a country where women may enjoy so much liberty, and are free from all reproach, as in Turkey. A Turkish husband that sees a pair of slippers at the door of his harem must not enter; his respect for the sex prevents him from intruding when a stranger is there to visit; how easy then for men to visit and pass for women! If I was to walk about the streets here I would certainly wear the same dress. (270)

Here again the contradiction between Craven's observation and conviction becomes apparent. She challenges her view of "walking mummies" with the great liberty and freedom of the Ottoman women. She believes that women have freedom in Turkey. Lady Craven thinks a Turkish husband cannot get into his "harem [house]" if he sees slippers on the threshold because the slippers imply that there are women guests inside the house. Actually, the slippers on the threshold imply that women and men are not allowed to share the same space. Therefore, a man cannot get into his house if there are women other than his wife inside. The custom may allow certain freedom to women. But it may also be interpreted as gender discrimination considering that women are denied equal roles and position.

Craven's interpretation of a headdress changes in accordance with the status of a woman. She was hosted by a Khan in Sevastopol, an aristocrat whose sister's headdress and clothes enchanted her: "her dress was magnificent, particularly her girdle, in the front of which were two circles like bracelet lockets; the centers of them contained two fine emeralds" (242). She saw a headdress on a noble Wallachian Lady. She says: "this head-dress was far from being ugly" (392). But she described a headdress on lower class females as follows: "The females among the lower class disgusted me much by their head-dress –their hair is strained up to a point on the top of their head, and fastened to a pin– judge what a figure an old grey-headed or bald woman must take" (85). As indicated, there is an obvious difference between Craven's observation and conviction. This difference is made clear by an anecdote. Lady Craven has less antipathy for a Greek woman. She attended a wedding ceremony of a Greek family in Constantinople and described the bride as follows:

> I have been to see two Greek brides in Constantinople; their custom is to receive everybody who has any curiosity to see their wedding clothes. These were very magnificent and the women very pretty; and looked prettier from a singular contrast in the turn of their features. One had a true Greek face, her head small, her nose straight, large blue eyes, with dark or black eyelids and hair, and her eyebrows straight [...] a soft and sad countenance. (306)

Having shared the same space and lived together long enough, it is natural that the Ottomans and other religious communities developed similar customs and habits.[15] The wedding ceremonies of Turks and Greeks, for instance, were very similar. Both Greeks and Turks begin celebration and accept their guests a day before the wedding. They both welcome everyone who wants to attend the wedding. However, Lady Craven does not write about the similarity between Turks and Christian in the Ottoman Empire.

As Adams states, fantasy may translate and signify the difference between one's own nation "here" and the other nation "there" (95). In Lady Craven's letters, a fantastic anecdote is conveyed from the wife of the French ambassador. Lady Craven writes about Captain Pasha, admitting that she

---

[15] Goffman takes the Orthodox navy association with the Ottoman as a good instance for the current policy. He states that when the Turkomen faced the water they took help from Greek shipbuilders and hired a Byzantium ship to cross the sea. Yet, the Greeks were supported by the empire as mariners, shipbuilders and fishermen. It is a very common instance in the travellers' accounts about Turkey to read about their journey on the Greek ships (2002).

wrote what the wife of the French ambassador told her. She writes that Captain Pasha

> is always accompanied by a lion, who follows him like a dog; the other day he suffered him to accompany him to the Divan, but the ministers were so terrified that some jumped out of the windows, one was near breaking his neck in flying down stairs, and the high admiral and his lion were left to settle the council of the day together. (276)

The anecdote, interestingly and ironically, but at the same time comically, brings the serious and the ridiculous together. A high Admiral with a lion[16] arouses fear and threat, but the lion is like a dog and they go together to the Divan, the most high-level meeting, where all the important decisions about the State are taken.

However, there were certain similarities between Lady Craven and Lady Mary. They both thought that absolutism in the Ottoman state order caused misery and corruption. Elizabeth Craven described the tyranny of the Ottoman Sultan with a semi-fantastic approach. She wrote that she employed a large telescope in the house to observe the Ottoman Seraglio carefully (268). She watched the Sultan through her telescope[17] in Pera and saw him in the Seraglio on a silver sofa. The Sultan had a livid and pale face and had dyed his beard black to look young and strong.[18] She learnt that the Sultan, by walking in the town with few attendants wanted to make people believe that he had no fears. She compared it to the children's habit of whistling in the dark to make the nurses believe that they were not afraid (300). She noticed that the ministers of the Ottoman court consisted of unqualified people. The Vizier was a water carrier to Hassan Bey, and Captain Pasha who had only been a servant in Algiers (273). Offices and official status were obtained and re-

---

[16] There is no account in the Ottoman history about any Turkish pasha who went everywhere with his lion.

[17] As we have stated in the introduction chapter, the telescope was thought to give a better picture of nature in the 18th century.

[18] The Ottomans believed that it was necessary to have a young, brave and grand appearance in the war. They dyed their hair and beard for this reason. It was not only to look younger, as stated by Craven.

placed by intrigues. Each Sultan had supporters; when a Sultan changed, the ministers and staff changed, too. There was also no confidence at the court; even the Sultan's confidence could not help one. Lady Craven writes:

> There is a recent example here, proving that the confidence of the Sultan is not the surest way to escape a sudden and unexpected death. One Petraki, a Greek, a kind of banker to the court, by his frequent access to Achmet, raised the jealousy of the ministry, who, upon various pretences, one day in council, desired Petraki's head might fall. (274)

Petraki was the secret agent of the Sultan. He kept the accounts of services but Sultan's confidence did not save Petraki's head. Captain Pasha and his supporters desired the head of Petraki, and Sultan Achmet could not resist the demand (275). Craven thought that revolt, idleness and the disposition of the sultans brought discomfort and chaos to the country. People were not happy with the situation. They looked for peace and comfort in dull moments of rest at home and in remote places like baths and coffee-houses (414). Elizabeth Craven, like Lady Mary, thought that the absolutism created violence and corruption.

Lady Mary and Lady Craven were both enchanted by the beauty of gardens and neatness of graveyards in Constantinople. Craven says that Turkey is a "beautiful, enchanting country, the climate, the objects, the situation of it, make it an earthly paradise" (284). Although frightening, graveyards in Pera "form very romantic walks, as the trees and gravestones are huddled together in a confused manner; both presenting great variety to those who ramble among them" (287). They both admired the Ottoman culture for its particular attention to the environment, especially to the harmony and tidiness of the graveyards. The architecture of the graveyards was one of the good aspects of the Ottoman world Lady Craven observed in Constantinople. Lady Craven was attracted by the ways the gravestones were curved and structured. She says: "each grave-stone is crowned with a turban, the form of which shows the employment or quality of the corpse when living" (288).

Like Lady Mary, she did not think that the Turk's advancement in the mainland and on sea was a matter of anxiety for Europeans. Lady Craven writes of her own perception of the long-held Ottoman threat. She says: "I am not of [the] opinion [that] I would not wish to surround my country with any defense than that which Mahometans' idleness could form –The Turks are faithful to their treaties and do not seek war under false pretences" (413).

Lady Craven admits that the readers should not expect "a very rational letter" from her. She admits that "the vulgar idle tale of real life never once comes into [her] mind" for which "she feels quite happy" (106). For instance, she says: "You must not suppose that I mean to murder any one, but I think of all the two-legged animals I have seen I should regret killing a Turk the least" (377). She considers Turkish women brutal in many aspects but admits that "the clothes and jewels of women are magnificent according to the quality of the husbands" (335). The ancient cities and all that they contain are left uncared because of the ignorance of the Ottomans, and unfortunately the Christians living with Turks are afflicted with the same moral corruptions (285). She complicates and blurs the difference between actual experience and epistolary narrative. She fabricates myth, stereotypes, and fantasy and travel experience. On the one hand, she challenges Lady Mary Wortley Montagu's *Turkish Embassy Letters*, which was very popular during the 18th century; and on the other hand, unlike Lady Mary Montagu, she remains on the threshold of the Ottoman world.

We can say, in conlusion, that Penelope Aubin, Lady Mary and Lady Craven all claimed a privileged female position. Penelope Aubin challenges the temptation of the Ottoman world in *The Strange Adventure* and argues that women have power to resist such temptations. Lady Mary makes use of female nearness to see things from a privileged point of view. Although she achieves this to a certain extent, it is difficult to find this attitude in Craven who can be located in between Lady Mary and Penelope Aubin. The difference between their perspectives might have stemmed from the way they wrote.

Conclusion

The present study has indicated that the representation of the Ottoman Orient in 18th century English literature has liberal and critical aspects. The new critical perspectives shed light on possible resemblances between the two worlds and foregrounded a less orthodox and more liberal attitude towards the other culture. There was a long tradition of historical, political, economic and cultural interaction between the two worlds; the Ottomans and the Europeans had had continual cultural and economic contacts with one another. Venetians, the French, Genoese, and English had ambassadors and merchants in the Ottoman Empire; the Ottoman merchants also travelled in Europe. They created bridges between the two cultures and indicated a possible form of conformity with the other society. Thus, political and cultural exchange went on unbroken for centuries.

However, political and cultural conflict and rivalry due to religion did not disappear for a long time between Turks and Europeans. Intellectual and cultural atmosphere began to change in Europe in the 18th century, especially after colonial interactions with the rest of the world. Developing colonial networks made it possible and even necessary for the Europeans to negotiate and learn about other societies and cultures. This necessity created a liberal atmosphere and made it possible for 18th century writers to move easily between the Eastern and Western world. The image of the Turks and the Ottoman Empire was replaced by less negative ones. The Ottoman Orient was evaluated from a critical perspective which shed light on cultural, political and social resemblances between the Orient and Europe. The new critical and liberal outlook drew attention to the similarities and differences between cultures. For instance, there remained only "few western Europeans" who referred "to the Ottomans as the terror of Europe" in the 18th century (Goffman 19).

As the 18th century progressed writers moved away from the belief that a person existed as a complete, fixed self to the realization that the individual identity was not a determined one (Zagrodnik 9). The 18th century perspective illuminated the aspects of cultural exchange; political and social similarities between the Orient and Europe. There appeared a negotiating and dialogic attitude. It has been indicated how the changing notion of history and the increasing information about the Orient created a new vision and consensus about the Oriental culture. The changing face of the interaction was also coincidental with the beginning of a peaceful period. After the siege of Vienna, conflict and war between the Ottoman Empire and Europe diminished. A peaceful situation developed and the orthodox ideas were replaced by liberal ones. Here, Berlin's argument about Giambattista Vico to explain the changing face of the attitude in the 18th century is illuminating. According to Berlin, Vico developed a liberal form of historical writing in the 18th century. He argued that each culture and each stage of civilization in a society, though they may be similar to each other, has its own light which forms a single process. Since the process of cultural development and change has different rules for each society, interpretation of each civilization by the application of criteria that hold only for the other civilization will end in cultural imperialism (qtd. in Berlin 76). Vico made it popular in the 18th century to look upon a different culture from a plural perspective which recognized the values of the different culture as equally genuine, equally ultimate above all equally objective.

It has also been emphasized by the present study that the developing critical perspective rejected absolute standards. Using a plural and critical perspective, 18th century writers like Marana, Montesquieu, Hume, Gibbon and Johnson embodied a "variety of values and attitudes, some of which one society, some another, have made their own; attitudes and values which members of other societies may admire or condemn but can always [...] contrive to understand" (qtd. in Berlin 79). They created a cosmopolitan and liberal character that considered himself a part of a larger world and negotiated the other culture he encountered. The negotiating critical attitude is significant because it anticipated the new historicism of the 18th century and rejected the idea that there was one, only one, true morality or equally similar systems of values in every society. How such a critical attitude was first used by Marana in the *Turkish Spy,* which initiated a popular tendency by creating an oriental observer to judge Europe from a distant perspective, has been explained. The foreign mask of the oriental-observer gave voice to and interanimated the Oriental and European culture. For instance, in the context of the *Turkish Spy* and the *Persian Letters* parallels were drawn between European states and the Ottoman Empire. The Ottoman ambition over Europe and the Middle East was compared to France and England's desire to develop colonial networks. Montesquieu's symbolic choice of the Persian seraglio as a context to discuss the notion of government and to criticize the developing debate upon the absolute power of the French King was not coincidental; like his contemporaries and other European intellectuals, Montesquieu played with the traditional idea of the Oriental state to exploit the French political context. His argument relied on consistent resemblances between the political context of France and Oriental Persia. It was implied that the French government resembled Eastern despotism. For instance, Mahmut and Rica identified the French King (Louis XIV) as the most Christian Turk. It was also argued in the letters that the Ottoman system that secured the heir of the throne was very attractive to Louis XIV who had an ambition to replace the monarchy with absolutism. European and Ottoman monarchies were compared to discuss political ideas rather than as accusations. Locke and Hobbes used absolutism and tyranny to refer to the current political events and gave the Ottoman State as a model from which the European could take certain political lessons (Aksan 214). The influence of the *Spy* went beyond the fictional boundary. Defoe created from the *Turkish Spy* an actual project to reform the *Defect of Intelligence* in England in 1704 (Brown 120).

The present study has illustrated that the critical distant perspective of the oriental observer was later imitated and transformed by 18th century periodical writers like Addison and Steel. The transformation of the foreign oriental observer into the distant local observer indicates that 18th century writers began to look at their contemporary society and the world outside Europe from a more pluralist and critical but at the same time negotiating and dialogic point of view than in the earlier centuries. This new attitude was discussed with reference to Mr. Spectator's observation about the Royal Exchange in the *Spectator*. Mr. Spectator makes the Oriental world look more real and concrete by identifying and naming commercial commodities of each oriental country. He symbolically moves in between the multi-layered Oriental world and Enlightenment England with a hybrid spirit as a citizen of the world.

I emphasized that the introduction of the Oriental tales to Europe at the beginning of the 18th century initiated a second phase of cultural interaction between the Ottoman Orient and Europe. The tales discussed in this study indicated a form of inquisitive enlightenment spirit which negotiated social, political and cultural differences between the Orient and Europe. Each culture actively interacted with the other and enriched its cultural heritage by borrowing from the other and by dissolving the traces of the other culture. The long held Orient-Europe division was deconstructed, became obscure and problematic through the inquisitive and critical perspective in the tales. The tales produced a hybrid identity. The world of the tales was two worlds: one was the Oriental world in which the tales were created and the other one was Europe where the tales were re-written. It was obvious from the discussion in this book that Johnson read a lot about the Orient before he wrote *Rasselas* as an Oriental tale. Beckford was an ambitious reader of the Oriental tales. His *Vathek* was a major Oriental tale written in a spirit closer to the *Arabian Nights*. In the tale, the boundaries between literary and non-literary discourse, between the Orient and Europe were carefully worked and the traditional cultural division was re-questioned. The tales established a new relation to both worlds and Beckford moved between the Oriental past and contemporary condition of Europe. Vathek was an Oriental figure in the tale but he was at the same time comparable to Faustus and a gothic character. The tales were borrowed from either world and created their own dialogic identity. The inquisitive spirit of the tales made the Oriental worlds actual and accessible to European readers.

The female perception of the Ottoman Orient was discussed as the last issue of the book. It has been indicated that Penelope Aubin's, Lady Mary Wortley Montagu's and Elizabeth Craven's writings about the Ottoman Orient display a significant critical attitude in the 18th century. Resisting simplification and male categories they established an alternative style to depict the world from their own point of view. The female perception of and observations in the Ottoman Orient were discussed with emphasis on the writers' claims to represent the Ottoman world in a manner different from that of male travellers. The Ottoman Levant was a fascinating and tempting new world and the Ottoman Empire was powerful until the end of the 18th century. Although there were risks, there were large profits for enterprisers and opportunities for adventurers. Tempted by the economic and worldly prosperity of the Levant, many European merchants and adventurers began to live in the Ottoman Empire. Aubin attacked those merchants and adventurers who were weak to stand against the temptation. She created female characters that resisted the temptations. Lady Mary criticized male travellers for misrepresenting the Ottoman world. She conversed with Ottoman people, attended elite female community meetings and described its world intimately. Lady Craven observed common Ottoman people and wrote in a manner different from Lady Mary. She challenged Lady Mary's observation of the high Ottoman culture by writing on common people and their lives. The female writings represented the Ottoman world from heterogeneous perspectives. The Ottoman Levant was a network of contacts, and an unstable meeting ground for cross-cultural encounter. English traders and travellers who went to the Mediterranean had to develop new forms of behaviors to cope with and negotiate the Ottoman practices (Vitkus 3-5).

It might have been illuminating to use Said's theory to discuss the aspects of "otherness" of the Ottoman Orient, which had been discussed by Conant, Ekthiar, Nassır and Kabbani. However, instead of reiterating aspects of the Orient or challenging Said's argument, I argued that there was a long cultural, political, economic, and social interaction between the Ottomans and European nations, which made the Ottoman Orient a familiar and knowable reality to the Europeans. It has shown how the Oriental knowledge was used to compare and contrast Europe and the Orient from a more critical and liberal perspective by writers likes Jean Paulo Marana, Montesquieu, Johnson and Beckford. From the perspective of the referred Ottoman-European interaction the present study has indicated that Edward Said's Orientalism did not take into account the developing critical and liberal perspective in the pseudo-oriental letters, oriental tales and travel literature in 18th century English literature.

The present study also suggests a further investigation: the critical perspective and the changing face of the interaction that took place in European thought in the dawn of the colonial period produced a dialogical and negotiating tendency in which the Orient and Europe collaborated to recognize the other not by denying difference but by articulating and exploring it. This critical perspective can be taken as an early phase of what Homi Bhaba describes as colonial hybridity. The hybridity in the 18th century letters, tales and travelogues emerged out of dialogy and negotiation. A conflict existed in these texts between the European perspective and the oriental world. The conflict can be evaluated as positive for the reason that at the end of this conflict a possible meeting-space and clashing-space between the European and the oriental culture emerges. In particular, ability and knowledge of the oriental observer to outwit the other can provide illuminating evidence in the development of a witty character of colonial literature.[1] The critical foreign voice anticipates the early encounter and conflict in colonial novels between the colonizer and the colonized. Like the oriental observer, a witty colonial agent goes to the colonized society for a mission and develops forms of behavior to outwit the opposite groups. His ability to hide his identity in another society and to outwit the other becomes available to erect political and economic power in foreign countries. He uses this to pit the colonized against one another or to divide them for the security of the empire. Rudyard Kipling's *Kim*

---

[1] Weight considers the foreign observer as a flat character; I consider it as a hybrid character. A flat character is fixed and remains the same throughout the narrative but the hybrid character changes and indicates development.

is a European observer who outwits the Indians. He is a colonial character in the service of the developing British Empire. A criticism of the colonial attitude can be found in Salman Rushdie's *Midnight Children* and E. M. Forster's *A Passage to India*. The outsider (foreign observer) of the letters and tales, then, anticipates a popular colonial character who outwits the hostile natives. In this sense, investigation of the 18th century oriental observer can be an interesting field for other studies.

From the argument it can be concluded that there has been a long process of interaction between the Ottoman Orient and Europe. The development of the critical orientalist tendency in Europe in the 18th century was not coincidental. The critical and liberal 18th century attitude emerged out of actual historical interaction. Contemporary writers crafted letters, tales and travelogues to interanimate the Oriental and European culture. Edward Said remarks the process of this interaction as homogenous in *Orientalism*. He constructs an argument and a critical attitude about the representation of the Orient upon the notion of the presumed continuity of actual Europe vs. fictional Orient. Thus, he has ignored certain facts. I tried to illuminate here that the representation of the Ottoman Orient in 18th century English literature —namely in pseudo-oriental letters, oriental tales and travel writings— relied on familiarity and knowledge due to a long process of actual interactions. From the Crusades to the Renaissance and to the 18th century, travellers, ambassadors, adventurers, missionaries and scholars visited the Ottoman Orient and observed the Ottoman world in its own context. They introduced the Ottoman religion, culture and society to Europe from various points of view. As a result the Ottoman Empire and Europe developed heterogeneous interactions in different historical periods from which 18th century writers inherited a valuable sum of knowledge. As Weight suggests, if the Ottoman Orient had been represented as imaginary and fixed, it would have been dismissible, derivative and unimportant (14).

References

Primary Sources

Aubin, P. *The Strange Adventure of Count de Vinevil*. 2002. Blackmask Online. 5 May 2002. <http://www.blackmask.com/books66c/devinvevildex.htm>.

Beckford, W. *The History of Caliph Vathek*. Oxford: Oxford University Press, 1983.

Craven, E. *A Journey Through the Crimea to Constantinople*. London: G. G. J. and J. Robinson Co., 1939.

Johnson, S. *The History of Rasselas, Prince of Abyssinia*. London: A. J. F. Collins and University Tutorial Press, 1964. <www.gutenberg.org>.

Marana, P. G. *Letters Written by a Turkish Spy*, ed. Arthur Weitzman. New York: Temple University Publication, 1970.

Montagu, L. M. W. *Turkish Embassy Letters*. Athens G. A.: University of Georgia Press, 1993.

Montesquieu, C. S. *Persian Letters*. Translated by C. J. Betts. Middlesex: Penguin, 1973. <www.gutenberg.org>.

Secondary Sources

Abrams, M. H. A *Glossary of Literary Terms*. New York: Harcourt Brace College Publishers, 1993.

Adams, G. P. *Travel Literature and the Evolution of the Novel*. Kentucky: The University press of Kentucky, 1983.

Addison, J. "The Spectator". *The Longman Anthology of British Literature,* Ed. D. Damrosch. Vol.1C- *The Restoration and the Eighteenth Century.* New York: Longman, 2003. 2410-2413.

Akalin, E. *Discovering Self and Other: Representation of Ottoman Turks in English Drama.* Diss. University of Toronto, 2001.

Akgündüz, A. *Kölelik ve Cariyelik Müessesesi ve Osmanlıda Harem.* Istanbul: 1995.

Aksan, V. "Is there a Turk in the Turkish Spy." *Eighteenth Century Fiction* 6 (1994): 201-214.

Aksoy, N. *Rönesans İngilteresinde Türkler.* Istanbul: İstanbul Bilgi Üniversitesi Yayınları, 1990.

Alderson, A. D. *The Structure of the Ottoman Dynasty.* Connecticut, USA: Greenwood Press, 1982.

Ali Rıza Bey [Balıkhane Nazırı]. *Bir Zamanlar İstanbul.* Istanbul: Tercüman Gazetesi Matbaası, 1981.

Ali Seydi Bey. *Tefrişat ve Teşkilatlarımız.* Istanbul: Tercüman Gazetesi Matbaası, 1981.

Almond, I. "Leibniz, Historicism and The "Plague of Islam""": *Eighteenth-Century Studies* 39 (2006): 463-483.

Aramaduvan, S. "Lady Mary Wortley Montagu in the Hammam: Masquerade, Womanliness, and Levantization": *ELH Spring* 62 (1995): 69-102.

Astell, M. "Some Reflection upon Marriage" *The Longman Anthology of British Literature.* Ed. D. Damrosch. Vol. 1C- *The Restoration and the Eighteenth Century.* New York, London: Longman, 2003.2356-2366.

Aytoun, E. *The Penny Universities A History of the Coffee-Houses.* London: Secker & Warburg, 1956.

Ayverdi, S. *Boğaziçinde Tarih.* Istanbul: Baha Matbaası, 1968.

Bakhtin, M. M. *The Dialogic Imagination Four Essays.* Trans. by Caryl Emerson and Michael Holquist. Austin: University of Texas Press, 1990.

Baum, E. J. *Montesquieu and Social Theory.* New York: Pergoman Press, 1979.

Beckford, W. *Dreams, Waking Thoughts and Incidents*. New Jersey: Associated University Press Inc. 1971.

Bent, J. T. *Early Voyages and Travels in the Levant. The Diary of Master Thomas Dallam, 1599-1600. II. Extracts from the diaries of Dr. John Covel, 1670-1679. With some account of the Levant Company of Turkey merchants. Edited with an introduction and notes*. New York: B. Franklin, 1964.

Berlin, I. *The Crooked Timber of Humanity*. New York: Vintage Books, 1990.

Bhaba, H. *The Location of Culture*. London: Routledge, 1994.

Bible, English. The Old and New Testaments: King James Version, 1611: New York: American Bible Society, 1967.

Bisaha, N. *Creating East and West Renaissance Humanist and the Ottoman-Turks*. Philadelphia: University of Pennsylvania, 2004.

Blount, H. *A Voyage into the Levant*. Amsterdam: Walter J. Johnson, Inc., 1977.

Bohls, E. A. *Women Travel Writers and the Language of Aesthetics 1716-1818*. Cambridge: Cambridge University Press, 1995.

Bon, O. *The Sultan's Seraglio*. Translated by Robert Withers. London: SaqiBooks, 1996.

Bond, D. F. *The Spectator*. Oxford: Clarendon Press, 1965.

Bond, P. R. *The Tatler The Making of Literary Journal.* Cambridge, Massachusetts: Harvard University Press, 1971.

Boswel, J. "Life of Samuel Johnson" *The Longman Anthology of British Literature.* Ed. D. Damrosch, D. Vol.1C- *The Restoration and the EighteenthCentury*. New York, London: Longman, 2003. 2843-2858.

Bowen, H. *British Contribution to Turkish Studies*. London, New York: Published for British Council by Longman Green & Co., 1945.

Braude, B. & Lewis, B. *Christians and Jews in the Ottoman Empire; The Functioning of Plural Society*. New York: Holmes & Meier Pub. Inc., 1982. 1-25.

Brown, S. A. *The Double Agency of the Clandestine in Late Seventeenth and Early Eighteenth Century Spy Narratives*. Diss. Emory University: 1997. 105-120.

Carleton, M. "The Case of Madam Mary Carleton" *The Longman Anthology of British Literature.* Ed. D. Damrosch, D. Vol. 1C- *The Restoration and theEighteenth Century.* New York, London: Longman, 2003. 2113-2122.

Clifford, J. *Dictionary Johnson: Samuel Johnson's Middle Years.* New York: Oxford University Press, 1977.

Clarke, J. J. *Oriental Enlightenment: The Encounter Between Asia and Western Thought.* London: Routledge, 1997.

Clery, E. S. et all. *Authorship, Commerce, and the Public, Scenes of Writing 1756-1850.* New York: Palgrave Macmillan, 2002.

Coles, P. *The Ottoman Impact on Europe.* London: Harcourt, Brace & World Inc., 1968.

Conant, M. P. *Oriental Tales in England in the Eighteenth Century.* New York: Octagon Books Inc., 1966.

Covel, J. *Early Voyages and Travels in the Levan*t (1670-1679). New York: Burt Franklin Publisher, (1964).

Cowan, B. Mr. "Spectator and Coffee-House Public Sphere": *Eighteenth- Century Studies* 37 (2004): 345-366.

Croutier, A. L. *Harem The World Behind the Veil.* New York: Abbeville Press, 1944.

Curley, M. T. *Samuel Johnson and the Age of Travel.* Athens: University Of Georgia Press, 1976.

Currie, M. *Postmodern Narrative Theory.* London: Macmillian Press, 1998.

Dallam, T. *Early voyages and travels in the Levant. I. The diary of Master Thomas Dallam, 1599-1600. Edited with an introduction and Notes.* New York: B. Franklin, 1964.

Defoe, D. *Defoe's Review, Reproduced from the Original Editions by Arthur Wesley Secord.* New York: Facsimile Book, AMS Press, 1965.

Demaria, R. "The Eighteenth Century Periodical Essay" *The Cambridge History of English Literature* Ed. John Richetti. Cambridge: Cambridge University Press, 2005. 530-550.

Dierks, K. "Letter Writing, Stationary Supplies, and Consumer Modernity in the Eighteenth-Century Atlantic World": *Early American Literature* 41 (2006): 473-494.

Dikkaya, F. & Yumul, A. *Avrupalı mı Levanten mi?* İstanbul: Bağlam Yayınevi, 2006.

D'ohsson, M. *18. Yüzyıl Türkiyesinde Örf ve Adetler.* Istanbul: Tercüman Gazetesi Matbaası, Istanbul, (1981)

Dryden, J. "Annus Mirabilis" The Norton Anthology of English Literature. Ed. M. H. Abrams. New York: Norton & Company, Inc., 1986. 1789-1791.

Ehrenpreis, I. Halsband, R. *The Lady of Letters in the Eighteenth Century*: Los Angeles: University of California Press, 1969.

Ekhtiar, R. S. *Fictions of Enlightenment, The Oriental Tale in Eighteenth Century England.* Diss. Breindes University, 1985.

Eliot, C. *Turkey in Europe.* London: Frank Cass & Co. LTD, 1965.

Ezel, M. J. *Social Authorship and the Advent of Printing.* Baltimore: John Hopkins University Press, 1999.

Fabricant, C. "Eighteenth Century Travel Literature." *The Cambridge History of English Literature.* Ed. John Richetti. Cambridge: CUP, 2005. 705-740.

Faroqhi, S. *Subjects of the Sultan: Culture and Daily Life in the Ottoman Empire.* New York: I.B. Tauris, 1989.

Fothergill, B. "The Influence of Landscape and Architecture on the Composition of Vathek". *The Escape from Time, Bicentenary Revolution.* Ed. Kenneth W. Graham. New York: AMS Press, 1990. 31-40.

Gardiner, M. *The Dialogics of Critique, M.M. Bakhtin and the Theory of Ideology.* New York: Routledge, 1992.

Garnett, L. M. J. *The Women of Turkey and Their Folk-Lore.* London: David Nutt 270-71 Strand W. C., 1890.

Garret, J. "Ending in Infinity William Beckford's Arabian Tale". *Eighteenth Century Fiction* 5 (1992): 15-34.

Gemmet, R. J. "Introduction". *Dreams, Waking Thoughts and Incidents.* New Jersey: Associated University Press Inc., 1971.

Gentleman Magazine, London: January-December, 1759.

Gibbon, E. *Decline and Fall of the Roman Empire*, Ed. J.B. Bury 3rd Edition Vol. 5-6. New York: Lovell Co., 1845.

Gill, R. B. "The Escape from Time". *Bicentenary Revolution,* Ed. By Kenneth W. Graham. New York: AMS Press, 1990. 135-145.

Goffman, D. *Britons in the Ottoman Empire, 1642-1660.* Seattle: University of Washington Press, 1998.

—— *The Ottoman Empire And The Early Modern Europe*: Cambridge: Cambridge University Press, 2002.

Greenblatt, J. S. *Learning to Curse Essays in Early Modern Culture.* London: Routledge, 1990.

—— *Renaissance and Self Fashioning: from More to Shakespeare:* Chicago: Chicago University Press, 1980.

—— *Shakespearean Negotiation: The Circulation of Social Energy in Renaissance England.* Berkeley: California University Press, 1988.

Griffin, D. *The Cambridge History of English Literature.* Ed. John Richetti. Cambridge: Cambridge University Press, 2005.

Hardy, J. P. *Samuel Johnson, A Critical Study*. London: Routledge & Kean Paul, and Henley, 1979.

Haynes, J. *The Humanist as Traveler.* New Jersey: Associated University Press, 1986.

Hawthorn, J. *A Glossary of Contemporary Literary Theory.* New York: Edward Arnold Press, 1994.

Hayward, M. *The Representation of Islam and Muslims in Eighteenth Century British Fiction.* Diss. University of Indiana. 2001.

Hobbes, T. *Leviathan,* From *Reason at Work, Introductory Readings in Philosophy,* Ed. M. Cahn et al., New York: Harcourt Brace Jovanovich Publishers, 1984. 169-181.

Hotham, D. *The Turks.* London: John Murray Pub. Ltd., 1972.

Howells, R. "The Secret Life: Marana's Espion Du Grand-Seigneur (1684-86)": *French Studies*, LIII (1999):110-129.

Hume, D. "The Problem of Induction, An Inquiry Concerning Human Understanding". *Reason at Work Introductory Reading in Philosophy*. Ed. M. C. Steven, New York: Harcourt Brace Jovanovich Publishers, 1984. 306.318.

—— *Dialogues Concerning Natural Religion*: Edit. By Selby, 02 October 2007. <www.gutenberg.org, 2003>.

James, J. "The Caliph of *Fonthill*": American Scholar 1 (2003): 65-71.

Johnson, S. *The Rambler / by Samuel Johnson with an historical and biographical preface by Alex Chalmers*. Philadelphia: E. Earle Press, 1812.

—— *A Dictionary of English Language: an Anthology*, Edited by Daniel Crystal. New York: Penguin, 2006.

—— The Vanity of Human Wishes: 02 October 2007. <www.gutenberg.org, 2003>.

Kabbani, R. *Europe's Myth of Orient*. London: Macmillan, 1986.

Kaiser, T. *The Debate on Turkish Despotism in Eighteenth Century French Political Culture*. Chicago: The University of Chicago online source, 2000.

Knolles, R. *The Generall Historie of the Turkes...* London: Printed by Adam Islip, 1621.

Lanser, S. S. *Towards a Feminist Narratology (1986)* Feminism An Anthology of literary Theory and Criticism. New Jersey: Rutgers University Press, 1996.

Laqueur, H.P. *İstanbulda Osmanlı Mezarlıları ve Mezartaşları*, Trans. By Selahattin Dilidüzgün. İstanbul: Tarih Vakfı Yayınları, 1993.

Lewis, B. *Islam and The West*. New York: Oxford University Press, , 1993.

—— *Istanbul and The Civilization of the Ottoman, Empire*: University of Oklahoma Press, Oklahoma 1989.

Lewis, R. *Rethinking Orientalism Women, Travel and the Ottoman Harem*. New Jersey: Rutgers University Press, 2004.

Locke, J. "An Inquiry Concerning Human Understanding", from *Reason at Work Introductory Reading in Philosophy*. Ed. M. Cahn et al., New York: Harcourt Brace Jovanovich Publishers, 1984. 292-305.

Lowe, L. *Critical Terrain- French and British Orientalism*. Ithaca London: Cornell University Press, 1991.

Macfie, A. L. *Orientalism: A Reader:* Edinburgh: Edinburgh University Press, 2000.

Mackie, E. *The Commerce of Everyday Life Selections from The Tatler and The Spectator*. New York: Bedford/St. Martin's Press, 1998.

Marzick, C. B. [Trans. by Sir Frank T.] *Vathek with the Episodes of Vathek*. London: The Abbey Classic, 2001.

Mattar, N. *Islam in Britain, 1558-1685*: Cambridge: CUP, 1998.

—— *Turks, Moors and Englishmen in The Age of Discovery*. New York: Colombia University Press, 1999.

—— "English Accounts of Captivity in North Africa and Middle East: 1577-1625": *Renaissance Quartley* 54 (2001): 553-565

—— "The Renegade in English Seventeenth-Century Imagination": *Studies in English Literature* 33 (1993): 489-491.

McBurney, W. "The Authorship of Turkish Spy": *PMLA* 72 (1957): 915-935.

Mclean, G. *The Rise of Oriental Travel: English Visitors to the Ottoman Empire 1587-1720*. New York: Macmillan, 2004.

Men's Answer to Women's Petition. London: The Rodale Press, 1954.

Mernissi, F. *Scheherazade Goes West [Haremden Kaçan Şehrazat]* Trans. by Zehra Savan. Istanbul: Alfa Basım Yayın Dağıtım Ltd. Şti. 2001.

Mohan, J. "Voltaire's Image of India": *Journal of World History* 16 (2005): 173-184.

Nassbaum, F. *Torrid Zones* ... London: The John Hopkins Univ. Press, 1995.

Nassir, G. Q. *A History and Criticism of Samuel Johnson's Oriental Tales*. Florida: Diss. Florida State University, 1989.

O'Brien, K. *Books and their readers in Eighteenth Century England New Essays.* New York: Continuum Press, 2003

—— "History and Literature" from *The Cambridge History of English Literature,* Edit. By John Richetti. Cambridge: Cambridge University Press, 2005. 365-390.

O'Connor, M. "Piracy Slavery and Redemption: Barbary Narratives from Early Modern England": *Albion* 35 (2003): 106-110.

English Coffee-Houses. London: The Rodale Press, 1954.

Ortaylı, İ. *Osmanlı'yı Yeniden Keşfetmek.* İstanbul: Timaş Kitabevi, 2006.

Ousby, I. *Companion to Literature in English.* Cambridge: CUP, 1992.

Ozkan, N. "Este Hanedanı Kıyısında Osmanlı Devleti", *EJOS Dergisi* 3 (2002): 108-120.

Pope, A. "Essay on Man", "Essay on Criticism", "The Iliad", *The Longman Anthology of British Literature, Vol.1C- The Restoration and the Eighteenth Century.* Ed. D. Damrosch. New York: Longman, 2003.2476-2550.

—— *The Iliad by Homer, translated by Alexander Pope,* Edited by Steven Shankman, London: Penguin, 1996.

Ranelagh, E. L. *The Past We Share The Near Eastern Ancestry of Western Folk Literature.* London: Quartet Books, 1979.

Richard, D. *Mask of Difference Cultural Representation in Literature Anthropology and Art.* Cambridge: Cambridge University Press, 1994.

Richetti, J. *The Cambridge History of English Literature.* Cambridge: Cambridge University Press, 2005. 40-390.

Roosbroeck, G. L. *Persian Letters before Montesquieu.* New York: Burt Franklin Press, 1972.

Rycaut, P. *The Present State of the Ottoman Empire.* Farnborough: Gregg International Pub. Ltd., 1972.

Saglia, D. "William Beckford's Sparks of Orientalism and the Material-discursive orient of British Romanticism", *Textual Practice* 16 (2002):75-90.

Said, E. *Orientalism.* New York: Penguin, 1984.

Sallis, E. *Scheherazade Through the Looking Glass*. Richmond: Curzon Press, 1999.

Sambrook, J. *The Eighteenth Century The Intellectual and Cultural Context of English Literature 1700-1789*. New York: Longman, 1993.

Sampson, A. K. *The Romantic Pilgrimage to the Orient: Byron, Scott and Burton*. Austin: A Dissertation Submitted to The University of Texas, 1999.

Shklar, N. J. *Montesquieu*. New York: OUP, 1987.

Sherman, S. and Zwicker, N. S. *The Longman Anthology of British Literature, Vol. 1C-TheRestoration and the Eighteenth Century*. Ed. D. Damrosch. London: Longman, 2003.2061-2084.

Steel, R. *The Tatler, The Longman Anthology of British Literature, Vol.1C-The Restoration and the Eighteenth Century*. Ed. D. Damrosch. New York: Longman, London, 2003.

Svilpis, J. E. "Orientalism, Fantasy and Vathek" from *The Escape from Time,Bicentenary Revolution*. Ed. By Kenneth W. Graham New York: AMS Press, 1990. 55-70.

Tinker, J. *William Beckford: The First English Homosexual*. Stanford: A Diss. Stanford University, 1996.

Tomorken, E. *Johnson Rasselas and The Choice of Criticism*. Kentucky: University of Kentucky Press, 1989.

Turner, S. H. K. "From Classical to Imperial: Changing Vision of Turkey in the Eighteenth Century", From *Travel Writing and Postcolonial Theory in Transit*. New York: St. Martin Press, 1999.

Vaka, D. *Haremlik; Some Pages From The Life Of Woman*. Boston: Mrs. Kenneth Brown Pub., (1965).

Vitkus, D. *Turning Turk, English Theatre and the Multicultural Mediterranean 1570-1630*. New York: Mcmillian, 2003.

Watt, M. W. *Muslim Christian Encounter Perceptions and Misperceptions*. New York: Routledge, 1991.

Watt, J. "Goldsmith's Cosmopolitanism": Duke University Press, *Eighteenth-Century Life* 30 (2005): 56-78.

Weight, M. G. *Oriental Correspondence, 18th Century Epistolary Fiction and Imperial Culture*. Diss. University of Delamore, 2002.

Weitzman, A. (editor) *Letters Writ By a Turkish Spy*. New York: Temple University Publication, 1970. i-xix.

Windet, J. *Letter Written from the Great Turke unto Holy Father the Pope*. Amsterdam: Theatrum Orbis Terrarum Ltd., 1971.

Withers, J. *The Sultan's Seraglio*. London: Saqi Books, 1996

Women's Petition Against Coffee. London: The Rodale Press, 1954.

Wood, C. A. *History of Levant Company*. London: Frank Cass & Co Ltd., 1964.

Wunder, A. "Western Travelers, Eastern Antiquities, and the Image of Turks in Early Modern Europe": *Journal of Modern History* 7 (2003): 89-119.

Zagrodnik, K. V. *Voyages of the Unknown, Voyages of the Self: Women in Early Eighteenth-Century Travel Writing*. Alabama: Diss. Auburn University, 1998.

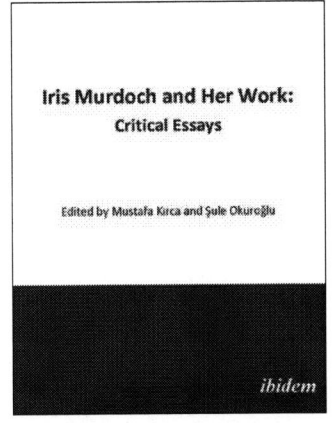

Mustafa Kırca and Şule Okuroğlu (eds.)

Iris Murdoch and Her Work

Critical Essays

240 pp., trade paperback, € 29.90

ISBN 978-3-8382-0020-0

Available at amazon
or directly from

ibidem

Iris Murdoch and Her Work assembles eighteen essays on the work of Iris Murdoch by scholars whose researches on Murdoch are already well-known. The book explores different aspects of Murdoch's work including her philosophy and fiction and focuses on a wide variety of issues ranging from reading Murdoch as a "fabulator" to the central role Murdoch plays in the "ethical turn". Approaching Murdoch's work from multiple perspectives, this book is of interest for Murdoch scholars and literature and philosophy students as well as for general readers.

The editors:
Mustafa Kırca holds his Ph.D. in English Literature from Middle East Technical University in Ankara, where he has been teaching courses in English language and literature. He has recently translated Richard North Patterson's *The Race* into Turkish (*Başkanlık Yarışı*, Artemis 2009), and his *Alan Ayckbourn in Chekhov's Footsteps* (*ibidem*-Verlag) has been published in 2010.
Şule Okuroğlu received an MA in English Literature from Middle East Technical University with a thesis on Metafictional Self-Reflexivity. She is currently working on her Ph.D. dissertation entitled "Identity Formation in the Female Writings of South Asian Diaspora in Britain". As a Research Assistant, she still teaches at Middle East Technical University in Ankara.

The contributors:
Bran Nicol, Frances White, A. Clare Brandabur, Gillian M. E. Alban, Fiona Tomkinson, Mukadder Erkan, Neslihan Ekmekçioğlu, Gökşen Aras, Meryem Ayan, Reyhan Özer, Minnie Matthee, Indira Nityanandam, Karan Singh Yadav, Jyoti Yadav, Joshua Lobb, Carla Fusco, Farzaneh Naseri-Sis, Ekin Şiriner, Ayşe Yönkul, and Kübra Çakıroğlu.

ibidem-Verlag • Melchiorstr. 15 • 70439 Stuttgart • Tel.: 0711/9807954 • Fax: 0711/8001889
ibidem@ibidem-verlag.de

***ibidem*-Verlag**

Melchiorstr. 15

D-70439 Stuttgart

info@ibidem-verlag.de

www.ibidem-verlag.de
www.ibidem.eu
www.edition-noema.de
www.autorenbetreuung.de